DIRECT SALES 101

By

Wayne E. Shillum

DEDICATION

THIS BOOK IS DEDICATED TO

MY DAD

ROBERT HENRY SHILLUM

Author's Comments

We consider a Direct Sales Person to be anyone who is selling to or for any Retail, Commercial or Industrial Business. It involves direct contact with the prospective purchaser to complete the sales process.

We have put together what we feel are the five most important areas that any person who wants to be successful in sales will need to learn and master. We have placed them in the progressive order (Parts 1 to 5) in which they should be learned.

Each part learned will be required before you will be able to properly understand and be fully equipped to handle the next part.

Part One – The Essential Elements for Selling Success

Part Two – Qualifying and Closing

Part Three – Overcoming Sales Objections

Part Four – Meetings and Sales Presentations

Part Five – Finding Prospects and Generating Leads

Wayne E Shillum – Author

Table of Contents

DIRECT SALES 101

PART ONE

THE ESSENTIAL ELEMENTS

10 KEY ELEMENTS

- You Must Have

- Your Company Must Have

- Your Customers Must Have

Written by

Wayne E Shillum

Part One is Dedicated to the Person

Who inspired me to start writing

My Sales and Marketing Books

My Daughter

Tracey Lynn Shillum

"Thanks Tracey for Your Continuing Support"

Overview of The Essential Elements

This is an area that is often not part of any sales training offered by others. We feel it forms the very nucleus of selling success.

Some new-to-sales people will doubt the validity of these elements as having any real value in sales; and because of this attitude, they will experience difficult times.

During my career in Sales, I have learned why these elements in the three areas outlined, are essential, to overcome the many obstacles that will challenge you on your sales journey.

The Essential Elements

1. The Key Personal Elements you will need
2. The Key Elements your Company/Employer should have
3. The Key Elements your Prospects/Customers need to have

These elements are essential if you wish to reach your optimum level in successful selling. Many people in sales will ignore these elements until they begin to experience failure after failure.

It is very important for people in the sales profession to be able to handle and overcome the many negative influences that they will face in their everyday selling activities.

WHAT YOU NEED AND WHY

The Elements You Need

1. Attitude: Having the proper attitude will create opportunities and successful outcomes to those opportunities.

2. Ethics: High ethical standards are essential in business, to build the confidence of your prospects.

3. Integrity: Without Integrity, you cannot create Trust.

4. Respect: You need to practice showing respect to get it.

5. Knowledge: The basis for building self-assurance and getting orders.

6. Enthusiasm: Enthusiasm is a game changer.

7. Goal Setting: Without goals you have no purpose or destination.

8. Commitment: You must be committed to achieve your goals.

9. Optimism: You must believe you will succeed, to succeed.

10. Persistence: Persistent creates success. Lack of it results in mediocrity or failure.

Why are These Elements Important?

Understanding and including these 10 key personal elements in your daily activities, will allow you to use all your sales skills and to achieve the full potential of the success you desire.

Your success or failure can be very much determined by how well you understand and put into practice these 10 Key Personal Elements.

Some of these elements are also the very things that apply to life. We are showing how they suit the conditions as they relate to sales, but they will bring success wherever they are applied.

You should use the 10 key personal elements outlined to form an infrastructure from which all your efforts will flow. They will become your greatest allies in your success journey.

Many new to sales; and surprisingly many who are more seasoned in sales, underestimate the valuable part that each of the 10 personal elements can play in their long term selling success.

Many people try sales and start full of enthusiasm, determination and full of hope for financial success.

They learn the skill sets required and begin their journey without creating or using this infrastructure to protect them from the hidden influences that will alter their journey.

They eventually leave sales in frustration and disappointment and never fully understand how these key elements could have made the outcome so much different.

Selling is not just about finding customers, making sales presentations, and knowing the many ways to close the sale or answer objections.

Yes, these are the skills required and very much needed to achieve the results you desire.

It is these behind the scenes elements that are all too often overlooked by many owners, trainers and those pursuing a sales career.

When these elements are utilized, they are often the biggest reasons for success; and if omitted, will invite failure.

In the following descriptions of each element, we will show you just how they will help you achieve a successful selling career.

Detailed Description

1. Attitude

It has been said: *"That it is a person's attitude at the beginning of a task, more than the task itself; that will determine the outcome."*

If properly incorporated into your sales career in a positive way, attitude will keep you traveling in the right direction. Many people over the years have commented on the importance of attitude and how it can affect and change our daily activities.

Your selling success will depend a great deal on adopting the right attitude. It means replacing any negativity held in your present attitude, with a positive one.

It is a known fact that a person can only hold one attitude at a time; therefore, if you are negative you cannot be positive. Reversely if you are positive, you cannot be negative.

Since positive thoughts attract positive results, you will know if you are on the right track, simply by monitoring your attitude or the results of your present task or undertaking.

In Sales, we are very much influenced by Attitude.

Thomas Jefferson once said: *"Nothing can stop the person with the right mental attitude from achieving their goals. Nothing on earth can help the person with the wrong mental attitude."*

Being either Positive or Negative are attitudes that very much affect our sales efforts every day. We can switch back and forth many times as good and bad things present themselves.

By understanding attitude; and how much being either positive or negative, can affect the results of your sales efforts, you will understand why and how things can quickly change the results.

This knowledge will allow you to have more control over the outcome of your selling efforts.

Controlling your Thoughts

Learning to control these thoughts can be very difficult until you train your thought patterns to accept only positive input and reject the negative vibrations that enter your life.

In sales, emitting positive vibrations and thoughts will reinforce your ability to stay positive and will influence the decision making of your prospects.

Attitude will also influence your ability to continue your selling efforts and stay on course.

In the beginning staying positive will be a challenge. You will find yourself changing back and forth from positive to negative many times, as good and bad events occur in your sales activity and your everyday life.

Be persistent and this phase will truly pass. Being positive is an acquired skill not an inherited one. It is like riding a bicycle. Many rehearsals will develop the acquired skills to ride.

Willie Nelson once said: *"Once you replace Negative thoughts with Positive ones, you'll start having positive results."*

We have heard much about being positive, and there have been many books written on this subject. One excellent book is *"The Secret."* Another *"The Power of Positive Thinking"*

Many scholars and writers have also produced famous quotes about positive thinking and the importance of overcoming negative thinking. We will be quoting many of them because they make the points intended so well.

Positive thinking creates positive results. Positive thinking sets the stage and allows you to extinguish the negativity that stands in your way to get a sale.

Winston Churchill once said: *"The positive thinker sees the invisible, feels the intangible, and achieves the impossible."*

Positive thinking is stronger than negative thinking and will conquer negativity every time. The secret is to replace negative thoughts immediately, before they can change the direction of your day.

It takes a determined mind to stay positive, as the untrained mind easily succumbs to negative thoughts.

Have you Ever Noticed?

When something bad or negative happens, it is often followed by many bad or negative things? This happens because the person did not make the effort to get back on track, by thinking of good or positive things.

Even a small amount of negativity creates more negativity and will soon rule your day. The wrong way to handle negativity is to fight it, as that brings more negativity into your life.

If someone upsets you or negatively confronts you, the best thing to do is to side-step it, by-pass it and forget about it. It is sometimes the hardest thing to do, because we are conditioned to immediately fight the opposing force.

Mother Teresa once said: *"Invite me to an antiwar demonstration and I will not come. Invite me to a Peace rally and I will be there."*

It is easy for negativity to creep into our thoughts because there is so much of it in the world today.

It is easy to become a negative person in our sales efforts because there are so many negative influences from first contact with the prospect to closing the sale and answering objections.

Our activities outside of sales also very much influence our thoughts and sales efforts. One or two negative happenings; if allowed, can change our approach to a sale and cause us to lose it.

Examples of Negative Influences

Example 1

- We might travel an hour or more to reach an appointment only to find they are not there.

- We then become angry and negative on our way to the next appointment, very much affecting the outcome of it.

Example 2

- We might not have been given all the information on our previous sales calls.

- We make a great presentation that does not solve the problem or meet all the prospects needs, because we lack that information.

- If we demonstrate anger or blame the prospect, we will lose the opportunity.

- Remain positive, apologize, correct it and make a new presentation. This time with the right information.

We will also hear the word "NO" many times or will be misled by many purchasers along the way. Staying positive is one of the biggest requirements in Sales.

The Biggest Result of Being Negative is Failure.

Ralph Waldo Emerson once said: *"We become what we think about all day long."*

It is important to know how to overcome the influences of negativity and become a source of positive vibrations. When one does become that source, they will notice that everything happening around them is good.

One way to become positive is to build a vision board, an inventory of the possessions and goals that you want to achieve. Place it where you will see it every day to remind you of what you are working towards and why.

See yourself as already possessing these items and enjoying them.

- Make a list of things you enjoy doing.
- Keep music that inspires you close by always.
- Be thankful about the good things you already have, and the good things that you will soon be enjoying.
- Build a list of things that you are thankful for and say them again and again.

History shows that all the great teachers and spiritual leaders all stress being thankful. Tell yourself over and over that: *"You are happy because, you will be successful because, you will achieve that goal because."*

Think those happy and joyful thoughts, and the world will soon change around you. Positive things will begin and continue to happen.

The Biggest Result of Being Positive is Success.

Dr. John Demartini once said: *"Whatever we think about and thank about we bring about."*

Some jobs can be done despite being unhappy but selling successfully while in a negative mood does not work very well, if at all. Your attitude of negativity will be felt by your prospective client; and when you believe you will not achieve positive results, you will not.

Fear, is one of the most dangerous forms of negative thinking. Fear soon creates doubt. Fear and doubt are the partners of failure. When we start to fear something, we change our ability to avoid or prevent what we fear, from happening.

Do not dwell on the fear, as it will surely change your life.

Fearing the outcome of a sales call or presentation will create a negative call or presentation. It will affect your performance and ability to achieve your goal.

An unknown author once said: *"Worry is a think-stream of fear; which if encouraged, becomes a wide channel into which all other thoughts flow."*

How Negative Attitudes Changed My Life

At one point in my sales career I was earning huge sums of money. I was investing much of it and was also making large sums of money in Real Estate.

I did things that everyone told me that I was crazy for doing. *"Stop taking chances,"* they would say, *"or you will lose everything."* In the beginning, I would laugh and brush the comments off and carry on.

Negative people are often jealous people

Negativity and jealousy are dangerous influences on those people harboring them, and to those who are around these people. Their influences often go unnoticed by the conscious mind, but unfortunately, these negative influences can do much damage to one's attitude before it is apparent.

What Happened to me

After a time of repeatedly hearing these things, negativity and doubt started to slowly creep in to my life. I started to worry about my decision making, my investments, not being able to make sales, losing my possessions and the financial success that I was enjoying.

That worry, and fear soon became so intrusive that it changed the way I thought, and the way I did things. I became fearful and negative, and soon my whole life was negative.

I started doubting every sales decision, every investment decision and every calculated chance that I took in my everyday activity. I started to worry about not making sales.

I did not realize what was happening at the time and for about six months, I let fear and negativity rule my life.

THUS...

I soon lost my focus, drive and enthusiasm for work and began to fear the outcome of every decision. My decisions resulted in a negative impact on my quality of life and the success I had once enjoyed.

Soon my income and success in my sales efforts plummeted and I went through some very difficult times.

Buddha once said: *"All that we are is a result of what we have thought."*

Things became so bad that I decided to take a break from the stress and negativity. I moved my family to a farm we owned on a lake in northern Ontario.

After a while, without the daily work activity that I had been used to, I started doing things that I enjoyed. They were little things at first like chopping wood, going fishing, cutting the grass and having camp fires down by the lake.

Without the Negativity

Without realizing what was happening, I began to stop worrying and started to enjoy life again. After a year of relaxing and having just plain fun, I started to get a little bored and started a small advertising business to promote tourism in the area.

The activities of my new business soon covered three counties and I started enjoying work again.

I then started to miss the bigger challenges that I had once taken head on. I returned to the career that I had left on hold. I went back to my positive attitude and began to enjoy success once again.

Dale Carnegie once said: *"If you want to conquer your fear, don't sit at home and think about it. Go out and get busy."*

Change your fear to joy and happiness. Think of yourself as already overcoming what you fear. Do it over and over.

See Success

Feel Success

And it will come

Lou Holtz once said: *"Ability is what you're capable of doing. Motivation determines what you do. Attitude determines how well you do it."*

We are often challenged by what others may consider to be huge or insurmountable tasks; that we have undertaken, as our goals. If we listen to those people; who do not have the same attitude, vision or goals that we have, we can begin to doubt our ability to achieve a successful outcome.

Always remember that Negative people fear positive thinking people. They are intimidated by them, and it often becomes their main objective, sometimes their obsession, to bring positive people down.

"Attitude" will change the way we look at things and the outcome. We must be able to recognize how one's attitude will change the events of the day and our selling results

Summary to Attitude

Eleanor Roosevelt once said: *"A stumbling block to the pessimist is a stepping stone to the optimist."*

Lao Tzu once said: *"What the caterpillar calls the end, the rest of the world calls a butterfly."*

Approaching things with the right or wrong outlook will see you end up with either the opportunity to enjoy success or going down in defeat. Your outlook can become a positive vehicle for your success, or one destined for failure.

William James once said: *"The greatest revolution of our generation is the discovery that human beings, by changing the inner attitude of their minds, can change the outer aspects of their lives."*

I personally consider Attitude to be the most important element of sales activities, because of what happened to me.

I know that I have placed a lot of importance on this element but having either a positive or negative attitude directly determines the outcome of your selling efforts.

Reaching your goals

Becoming successful in sales all starts with having a positive mental attitude.

Know that you are at this very moment, the person that you have asked yourself to become, with your past and present thoughts, and your existing attitude.

Just as your present position is a sum of all your thoughts to date; the greatest knowledge you will acquire, is that you can become whatever you wish to become, by changing your attitude from negative to positive.

Success or Failure in Sales will reflect Your Attitude.

2. Ethics

Business Ethics is sometimes described as: *"The system of moral principles or rules of conduct in one's profession."*

Good ethics should be your guiding philosophy in your business endeavors.

Ethics can be written or unwritten codes or values that govern decisions and actions within a company or profession.

In this case, we are in

"The Sales Profession"

Potter Stewart once said: *"Ethics knows the difference between what you have a right to do, and what is right to do."*

Morals are said to be socially imposed rules of behavior and teachings for society in general.

Ethics have been referred to as the personally imposed rules established and implemented by one's own choice.

In the business world

The various businesses and professions set standards for determining the distinction between good and bad decision-making behavior. Knowing what the difference between right and wrong is; and choosing to do what is right, is considered good ethical behavior.

Alexander Solzhenitsyn once said: *"Even the most rational approach to ethics is defenseless if there isn't the will to do what is right."*

Ethics are the Guidelines that you will Set to Follow

They Become your Book of Behavioral Codes

Moral Principles are the Tools used to Achieve the Results

"Having scruples" is often used as a synonym for either having ethics or having morals.

Scruple means anxiety or pang of conscience.

Loosely translated a scruple is a sharp point which will prod your conscious mind to say when you are not following good ethical judgment.

Albert Schweitzer once said: *"Ethics is nothing less than reverence for life."*

The business world will be very focused on whether you have good business ethics, morals or scruples or do not have them.

You will be very much under the microscope until you have shown that your personal rules of conduct, will provide a haven where your prospects can safely do business.

Example: The client views your ethics as questionable

Result: As the sales representative, you are the liaison between the customer and your company. The client will question doing business with you, even if your company is known to be ethical.

The Other Side

If you; as a sales person, are ethical, and your company has a questionable history of ethical practices, you will become tainted by the reputation of your company.

It will make your job extremely difficult to convince the potential client that their business is in safe hands.

Competition

The world of sales is extremely competitive, and you will find yourself battling with unethical competition many times. You will also loose orders because of the unethical practices of others and you may be tempted follow the same path as them.

Emmanuel Kent once said: *"In law, a man is guilty when he violates the rights of others. In ethics, he is guilty if he only thinks of doing it."*

There is a difference between joining the ranks of the unethical and doing the right thing about it when an unethical situation happens to you. If someone has maligned you or your company, you **do have** the right to set the record straight.

Be very careful how you do this. Point out where the accusation is wrong - because you have a right to do this. Do not attempt to smear the reputation of the person or company that has committed the act.

If you do this

You will end up being the one

Who is Labeled Unethical

It is a very precarious journey that one begins when correcting these issues and one must give it much thought before proceeding. If these issues are left unchecked; these untruths can soon become accepted as fact in your professional world, and you will have a difficult job to reverse the damage done.

Valdemar W. Setzer once said: *"Ethics is not definable, is not implementable, because it is not conscious. It involves not only our thinking, but also our feelings."*

At one point in my career, I made the mistake of shrugging off and ignoring the misleading comments made by competition. I felt that my good actions spoke for themselves.

That proverbial saying *"If enough mud is thrown at the wall, some of it will stick"*

Consequently - I started losing orders before I began to ask questions and dig below the surface.

Most purchasers do not want to be dragged into these kinds of circumstances. They will often not provide the real reasons for not choosing your product or service.

They find it easier; simply to remain silent, and not take a chance with the person or company where ethics are in question. They usually will not say anything to the accused company or person.

Most purchasers will avoid getting caught in the middle of a dispute.

It took a while for me to overcome the damage created by my competitor's unethical accusations and lies. I soon realized that I had to fight hard to keep my reputation intact.

Practicing it Alone was Not Good Enough

Maintenance is also Required

Do it in an Ethical Way!

3. Integrity

In ethics, integrity is regarded as honesty and truthfulness or the accuracy of one's actions. Much has been said and written about integrity. Integrity has been said to be an ingredient of good Ethics. Integrity is not a conditional word. It does not blow in the wind or change with the weather.

Some Dictionary Explanations of Integrity are:

- "Soundness of moral character, a sound unimpaired condition, wholeness or completeness"
- "The refusal to engage in behavior that evades responsibility"
- "A concept of consistency of actions, values, methods, measures, principles, expectations and outcomes
- "Adherence to moral and ethical principles, soundness of moral character, honesty and incorruptibility

In demonstrating Integrity, one must act per the values, beliefs, and principles that they claim to hold.

If one is said and known to have Integrity, it will create trust and the ability to move forward in a positive way.

Trust is Essential in the Business World.

Building trust with your prospects is an indispensable part of the sales process. You must strive for integrity and know that your values in life will cause you to behave in a way that is consistent with your beliefs.

W. Clement Stone once said: *"Have the courage to say no. Have the courage to face the truth. Do the right thing because it is right! These are the magic keys to living your life with integrity."*

Persons, who have low or no integrity, will demonstrate dishonest behavior and then try to justify it. These people also believe others will commit deceitful behavior when and if it is required to get the order.

This Belief Becomes their Justification

To act without Integrity

So, it is easy to see why it is very important not only to have integrity, but to be seen, as having it. We all have heard the saying *"to see is to believe."* That is why it is important to show integrity always.

Dr. Laura Schlesinger once said: *"People with integrity do what they say they are going to do. Others have excuses."*

If your client knows you are a person with integrity, they know you will follow through on your promises to them.

There is always a great deal of trust involved in any sale or transaction as it is almost impossible to cover everything in the terms and conditions of an agreement.

Trust is Essential

When dealing with a salesperson or the company they represent, the element of trust is very high on the requirement list of the purchaser. Your integrity will never be questioned, if it is not questionable.

There are many sales people who will promise anything to get an order; and once they have it, they have a hard job remembering all the promises, unless they are in writing.

Do not Become one of these Types

The client also depends on your full understanding of their needs and knowing that your product or service will deliver and satisfy all their expectations, if you have said that it will.

There is nothing worse than guessing or hoping that your product or service will do the job that is in question. You have a responsibility to make the right fit when proposing something to your prospect.

Spencer Johnson once said: *"Integrity is telling myself the truth. Honesty is telling the truth to other people."*

Dwight D. Eisenhower once said: *"The qualities of a great person are Vision, Integrity and Courage."*

4. Respect

Respect is said to be the result of good ethics. It is an element that needs to be given to others first. It is also something that needs to be earned and should not be taken for granted.

Respect can be shown through behavior and can also be felt. We can act respectful or we can feel respect from others.

Some Dictionary explanations for Respect are:

- It denotes a positive way of feeling of esteem for another person or entity
- To avoid violation of or interference with
- The state of being regarded with honor or esteem
- To show consideration or hold in high opinion

Showing Respect is a Key Element.

Respect can be given to others, shown to others and is enjoyed by others. It is often a courtesy extended when meeting someone for the first time and is expected by your new prospects.

If an employee, you have already shown it to the people that hired you, or you would probably not be employed by them.

Respecting your co-workers

Whether you are the owner or an employed sales person, it is essential that you show respect for everyone. It is the first step in earning it for you.

Respect everyone's time in your company and do not expect them to automatically do things that interfere with their lunch, their breaks, or their right to leave at the end of the day.

You will often need the assistance of many of the people that you work with; so always show them the respect they deserve in these areas. By showing respect and appreciation for their time and efforts, you will earn their respect. You will also get their support when it is needed.

Mark A Clement once said: *"Leaders (People) who win the respect of others are the ones who deliver more than they promise, not promise more than they deliver."*

Treat your prospect with respect.

If you have set an appointment always arrive a few minutes ahead of time. Do not get there 30 minutes early and expect them to see you. They have a schedule, and you may upset them if you impose on it in this manner.

Also, if you see that you will be late for your appointment; even if it is five minutes, call and let them know when you expect to be there. They will appreciate your call and may finish something they are doing instead of rushing to get prepared for your meeting.

If you are late, make sure that when you arrive, you apologize and show them that you respect their time, and are sorry for your tardiness.

Avoid being Someone who is Always Late

Even a call and Apology doesn't work after a while.

When you first meet someone, never use their first name, without asking their permission to do so. Yes, it may seem like old school; but good manners, are ageless.

People like getting respect because it boosts their own self-image and confidence. If you show respect right from the beginning, you will create that very important first impression.

First impressions are a onetime thing

And can never be done over

Respect requires an ongoing effort, or it will surely fade away. If you have lost the respect of your co-workers or they have lost your respect, it is best to try and resolve your differences.

Do this to be able to continue working in a harmonious working environment. Even if it requires the intervention of someone else to get things back on track, it will be better than continuing in a dysfunctional environment.

Never be a fake or go overboard when showing respect, especially if it has not been earned by the other party. You should "out of courtesy" always show it to your prospect unless they have violated that right.

In this case, it is best to confront them with your concerns and if the situation cannot be resolved you should take it to a higher level or consider discontinuing doing business with them.

Business will Seldom Be Conducted where there is No Respect

5. Knowledge

This is another cornerstone of being successful in sales. Without knowledge, you cannot ask the right questions, do the right research, make the proper recommendations.

You cannot ask for the order properly or answer your prospect's questions or objections.

I will never forget a comment made by someone in a sales meeting when challenged by the sales manager on their lack of product knowledge.

In their own defense, they said: *"Product knowledge is not really that important! That is why we have great catalogs and brochures that we can provide to our customer."*

"I always have lots of material with me to provide that information."

To this person, it made perfect sense, but perhaps it explained, why they always had the lowest sales figures in the room.

Some Dictionaries say this about Knowledge.

- Acquaintance or familiarity gained with experience
- The state of knowing
- A familiarity with someone or something, which can include facts, information, descriptions, or skills acquired through experience and education
- Acquaintance with facts, truths or principles as from study

Henry Ford once said: *"The only real security that a person will have in this world is a reserve of knowledge, experience, and ability."*

Lee Iacocca once said: *"There is no substitute for accurate knowledge. Know yourself, your business and your men."*

Where you will need Knowledge

As a sales person, you will need considerable knowledge in many areas if you expect to become successful. Many people underestimate what is involved when they represent a company as a sales person.

There are seven areas that we will outline that one should make the effort to become knowledgeable in.

1. Knowledge of your Company

As a new owner of a business, or a new employee looking after sales, you will need to know the following:

- Who started the company?
- When it was started and why?
- Its history and changes?
- Who is running it now? (if an employee)
- What is the company's position in the marketplace?
- What is its vision, mission, its goals and objectives?

What is your companies brand strategy, its brand vision, the brand target and the brand position in the marketplace?

- Full knowledge of all your products and services (offerings)?
- What are all the benefits and features of your offerings?
- What are the weaknesses of your offerings?

If an Employee

- What is the overall marketing plan of the company?
- Know all the people in your company and their functions.
- Know how you fit into this picture.

Why do you need to have these things ready to use?

If you are going to represent a company; or even as an owner, you will need to talk with authority about these things. Every item just listed is important, because you never know when you will be tested on the subject matter of *"Your Company."*

Some people will test you to see if you are just working to put money in your own pocket or if you know and believe in your company. If you know and believe in your company, your prospect will usually follow your lead.

The potential customer will have more trust in a person who knows every aspect about the company that they are selling for, and they will be more comfortable purchasing from them.

If you are an employee, make the effort to learn the above and it will show your employer that they have chosen someone who is committed to doing a good job. If you are the owner, there is no excuse for not knowing.

2. Knowledge of your Competition (all of them)

- Who started the company?
- When was, it started and why?
- Its history and changes?
- Who is running it now?
- What are their products and services (offerings)?
- What are their benefits?
- What are their weaknesses?
- Who are the people in the company and their functions?
- What are their good points and weaknesses?

Why do you need to know your Competition?

When you start quoting your prospects, you will not be alone. You will find that you will probably be quoting against many of the same companies each time you find a new opportunity.

You should be asking each time who you are quoting against. Your prospect may not tell you, but if they do, your knowledge of those competing, will provide an early indication of what you are up against and what your chances are.

The approach you will need to take to get the order, will be partly based on your knowledge of your competition.

To have the best chance of getting the order you should learn everything you can about your competition. When you find a new competitor, thoroughly check them out immediately.

The Challenges

Each of your competitors will create a different challenge for you. One may have some product features that you do not have but you may feel your other features are better suited for the customer's requirements.

You will need to point out why your features are better, without knocking you're your competitor. Knowledge will allow you to do this in a subtle way.

Pricing

Pricing is always an issue, and no one likes to think the higher price is just that, and there are no additional benefits because of it.

You will need to demonstrate why your price is higher than X company and show why your benefits more than justify the price difference. It could be improved performance, increased quality or the savings generated.

Knowledge allows you to show Value

Knowing and explaining your features and benefits will often beat a lower price as well, when you are challenged with this situation.

Knowing your competition better than they know you

Will give you a competitive edge

Be assured; that once you start winning a few orders, your competition will want to know all about you and your company as well.

3. Knowledge of your Industry

- Why are your offerings needed?
- What is your target market?
- Where are your growth markets?
- Where can you develop new markets?
- What new products are being developed by your company?

Why do you need to know your Industry?

- You will not only need to know who and where all your existing customers are; but, why you still have them.

- Why and when did they start doing business with your company?

- Are there other business types that have the same needs as your present clients that you might explore to obtain new business?

- Is the market for your product growing or is it shrinking and why?

- What new products will your company be introducing to the marketplace.

Do not wait until new products arrive before you start promoting them.

Find out what your competition is doing in the new products area and keep your R&D informed of these new products or services on the competition horizon.

Knowing the answers to these questions will keep you selling when others are not.

4. Knowledge of How to Qualify your Prospect and Close a Sale

- Why is closing a process and not just something at the end.

- What are Qualifying questions?

- Why are Qualifying questions so important?

- What are Closing questions?

- When do you use Closing questions?

- When do you ask for the order?

- How do you Close?

- How often should you close?

Why you need to know *"How to Qualify your Prospect?"*

Without this knowledge, you will waste a large amount of time with people who have no need, no interest or no money.

Qualifying is the first part of the Closing Process.

Why you need to know *"How to Close?"*

If you do not know how to close you will find yourself totally adrift during and at the end of your presentation. Very few prospects will volunteer a purchase order without being asked for it first.

There are many ways to ask for an order and many times when closing questions should be asked. Each situation may present a different approach to get the order.

Not knowing when or how to ask will often mean leaving without a sale even if the client was prepared to buy.

If you know only two closes and have used both and neither of them has been successful, you will quickly realize why successful sales people know ten to fifteen closes and use most of them all the time.

You need to ask for the order.

The client will Rarely say YES before you Ask

5. Know "How to Overcome Objections"

You should know why objections occur and how you answer them. You will need to know the difference between a condition and an objection.

Knowing both; why they happen and how to answer them, is Critical!

The first thing a sales person needs to understand is that answering objections is really finding out why the customer is not ready to proceed or make a purchase at that point in time.

An Objection Usually Shows

That there is Further Information Required

The client needs to know something that is important before they will purchase your offerings. Your knowledge of how to handle their objection, will help you find out what they need to know.

This is not Trickery as some may feel.

The Process for "Answering Objections"

It is simply a blue print to follow to answer their questions. There are many reasons why the customer is hesitating and just as many ways to find out their real reason is for the objection.

If you cannot discover the reason for their hesitation and are not able to answer their questions, you probably will not get the order.

6. Knowledge of Presentations

Before preparing your quotation what you need to know

- How do you get the required information?
- What do you need in your presentation?
- Who do you make the quotation to?
- How do you deliver it?
- What do you do at the end?
- What will be your "Call to Action"?

As well you will need to be a good communicator and fully understand the three levels of Communication. You must know how to both deliver your presentation and read your clients reaction.

Preparing for your Presentations

Before you can make a sale, you must find a need for your product or service.

In your prospecting, there will be key questions to ask to uncover such a need. These questions usually take place on your first contact. Your first meeting or second visit will uncover more information and needs.

You will require the answers before you can quote or make an accurate presentation outlining your recommendations. Once you have the answers to your questions, you will prepare your quotation (presentation) so you can get the order.

The presentation will follow a required format if you expect to create the best opportunity to get the sale.

You will need to know the different types of meetings, the purpose of each and the different agendas and timelines.

What You Need to Know for your Presentations

1. How to catch their attention

2. How to hold it long enough to deliver your message.

3. The best way to show benefits and the reasons why your products or services will solve the need(s) that your client has.

4. How to construct your presentation with the ability to easily close when you are done and do it within the proper time line.

5. How to find right people to make your presentation to.

Your presentation; if it is done correctly, will carry right into the opportunity to ask for the order.

7. Knowledge of Prospecting

Some companies will often provide this service through their marketing as it is a function of marketing. If this is the case, you may not be called upon to find clients. Do not ignore this important skillset as it is required for most higher professional sales positions.

For the most part; especially in small and medium sized companies, prospecting will be part of sales and you will need to know how to do it.

- Where to find your prospects?
- Who do you need to contact to get the best results?
- When is the best time to contact them?
- How do you reach them?
- How do you set appointments?
- What do you do on your first visit?

Why you need to know "How to Prospect"

If you have not learned *"how to prospect"* before you start working in certain sales positions, you should get ready for a rough beginning. You will find yourself with appointments to make and not knowing how to make them.

You will not know where to start or even when to prospect.

Prospecting is the key to being successful in sales. Just as the early prospector needed to know where and how to pan for gold; you will also need to know, where to look for clients and how to make appointments.

You will need to know what to do and how to recognize a good prospect when you talk to one. Starting sales without knowing how to prospect is like starting on a long journey without a road map that outlines a pathway to follow.

Summary of Knowledge

If you do not become a master of these areas and obtain a full and an in-depth knowledge of them; you will probably become a mediocre sales person - at best.

You will probably never reach your full potential

Peter Drucker once said: *"Knowledge has power. It controls access to opportunity and advancement."*

Dale Carnegie once said: *"Knowledge isn't power until it is applied."*

It takes a lot of hard work and dedication to learn and master these seven areas of knowledge.

While your company is developing new products, product features, and new and improved services, your competition is doing the same. This acquiring of knowledge is not a onetime thing. Your work place is forever changing, and you must develop a way to keep up with changes.

Brian Tracy once said: *"Those people who develop the ability to continuously acquire knowledge that they can apply to their work and to their lives, will be the movers and shakers in our society for the indefinite future."*

6. Enthusiasm

Adding Enthusiasm is the increasing of an action that will create a greater reaction. When our enthusiasm is positive, and we are passionate about it, we have already sown the seeds for success.

When we add enthusiasm, we pump up the volume, we increase the intensity, we turn a duet into a choir, and we turn a good presentation into a great presentation.

The Dictionary offers the following definitions for Enthusiasm:

1) Lively, absorbing, keen interest
2) Intense and eager enjoyment, interest or approval
3) A source or cause of great excitement or interest

Enthusiasm is the perfect companion to travel with. Watch for the amazing results of this extraordinary cohort.

You will not only be traveling in the right direction, you will have increased the speed and lessened the time it will take you to get there.

Enthusiasm is Contagious

It increases the vibrations and frequency around you. It increases your energy level. It adds power and drive to accomplish your goals.

Be enthusiastic, be excited, and be passionate about your goals and your dreams, and they will surely become a reality.

Ralph Waldo Emerson once said: *"Nothing great was ever achieved without enthusiasm."*

Speeches Without Enthusiasm

Have you ever watched the reaction of an audience when a speaker is talking in a monotone? The audience is twitching, they are looking around, and maybe some are even falling asleep, or leaving the room.

When the speaker is done, maybe the main reason for the crowd's applause is because it is finally over.

Speeches with Enthusiasm

Have you ever watched a crowd or perhaps the same crowd when a new speaker addresses them with enthusiasm? The crowd becomes attentive, they become excited, and no one is sleeping now.

The audience becomes reactive to the message. They may laugh, cry, cheer, and maybe even a produce a jeer; but, they will never be indifferent.

Norman Vincent Peale once said: *"Enthusiasm releases the drive to carry you over obstacles and adds significance to your life."*

About Enthusiasm

Enthusiasm is not always present automatically.

You must summon it.

You must build on it.

You must learn how enthusiasm alone can change the outcome of a sales presentation or situation.

You must work at keeping it with you always, as a partner and as your opportunity to do great things.

Some people may start something with enthusiasm and become discouraged if they do not see the results they desire immediately.

Often the Success They Seek

May lie Just Beyond their Impatience Threshold

Often their concept of immediate might just be minutes, hours or days. Success arrives when it is earned. Enthusiasm can shorten the time that is needed to achieve success, because of its nature and catalytic properties.

It cannot be a synthetic expression looking for a quick result. It must become a raging fire continuously fueled by one's desires. Success takes sustained effort and enthusiasm that comes from within.

Enthusiasm is an Essential part of Sales

It is the Accelerator that Changes

A Mediocre Situation - Into a Great Event

Enthusiasm will help change a prospect's indifference, and their willingness to see you, and hear what you want to say, when you are trying to get appointments.

If you are that enthused about an appointment, they will feel that what you want to say, must be good. When you greet people, show that you are genuinely very happy to meet or to see them. You will notice that your meetings will become exciting and produce greater results than you ever expected.

When you make a presentation, deliver it with enthusiasm, get excited.

Show passion about your company and its product(s). You will instill confidence in your prospect, and a desire to have some of that enthusiasm themselves.

Below is a passage taught to my two brothers and myself by our father - and rehearsed many times in our kitchen and household. It was recited both alone and in competition with each other, to demonstrate how to deliver a message with Enthusiasm.

Try Reciting It Yourself and Add the Enthusiasm

————

"Get into the thick of it

Wade in

Whatever your cherished goal

Brace up your will, till your pulses thrill

And you dare to your very sole

Do something more than make a noise

Let your purpose leap into flame

As you plunge with a cry

I will do or die

Then you

Will be playing

The game"

7. Goal Setting

Without a goal, your efforts become vague and without purpose. Your goal is your vision of what you wish to achieve and enjoy in your job or in your life.

The dictionary describes a goal as:

- The purpose toward which an endeavor is directed
- The finish of a race
- An observable and measurable result having one or more objectives to be achieved within a fixed time frame

There are usually two types of goals.

1. One type is a long-term goal and it can be months, years or even a life time goal.
2. The other type is a short-term one which is usually something to be accomplished within hours, days or weeks.

A Description of "Goal Setting"

Goal Setting is the process of deciding what you want to accomplish and delivering a plan to achieve the result you desire, within a set time.

How often have you heard the following?

"If you want to succeed in life, you must first have a goal."

If you want to be Successful in Sales,

You need to Set Goals.

Seneca once said: *"If one knows NOT what harbor they seek; any wind is the right wind."*

Mary Kay Ash once said: *"A goal is like a strenuous exercise; it makes you stretch."*

In setting goals

Grabbing the first thing that enters your mind might be right, but it could also be wrong. It could be wrong if you are more concerned about having a goal, than having the right goal.

Think of yourself as being single.

You are sitting in your living room one day and a friend says,

"You should get married."

Do you jump up, and run outside, and ask the first person you run into; to marry you? They could say yes, and you better be right, because you will be with that person for the rest of your life, or until a thing called separation or divorce.

Fortunately Making or Changing a Goal is a lot Easier.

Another Example

When you go shopping for an item, do you buy the first one you see, or do you check around and compare and evaluate, so that when you do purchase the item, you know you will be happy with your choice.

I'm not talking about grabbing a coffee or donuts!

Choosing the wrong goal happens more often than you think, and it usually happens when you have not been definite or careful in your original goal-setting.

- It could also be that your original goals were based on insufficient information, and new knowledge has caused you to reconsider them.

- It could be that your original goal was what someone else said or wanted for you, and you now know what you want.

The one thing that will happen is that, if you have chosen the wrong goal, your inner voice will usually tell you.

Listen to that voice that says: *"I have made the wrong goal choice, and I should change it"*

Do not stay with it because you are afraid to say you made a mistake

If it does not feel right

Change it!"

An unknown author once said: *"Though no one can go back and make a brand-new start, anyone can start from now, and make a brand-new ending."*

Goal Setting

Success is already halfway achieved when you get in the habit of setting, striving for and achieving goals. Each step you take toward your goal should be made with the conviction of achieving its successful outcome.

Goal setting is a very important part of your journey as it allows you to clearly see your destination always. Even during the boring tasks or little steps that might seem insignificant, you will see and feel your progress because you are moving toward that goal.

Goal setting is a two-part process.

1. First – You must decide what you want to do.
2. Second – You must devise a plan to achieve it.

The first part is usually easy - but the mistake that is most often made, is that the goal is "too general" to know when you have achieved it.

Examples of too general:

- I am going to increase my efforts
- I want to increase sales.

The right way:

- I will increase my sales calls by 10% starting tomorrow.
- I will increase my sales volume 20% by the end next month.

The How?

The second part is usually more difficult, and it is here that most people have the real problem.

Goals without an action plan or strategy become just words expressing a desire.

You must decide your goal and lay out your plan of action stating how you will reach your goal and when.

The Five goal-setting Ingredients

1. You must be specific in describing your goal and strategy.
2. Your goal must be measurable.
3. It must be attainable.
4. It must be relevant.
5. It must be time sensitive.

A proper Goal Formula Example

"I want to increase my monthly sales by 25% over my current average monthly volumes. I want to achieve this by the end of next month.

To do it I will offer an additional 5% discount over our normal quantity breaks on all merchandise purchased from now until the end of next month. I will use my email lists and social media marketing to achieve it.

Every goal you set, needs to follow this same basic pattern

As previously stated, there are two types of goals.

1. The long-term ones

- The major tasks
- The big ones

2. The short-term ones

- The daily ones
- The weekly ones

1. The Long-Term Goals

These are the main ones, the big ones that are career changers. They can be life-changing and take six months, a year, two years or longer to realize.

Examples

- They might be to earn enough to be able to buy a house in one or two years.
- Maybe you want to become the highest paid sales person in your company.

(Examples Long Term Continued)

- Maybe you want to increase your sales next year by three times this year's amount.

- You might even want to become a sales manager in your company

- Maybe you want to become the Vice-President of Marketing and Sales.

Make sure your goal has the five ingredients mentioned earlier.

An unknown author once said this about goals: *"The greatest danger for most of us is not that our aim is too high, and we miss it, it is that our aim is too low, and we reach it."*

Setting the long-term ones

Setting the big goals should be done with great care.

One should be very clear in what they are setting as their main or big goal(s), because they will become your declaration and your vision of what you wish to achieve.

They will become the beacons that will guide you and provide the constant destination for your efforts. They will be the focal point that will keep you from drifting aimlessly on a sea of uncertainty or doubt.

Keep these points in mind:

1. "If you aim for nothing, you'll hit it every time."
2. "If you do not have something to aim for, you will probably hit everything."

Put your goals in the forefront

Do not just write them down and then put them in a drawer. Put them on your office wall, on your bedroom wall, or over the mirror in your bathroom.

Place them wherever it makes Sense

Look at your goals Every Day

Say your goals out loud with a positive attitude, enthusiasm and commitment.

Out of sight, becomes out of mind, and eventually that unseen goal will lead to a loss of purpose.

Burn your goals into your sub-consciousness by reading them constantly, viewing them every day.

Look at them when you are Starting the day

And at the End of it

Some Examples

Question - Does the captain of a ship begin a voyage without first determining or charting the course the ship must take to reach its destination?

Answer - Unless the captain commits to his destination and the path to follow the ship will become lost at sea or reach any random port.

Question - Does a runner start a race without knowing where the finish line will be?

Answer - Not if they want to complete or win the race.

Most people do not jump out of bed in the morning and look to see which way the wind is blowing and start off in that direction. So, why do so many people, work without a goal and a plan to achieve their goals?

Establish the long-term Goal

The Big Sales Plan

Know your goals intimately, or you will not be able to chart the course.

If employed

Find out what goals your company needs you to reach in the first month, the second or third month, and by the end of the first six months or year.

There is nothing worse or more demoralizing than being wrong in your assumptions, when it comes to what your company needs you to achieve.

Once you know what the company needs, set your own goals. Make them higher than what your company is asking for.

The same Concept Applies!

If you Own the Company

Setting Long Range Goals Involves

- Setting your short-range plans

- Setting your daily plans and goals

- Setting your weekly plans and goals

- Setting monthly Plans and goals

You will need to do this, to reach the longer-range sales plan that you want to achieve.

Always

1) Chase your goals with a passion.
2) Be dedicated.
3) Do not let things keep you from reaching your goals.
4) Apply all the elements you see here.
5) Make this knowledge part of your daily blueprint for success.

Yes, you will have set-backs and failures on the way

If you keep your goal firmly planted in your mind, each time you get up to resume the challenge, you will be pointed in the right direction.

Henry Ford once said: *"Obstacles are those frightful things you see when you take your eyes off your goal."*

2. The Short-Term Goals

These are the smaller projects or steps in a much larger picture. They are your mini goals, and the components of your overall big plan.

They give you the opportunity to measure your progress and they will keep you pointed in the right direction.

They are essential, if you wish to track and obtain the results, that you or your company needs to see.

They become the stepping stones that you must take, when moving towards the big goal. It could be a significant journey to reach your main goal, so it will be necessary to set a few of these markers to pace yourself.

Often mini goals are set by the company's needs, but, it is better to aim higher than the minimum targets; because, that is exactly what they are, MINIMUMS!

To Reach your Goal

The following might be in the Action Plan

1. I will make 150 prospecting contacts by next Friday, and that should result in 5 to 6 prospects for me to see. (per the law of averages)

2. I will schedule the 5 to 6 appointments for the following week for Tuesday, Wednesday and Thursday at 10:00 and 2:30 to allow enough time to gather the information I need.

3. I will draft a presentation outline for each of the prospects seen that day. I will include all the information gathered as well as listing all their needs.

4. After seeing all the appointments that I set for the week, I will establish my plan and timing to finish the presentations for all of them.

5. I will finish preparing my presentations starting with the ones closest to completion while allowing more time for the ones requiring more work and research.

6. I will start setting my follow up appointments for the sales presentations once I have finished preparing the first two.

7. I will keep working until all presentations have been finished, and appointments have been made.

8. I will reserve enough time (approximately one week) to make my presentations to get the orders or schedule my follow ups.

9. Then I will begin the process all over again, while servicing the previous contacts for business obtained and until orders are obtained for the rest.

Thomas Huxley once said: *"The rung of a ladder was never meant to rest upon, but only to hold a person's foot long enough to enable them to put the other one somewhat higher."*

Set Deadlines

A goal without a deadline is like a story without an ending. It is like saying; I will be at your office sometime in the future. Setting a deadline gives the whole journey a sense of purpose and urgency.

"We will meet in your office next Tuesday at 10:00 AM."

Diana Scharf Hunt once said: *"Goals are dreams with deadlines."*

Ralph Waldo Emerson once said: *"We aim above the mark, to hit the mark."*

Success is what you expect to achieve, when you set Goals

One of the biggest prerequisites to becoming successful is doing something you enjoy. You must be happy in your life's undertakings and be excited every morning to get started on your daily endeavors.

You will surely be well on your way to the success you seek, if you enjoy what you are doing.

On the other side

If selling becomes a pathway that that is unpleasant and painful to think of when you get up each day, or causes anger or frustration during the day, sales may not be for you.

Unless it is because you don't have the knowledge that you need, and should learn more, or you have an attitude problem that you can correct, - give your sales path more thought.

If you are always miserable, nothing works, and you hate what you are doing, you may have chosen the wrong profession.

Malcolm Forbes once said: *"Success follows doing what you want to do. There is no other way to be successful."*

Dale Carnegie once said: *"People rarely succeed, unless they have fun in what they are doing."*

What is Success?

I adopted this phrase early in my sales career. It has served me well to always be able to continue my journey, after any setback.

"Success is the progressive realization of a worthy ideal."

Success should be viewed as a journey, not just a point to be reached as one might consider a goal.

If one thinks of, or measures success as a point, a goal, a destination to be reached; they will become discouraged with any failure. The beginning for achieving success is the actual undertaking of *"The Journey"* to reach your goals.

Winston Churchill once said: *"Success is going from failure to failure without the loss of enthusiasm."*

We begin to achieve success by taking the first step on our journey to reach our goals. Every time we continue with that journey after a failure, we are on the right pathway to achieve success.

Striving to reach one's goals, no matter what the setbacks may be, becomes one's own personal success journey.

When a Goal is Reached, - You Are Successful

It means the Completion of that Chapter

It is then time to set new goals, seek new horizons and move on to the next part of your journey.

What many people do not realize is that we are already successful, when we are creating successful thoughts and actions. The result will be reaching our goals every time

Robert Collier once said: *"Success is the sum of small efforts, repeated day in and day out."*

When you Treat Success as a Goal and not a Journey

The results are "NOT GOOD"

What Happens?

- Too many people stop with the first failure and accept it as the outcome of their efforts.

- They allow themselves to fall backwards into the abyss of self-pity and disappointment.

- One must become fixed on their goals and believe they will eventually reach them; no matter what failures happen along the way or how much effort it takes.

Ralph Waldo Emerson once said: *"Our greatest glory is not in never failing, but in rising up every time we fail."*

If one has set meaningful goals, small defeats along the way should be expected. If you look; you will find that in every defeat, there is a message for your success.

If one views the success journey as a smooth path without recognizing, there may be some difficult times; then they may not be prepared for the challenges, that will occur along the way.

Success Comes

✓ With the confidence gained from knowledge

✓ The willingness to work hard

✓ The determination to overcome all obstacles

✓ The persistence needed to finish the task

✓ The readiness to always learn more.

It is the Commitment to Overcome Failure

And not Fear it

Henry David Thoreau once said: *"If one advances confidently in the direction of their dreams, and endeavors to live the life which they have imagined, they will meet with a success unexpected in common hours."*

If we find ourselves in the situation of a failure, it is not the end, but the beginning of creating a renewed pathway for the success we seek.

One Should not be Afraid to Fail

It is a fear of failure itself that will keep one from their greatness successes in life.

Thomas Edison once said: *"Many of life's failures are people who did not know how close they were to success when they gave up."*

Embrace a failure and endeavor to find the positive message that it will contain. Analyze the failure and begin your journey again with this new knowledge.

Mary Pickford once said: – *"You may have a fresh start any moment you choose, for this thing that we call failure is not falling down, but the staying down."*

One thing is for certain. If we give up and accept defeat after any failure, we will surely have no chance for success.

It is the giving up and the acceptance of a failure that will deprive you of your dreams, the joys you want in life and all the goals you seek.

Thomas Edison

It is said; that in his experiments, he failed over 10,000 times before he invented the light bulb.

Where would we be today if he had given up after failure #9,992 and gone on to other things? Instead, he worked until he achieved the goal; that he knew and expected in his mind, would be the outcome of his efforts.

Having strong and unflinching perseverance; is a prerequisite of going the distance to accomplish your goals and reaching the success you desire.

Summary

What we can gather from the words of the sages who have been quoted here, is to expect failure, because it is an integral part of success.

Learn from failure; get up and continue as many times as it takes, to reach the goals we are looking to achieve.

We come back to Attitude and Staying Positive

No matter what happens along the way

A very successful man was once asked: *"When did you know that you were successful?"*

The man Immediately Replied:

"I was successful when I knew what I wanted to achieve in life and asked for it. I knew what I wanted, and I knew that I would get it, if I kept making the effort to get there."

"I set out on my journey knowing this and feeling that I was already in possession of the success I desired."

"I accepted that feeling into every part of my being and rejoiced in my success."

"I knew that I would be successful when I was sleeping in back alleys, living in cardboard boxes, and every time I failed in an endeavor."

"I knew, because I could already see myself reaching my goal, and feeling the joy and happiness that came with it."

Ralph Waldo Emerson once said: *"We become what we think about all day long."*

- If we see ourselves as a failure - we will be one.
- If we see ourselves successful, and we expect it, and know it is ours, then it will be.

This is a natural law of the universe and is spoken in many ways. It is fueled and assisted by all the elements that we have been discussing.

Some other quotes about Success

George Elliot once said: *"It is never too late to be the one you might have been."*

Abraham Lincoln once said: *"Always bear in mind that your own resolution to succeed is more important than any other one thing."*

Winston Churchill once said: *"Continuous effort, not strength or intelligence, is the key to unlocking our potential."*

Malcolm Forbes once said: *"Victory is sweetest when you've known defeat."*

Doug Larson once said: *"Some of the world's greatest feats were accomplished by people not smart enough to know they were impossible."*

Elbert Hubbard once said: *"There is no failure except in no longer trying. There is no defeat except from within, no insurmountable barrier, except our own inherent weakness of purpose."*

Andrew Carnegie once said: *"Don't be afraid to give your best to what seemingly are small jobs. Every time you conquer one, it makes you that much stronger. If you do the little jobs well, the big ones will tend to take care of themselves."*

8. Commitment

It is through commitment that you will create a combined force that will ensure success.

The element of commitment is the catalyst that will bond the other elements into a new higher form that will repel negativity and failure.

The Dictionary Describes Commitment this way:

1. A contract or legally binding agreement
2. The basic philosophy, spirit, and drive of a person or an organization to complete a task

Vince Lombardi once said: *"The quality of a person's life is in direct proportion to the commitment to excellence regardless of their chosen field of endeavor."*

Napoleon Hill once said: *"There is one quality which one must possess to win, and that is definiteness of purpose, which is the knowledge of what one wants, and having a burning desire to possess it."*

There is a Big Difference Between

Being Interested in Doing Something and

Being Committed to Do it

The Difference

- If you are interested in doing it, there is no urgency and you will do it when and if circumstances permit you to do it.

- If you are committed to do something there are no reasons or no excuses that will keep you from the end results.

Your commitment to do something will unlock and open doors for you and turn your desires into reality.

Vince Lombardi once explained an individual's commitment relating to a group effort this way: *"Commitment - That is what makes a team work, a company work, a society work and civilization work."*

9. Optimism

This is another element that you will need to be successful and reach your goals. Without the belief that you will overcome all difficulties to reach what you desire, you will become stalled on the journey to succeed in any task.

Being optimistic about your appointments, your quotations and reaching your goals is your ultimate expression of faith in your ability to finish what you have started.

The Dictionary Describes Optimism this way:

1. Hopefulness and confidence about the future or the successful outcome of something
2. A tendency to expect the best possible outcome or to dwell on the most hopeful aspects of a situation
3. The belief that good ultimately predominates over evil

Optimism is the ability to look at the bright side of any situation and expect the best outcome possible. Optimism is a powerful motivator and is one of the cornerstones of selling success.

Optimism cannot be over-rated as a positive factor in your selling efforts. It allows you to see the positive aspects of any situation and allows you to make the most of any possibility.

It will be Difficult to Succeed

Unless you Believe that you Will

When the self-doubt creeps into a situation, it is the voice of optimism that will change your negative feelings into the expectancy of a positive outcome.

Nicholas Murray Butler once said: *"Optimism is essential to achievement and is also the foundation of courage and true progress."*

Robert Brault once said: *"The average pencil is seven inches long with just a half-inch eraser – in case you thought optimism was dead."*

10. Persistence

If you have set your goals, then do not waiver from the pathway that you have set. Even though there will be many influences along the way that will tell you to give up your cause.

You must Remain Persistent!

Hal Borland once said: *"Knowing trees, I understand the meaning of patience. Knowing grass, I understand the meaning of persistence."*

You have not Set your Course

Just to Abandon it

When the times get rough; and there will be those times when you are in sales, it will take a determined effort to stop yourself from giving up. It will be your optimism, your enthusiasm and persistence that will allow you to complete your task successfully.

Benjamin Franklin once said: *"Energy and persistence conquer all things."*

The Dictionary Says this about Persistence:

1. The act of continuing despite opposition
2. To continue steadfastly, to endure tenaciously

It is said that the persistent salesman gets the order. This is supported by the fact that an average order is often obtained on the 4th, 5th and even higher closing attempts.

This fact also enforces why it is important to know a lot of closes and answers to objections. It is also said that persistence borders on annoyance, so it becomes a thin line between the two.

Since it is your Job to get the order

You will Find that….

Persistence is a necessary ingredient if you wish to obtain what you set out to do, even if it means going to the brink of annoyance.

Persistence is the last of our 10 personal elements that we are presenting. You will need to overcome the many obstacles along the way and clear the roadblocks ahead. With persistence, you will reach your destination.

Dale Carnegie once said: *"Flaming enthusiasm, backed by horse sense and persistence, is the quality that most frequently makes for success."*

Summary of the Personal Elements You Need

Selling is not easy. If you are not armed with the skill sets and the knowledge of the elements you need to have, you invite Failure.

The greatest confidence comes with the knowledge of how to achieve your goals and overcome the negative influences along the way.

You will know; at the beginning of any task, that you possess the knowledge, the ability and the drive to successfully complete it.

Our explanation of the key elements is all about what you need to know behind the scenes to become successful in selling and be able to maintain that success.

Keep these Personal Elements as part of your everyday efforts. If not practiced and maintained, they will not continue to serve your efforts.

These personal elements will be the elements that you have control over. Your success will be affected by how you use them.

WHAT YOUR COMPANY OR EMPLOYER

NEEDS AND WHY

Overview

In this section the elements apply to the company; whether it is yours, or you are employed by the company.

1. A Good Reputation

Your company or employer must have a good reputation to attract clients. No one wants to do business with a company with a bad reputation especially if it is their job or their company that will be affected by the outcome.

If you start working for a company with a questionable reputation; you have little chance of reversing any concerns or doubts your prospects might have. Even if you bring an untarnished image and history, it is your company or employer that will make the final decisions, and everyone knows it.

How it Affects you

If the company you represent is in question, your reputation will also become tarnished by your choice of employment. Any clients that you have brought with you may begin to question your judgment.

Getting hired by a company with a bad reputation will often be reasonably easy. You may find it very hard to find clients who are not aware of the company's reputation.

These types often do not care

These types of companies will always need to keep finding new unsuspecting customers and need to hire new sales people to replace the ones who have left.

This will make your job extremely difficult as you find door after door closing in your search for someone who will be comfortable doing business with you and your company.

As an owner looking after sales, the same conditions will apply to your efforts. Make every effort to change or improve your reputation. It will Affect your Sustainability as a Company

2. Ethics and Integrity

Your company or employer will need proven high ethical standards to create an image of dependability. They must have Integrity to create Trust.

Possessing ethics and integrity yourself will not overcome a situation if your employer does not have them. You will soon find that you're Business Ethics and Integrity will also be in question.

Guard your Integrity

You are entering dangerous territory for your career when you are associated with a company that has little or no ethics or Integrity, and you will soon find yourself painted with the same brush.

Even if you eventually leave this company (which you should) your tarnished reputation will become a difficult item to repair.

Do some Research

That is why it is best to do a little research before joining a company. A little investigation goes a long way in preventing what could become a huge negative mark on your career and future.

If your employer does not possess these elements, your job will always be a hard sell to your clients.

3. Quality Offerings with Benefits

Without some level of quality there is no future. Without benefits, there is nothing to offer your prospects.

You may own or work for a company that does not have the best of both elements; or maybe, not even the best of either of these elements. It is very important to know where the Quality and Benefits of your offerings will be positioned in the eyes of your prospects.

Do they meet an acceptable level that allows you to get sales?

You will probably have a price advantage with a lower quality item. Do not forget that the purchaser will be judged by his or her superiors, on the outcome of their buying decisions.

Once burned, purchasers will avoid making the same *"price based"* mistake again. It may not have been your company or product where they had the involvement; but, the bad experience is all that they need.

It is said by many seasoned purchasers: *"The damage created by a bad product or service choice, is remembered long after the joy or excitement of getting the lowest price."*

If the Quality is Comparable or Close

You will have a good Chance with a lower Price

There is always a demand for products that are price competitive even if the quality is not the highest or the same as others that are being considered. Often getting the best quality is not what your customer is looking for.

The first question should be: *"Will it do the job required and satisfy the customer's quality needs?"*

If the answer to this question is yes; and you also have a price advantage, that's a winning combination and the order should be yours.

A price advantage does not always mean lower quality or fewer benefits. It could simply mean better sourcing or more efficient management practices by your employer.

If the quality is below others; but the prices are the same, you will probably need an extra benefit that will overcome this quality situation. A benefit could be that your company provides better service and back up for their products.

Service More Important

In some cases, service will be more important than the difference in quality (if they are at all close) and could become the reason for choosing you.

In the end; if your company's product or service does not offer a benefit that will improve or solve a customer's needs, then even a lower price does not justify a purchase.

It is better to build or find a company that has a level of product or service quality and benefits, that will allow you to compete in the marketplace.

4. A Commitment to Help

Companies must be committed to help their customers. It is important for your company or employer to be committed to find solutions for problems that might exist to get the order.

Their products must be able to meet the ongoing needs of their customers. This is what will give your company strength and longevity.

Finding a need and filling that need is the key to your company's success as well as your own. Solving problems for their clients will create a secure and permanent place for your company in the business environment.

Beware of these types

a) The only purpose of the company is to make sales or money regardless of what their offerings are doing for their customers.

b) They are hit and run, and make no attempt to solve problems, relating to the performance of their offerings,

They will not Survive for very long

Prospects will soon identify the people and companies who are out to line their own pockets and have no real desire to help their clients.

These companies and salespersons are eventually found out and labeled accordingly.

5. Service Oriented

You will be judged by the service that your company or employer provides. Providing excellent service can often represent a primary need for your clients.

As the saying goes *"Time is Money"* and it is very difficult to replace lost productivity due to poor service.

Many customers place services ahead of price depending on the nature of the offerings.

- Companies who focus on looking after the needs of their customers in a time sensitive manner are always in demand.

- Companies who do not respond quickly or cannot fulfill the servicing requirements are soon abandoned.

6. Happy Satisfied Customers

If you do not own the company, do a little research and find out if your potential employer has happy and satisfied customers.

Happy, satisfied customers are usually loyal customers and provide repeat business. They also are willing to provide good references or refer new business to you.

A company that cares about their clients and looks after them will not always be looking for new prospects to replace the exodus of the unhappy ones.

Beware of a company with a hit and run business model. It will be based primarily, on finding new clients and providing little service or follow up after the sale.

This could mean that they will eventually run out of potential new business in your territory and you will be faced with starting over in a new territory or maybe a new company.

7. Good Marketing

This is essential for success. Eighty percent (80%) of small businesses do not have or use a good marketing plan. This may not always be evident; but, it is a very important element to look for.

Most will probably be doing some type of advertising or marketing and are getting some results. In smaller companies without a structured marketing plan in place, it will probably become your responsibility to provide the marketing or prospecting, as part of your sales duties.

You will solve part of the problem if you are good at it. Without a strong marketing support base behind you, your job will be very difficult.

If you become the companies only sales and marketing efforts, then you have taken on a very large task. The absence of a good marketing plan is the cause of many small and medium sized business failures.

A marketing Plan; if done right, will force the company to establish a procedure to:

- Provide information for you and your prospects about the company's history from the beginnings to present day status.

- Review their company, product or service strengths and weaknesses in the marketplace on a regular basis.

- Review their present and future market possibilities.

- Review their competitors in the same way and find how to compete with them in the marketplace.

- Establish a vision, a mission, set goals and action plans with deadlines.

- Implement or emphasize Branding.

- Establish a good marketing mix (advertising) to reach their prospects.

These are just a few of the areas that will be found in good marketing plans that are important. This explanation of marketing plans is not meant to be any more than making you aware of how important it is for a company to have a good marketing plan.

If they leave everything to you; and they are not committed to providing marketing support, you should think long and hard about working for this kind of company, unless you are up for the task.

8. A Good Work Environment

Happy employees create happy customers. Who wants to work with or for a company where everyone is unhappy or discontent?

How employees are treated will usually be passed on to how the customers of that company are treated.

If management looks after its employees, their employees will almost always look after their customers in the same manner. As a sales person, the results of your job efforts will largely depend on how well your clients are looked after and treated by your internal support team.

9. Loyalty to You

If you are a conscious and loyal employee, you will be putting a lot of time and effort into doing your job to the best of your ability. You will want to know that the company that you are working for will look after you in the same manner.

10. Dependability

Unless the company you are working for is dependable and continuously demonstrates this important element; you will always be trying to make up for their lack of it, with your clients.

Summary to What Your Company Needs

How the company views and handles the 10 Key Elements shown, will have long term effects on keeping both customers and employees.

As an owner; or as an employee, one will be continually faced with overcoming the negative aspects if they are present and not changed. As previously mentioned; as an employee, you have little control here.

WHAT YOUR PROSPECT NEEDS TO HAVE

1. A Genuine Need

Without a need, there is no reason to buy. The most important requirement that you should be looking for in a prospect is that they have a genuine need for your offerings.

The need can come in many forms – 4 examples

1. It could solve a process or production problem
2. It could solve a quality problem
3. It could solve an office procedure problem
4. It could solve a costing problem

The most important responsibility you will have is to find their needs and look after them.

There are many other need types besides the four shown above. We will cover more of them in our other parts of this course.

2. Enough Knowledge to Make the Right Decision

How can you expect your client to purchase your product or service without providing them with enough knowledge to make the right decision?

Your duty is to fully inform the prospect of all the features of your product or service and fully explain how it will help them. Unless you can do this, you will not gain their confidence or trust.

Without confidence and trust, they will not give you their business.

A decision to work with you requires that the client has enough knowledge about your company, its offerings and the benefits they will obtain as a customer, before they can make an informed decision.

3. A Desire or Willingness to Change

There must be willingness to Change. You can be quoting continuously and keep closing until you have no more closes to try.

Unless the customer wants to make a change to a new supplier or try a new product, you will not be successful.

4. The Authority to Act

Without authority, there can be no purchase. This is another big mistake that many sales people make. They put together and deliver a great presentation, only to find out they have made it to the wrong people.

They have no Authority to Purchase

Be sure you are working with the right people and that they can make or greatly influence the final decision.

5. Ethics and Integrity

The company and contact must be ethical and trustworthy. Unless your prospect is ethical and has integrity, you may find all your hard work will benefit others.

- Your presentation and solutions may become the outline to request quotes from others.

Sometimes there is no order and they are just building knowledge to do the project themselves or just impress their superiors with their own knowledge.

The good part is that most customers are ethical and will work with you and give their orders to the people who provide the most service, help and benefits for them or their company. Find out which type they are before spending a lot of time.

6. Honesty

The prospect needs to provide honest information and responses. A customer that cannot provide an honest answer or provide you with honest feedback on your efforts is a customer that you are better off without.

You will always be second guessing their motives and your ability to expect an order. Others may fail to inform you; if changes in the specifications have been made, and your quotation is outdated.

It could be as simple as asking: *"What is most important to you, performance or Price?" or "How does our proposal look? Are we being considered?" or "Have we included everything you asked for?*

Honesty is important in both directions and should not be one sided. Confidence and trust must exist on both sides seller and purchaser or the results will not be beneficial.

7. Appreciation of Your Time

You do not want prospects that do not respect your time. Too often a purchaser will request five or six quotes just to educate themselves on all the possibilities for their project.

This might be good for them; but. there is no consideration for the time that all the vendors are spending in pursuit of the order. All of them are kept on the hook until the end for leveraging and knowledge purposes.

It is often difficult to establish these intentions; but if you feel the validity of an order or project is in question, you need to verify the following:

- Is there a project or an order to be placed?
- Is the prospect prepared to act if all requirements are met?
- When will this happen?
- Does your final quote incorporate all the requirements?

Find out Early

You should establish as early in the game as possible, if they are wasting your time. They should be willing to provide some feedback at various points; to allow you to decide, if more time should be spent.

Some large projects can take 200 to 300 hours to assemble and present. You do not want to spend all this time; only to find, that you are not even in contention or there is no potential order.

There are many other ways that prospects will waste your time only to benefit their own purposes. Be aware of the early indicators of such prospects and move on.

8. Commitment to Act

They need to demonstrate their Commitment to act. Too many prospects will just be gathering information for future planning and that is OK if it is stated up front.

The choice is then your own as to how much time you will spend. You should establish these parameters early in your efforts.

1. Have all the specifications been provided for you to quote?
2. When are the quotations due?
3. How long before they will decide?
4. When will the project commence or order be placed?

Unfortunately, there are many who have no intention to act upon the project even if all the conditions are met.

9. The Ability to Pay

The prospect needs to demonstrate their financial ability to pay. The easiest prospects to sell your offerings to; will often be the ones, who cannot afford to pay or do not intend to pay.

They provide excuses or find reasons not to pay your company; once your products are delivered, or your services are completed.

Make sure your company's financial department does a credit check before you waste a lot of time in pursuit of this kind of business. If you do not ask in advance; it may be your job that is on the line if a lot of time is wasted or you get the order, and the client does not pay.

The Excuses

There are many excuses that can be presented for nonpayment. These companies usually have a history of these kinds of occurrences and are experts at coming up with the excuses.

If you ask and your company fails to do a proper credit check, then at least all the fingers are not all pointed at you.

There are usually indicators along the way, and you must act upon any suspicions you may have. Failure to do so, could possibly cost you your job and may affect your reputation as well.

10. Loyalty

Without customer loyalty, there is no future. You and your company should be looking for sustainability. If both you and your company look after your customers, you both should expect to be able to make a profit and can have them as loyal repeat customers.

Beware of those who are only after a one-time price or delivery advantage. Loyal customers should be what every company is after to stay in business. If your prospect is a price shopper and looking for the bargain of the day, there will be signs.

Your job is Not to Convert

Do not waste your time or your company's time to try and convert these types of prospects. Yes, quote them and make sure you make a profit for your company when you do quote.

Unless you can continue supplying bargains, you will probably find that price is their only loyalty and could be a onetime sale for you, often involving very little profit.

Most customers will reward your efforts with the order, their loyalty and repeat business. It is up to you to be able to recognize the ones who are only out for a one-time price advantage and will not become Loyal Customers.

SUMMARY TO THE ELEMENTS

We believe that recognizing and accepting the importance of these three areas of key elements for success, is the first step in the process of learning the art of selling.

They are all components that you will need to learn, accept and make part of your selling activities all the time, to be fully successful in sales.

You must be totally prepared to incorporate them into the everyday efforts of your sales career.

Often Ignored

As we indicated at the start of this "Part One" of our sales training, these elements and principles are often ignored by other sales trainers. They are also often ridiculed by many as platitudes, hype and not relative to success in selling.

Thus, many *could-be* sales professionals will obtain mediocre results or experience failure even if they possess the other kill sets that they need.

They will lack the basic structure to protect them from all the negative aspects that they will run into during their journey.

Recognize the importance of these elements. Utilize the knowledge that we have provided and enjoy a successful career.

END OF PART ONE

DIRECT SALES 101

PART TWO

QUALIFYING AND CLOSING

Written by

Wayne E Shillum

INTRODUCTION

QUALIFYING IS THE FIRST PART OF

THE SELLING PROCESS

THE SELLING PROCESS is a journey that involves creating the complete transformation of a stranger or potential prospect into a buying customer.

Your selling process begins with the qualification of the client's needs and their willingness to genuinely consider your offerings.

The qualifying continues with the verification of their interest throughout the entire journey and reaffirming your accuracy in providing the solutions to meet their needs.

It is also Confirming that they meet your Company's Needs

Closing is not just something that comes at the end of your efforts. It is a planned course of action structured to reach a positive result, which is "the completion of the sale."

The common references that are made to "Closing the Sale" will usually describe it as the point in time; when you are in front of the prospect, at the end of your sales presentation, and you are asking for the order.

Not Completely True

The Close is not just a point to be reached. It does not come only at the end of your sales presentation. "Closing the sale" is the journey you take to reach the final confirmation of your efforts.

Both Qualifying and Closing

Allow you to Accomplish "The Selling Process"

The Beginning

You should be shaping your final close right from the minute you open your mouth and the first time you contact or talk to your prospect.

1. The process starts with establishing that there is a need and interest in your products or services (offerings).

2. You will then learn how the client will benefit from your offerings through your meeting(s), before you make your final presentation.

3. At the end of your final presentation, you will ask for the order and Answer any Questions to secure it.

Whenever you ask a closing question, you will often get a question or objection to placing the order with you.

Closing and Overcoming Objections are a team; (which we call the "Dynamic Duo"). We will cover them in two separate parts of our training for clarity sake. *(Overcoming Objections is our Part Three.)*

Some people may think that teaching the skill sets of Closing and Overcoming Objections this early in the sales training, is out of sequence.

Yes, prospecting or finding clients is usually what you will do first in your sales efforts. Holding introductory and fact-finding Meetings is also an activity early in the process.

However; both the knowledge of Closing and the Overcoming of Objections are essential skill sets that are required, before you are able do anything else in the selling process.

They Will Be Needed

- As soon as you start prospecting
- When you contact your first prospect
- During your introductory and fact-finding meetings
- In your final presentations.

Qualifying, Pre-Closes, Final-Closes

There are many ways to qualify, pre-close and make your final closing attempts. You should know as many closes or closing questions as possible, because each situation will be a little different.

1. **Qualifying** a prospect is achieved by asking closing questions.
2. **Pre-Closing** questions are also needed to confirm that you are moving in the right direction in your information gathering meetings and during your final presentations.
3. **Final Closing** – These attempts should get the order.

The Prospect's Answers will show if your efforts are successful

There will be similarities to many closing attempts. With knowledge and practice, you will be able to select the right qualifying questions or closing method.

The Real Purpose

Memorizing the sample questions or the closes that we will be providing, does not mean you will need to recite them verbatim. The secret is to learn them, understand how they work, and why they work; so, you can put them into your own words and everyday use.

- The closing process must become you
- Not a robot that is repeating someone else's words verbatim.

What the Qualifying and Closing Process Involves

It Determines if you have a real potential client by:

1) Establishing Needs
2) Finding Solutions
3) Creating Interest and Desire to Purchase
4) Having a Compelling "Call to Action"
5) Getting the Order when you are done
6) Staying on course during the entire process

The Closing Process

1) Qualifying

In Part One, we outlined the key elements that need to be present in a prospect. Qualifying verifies that these elements are there. Qualifying is essential, and it is the first part of the closing process.

Qualifying establishes a prospect's needs, their willingness to consider your offerings, and the desire and ability to pay. It is better to miss one potential client by over qualification than waste time with 10 or 15 who have no potential.

The best part about taking this qualifying approach is; that if you feel afterward that you have missed a good potential client in the process, you can always call them back and have a second chance.

In the meantime, you have saved a lot of time by removing prospects with no potential. Not everyone will become a customer!

2) Pre-Closing

When you make, your follow-up calls to gather more information for your sales presentations, you should also be asking questions that further shape your final close.

Too many sales people visit the prospect and tell them what they are selling and try to convince the client to purchase their offerings without finding out if their offerings will meet the prospects needs.

They Spend Too Much Time Telling

Not Enough Time Asking and Listening

The goal of a sales person, is to discover where they can help their prospect achieve what they are looking for. You must show the prospect that your mission is the same mission as theirs.

This mission is to find a solution to any problem they have or meet any requirements that they have and provide the benefits of your offerings in the process.

The Procrastinators

The questions that you will ask during your initial meetings are all mini closes to determine if the prospect has a need, any interest in trying your offerings and often missed, the intent to buy or ability to pay.

The procrastinating sales people who wait until the end to ask any qualifying or closing questions will waste a lot of time. They are often so afraid of hearing a NO, that they will postpone any attempt that will Create one.

They rush through their presentation covering all their features and benefits without giving the prospect a chance to say anything. They are then surprised when they are done, when the prospect thanks them for coming and says they do not have a need and are not interested.

Meetings or sales presentations without interaction between the client and the sales person are monologues without direction or purpose. They are usually a waste of everyone's time. If there is no need or interest, there is no reason to present your offerings.

3) The Final Close

People who feel that the customer will automatically place the order without being asked; are doomed to mediocrity or failure. In most cases; even when making a great presentation, there will still be a need for a closing question to complete the mission.

Prospects Expect you to Ask

The fact is that most clients expect a close at the end of any presentation. If there is no closing request, they are usually surprised and perhaps happy there is no commitment requested.

Some people starting out in sales expect that an order automatically comes after a good presentation, and they do not know any closes. Some will know two or three closes and feel prepared.

The truth is that most sales are made on the fourth or fifth attempt to close. Some may even take six or more. If a person knows only two or three closes, how successful do you think they will be?

ESTABLISHMENT OF NEEDS

As Previously mentioned, the mistake often made by many salespeople is that they fail to qualify their prospect and establish if they have any needs or desire to consider a change.

They waste their own time, their company's time and their client's time by delaying the first part of the closing process which is to *"qualify the prospect."*

The Fear of a "NO"

Often it is just the fear of hearing a *"NO"* that holds the sales person back from qualifying their prospect. Many sales people feel secure in having many prospects who have not yet said either yes or no.

Surrounding oneself with many *Maybes* is dangerous because it creates a false comfort zone. Unfortunately, these comfortable salespeople do not realize that getting a NO is good, because it allows them to move on to the yes's.

The removal of the No's allows the sales person to concentrate totally on the real potential.

Too often the salesperson does not qualify. They oversell themselves and their company and the appointment is made. The presentation is given to someone who has absolutely no need for their offerings and no desire to purchase them.

Why are we placing so much emphasis on this? The reason is that sales people keep making this mistake repeatedly. Perhaps they feel they are giving up too soon and the prospect needs convincing. Success in prospecting does not always mean an appointment is made.

A Positive Result can be a:

- No - No need - Not interested - No desire to change

Yes, your list of potential clients may drop significantly; but, you now have more time to spend with your qualified prospects.

Eliminating the No's should be viewed as a huge success. When you treat a No as a positive thing, you will not fear one. You will then able to concentrate on the people with the real potential to buy your offerings.

They are the ones with the yes's.

You just say to yourself *"That's great another NO out of the way, I am now getting closer to the Yes's."*

The yes prospects will eventually say: *"YES I will purchase your offerings*

"If you do things right"

Qualifying a Prospect's Needs

This is the first part of your closing process; and like the early pioneering prospectors crouched over a river, it involves removing the debris, so you can get to the gold (the order).

Do not fear the "NO" Responses

They are Necessary to get to the YES ones

Create a list of Qualifying Questions

Each type of offering (product or service) will have many qualifying questions you can use. Make a list of as many simple questions that will qualify your prospect for a need or interest.

Your Opening Remarks

Create a compelling introduction of yourself and your company. Do not babble on about nothing.

Quickly state the reason for your call in a manner that will get their attention and create interest and a desire to hear more.

Remember that you are not calling for your needs, you are looking for prospects who can benefit from your products or services. Once the interest has been created, do not waste time. Get right into your questions.

Some Sample Questions for Industrial Sales

You Ask – "In your manufacturing process:

1. Do you paint your product or send it out to be painted?
2. Do you do any welding?

3. Do you exhaust any contaminants to atmosphere?

4. Do you use packaging materials?

5. What type of material handling equipment do you use?

6. What types of software do you use?

Let the client know that you are asking these questions to qualify if they could possibly benefit from your offerings before you make an appointment and waste both of your times.

You are not only showing respect for their time, you are showing that you are organized and thorough in your efforts to help your clients. You are not available unless there is some interest and a reason for a visit.

Structure your questions and information provided; so, that the reason for your appointment, is very clear to your prospect. This method of Qualification will eliminate most of your wasted calls where there is no need or interest.

It is better to quickly eliminate 10 prospects with no need or interest through these questions, rather than make 10 appointments and waste gas, and perhaps 2 – 3 days doing the qualifying in person.

Prospects will often be surprised if they need to qualify for a visit. You should phrase it so that it appears to be respect for *"their time."*

Finding More Needs

Needs will take many forms and can be as simple as supplying a product or service. It could be a more involved process which may require finding the solution to a complex problem.

It might be price related or quality, service, size and maybe even appearance. Each type of direct sales will have its own requirements.

You should develop a complete inventory of ways in which your offerings can satisfy your prospects interests – whatever they may be. Your offerings will determine the questions that you will ask.

Each type of direct sales will involve different questions and different client needs. It will be your job to find the right qualifying questions for the type of direct sales company that you represent.

You will then guide the prospect through the complete process

Here are just a few examples of needs that you might look for. They all can become trial closes to qualify your prospect when you ask if they want to achieve something.

The Questions below can relate to many client types

You Ask – Would you like to:

- Save energy?
- Reduce labor costs?
- Increase quality?
- Reduce noise?
- Remove odors, smoke or harmful particulates?
- Solve a safety infringement?
- Reduce water consumption?
- Reduce the time to complete a repetitive task?
- Increase Production Efficiency?
- Save on process material costs?
- Reduce floor space?
- Replace old equipment with better technology?
- Improve service response time?
- Cut costs of office products, or shipping costs and time?

Each yes to one of these questions about needs, will become a key point in your introductory meeting and your final presentation.

Willingness to Change

Along with establishing a need, you will be faced with the prospects willingness to make a change.

There is no sense in proceeding if the prospect is absolutely opposed to making any changes to their present suppliers. Make the effort however, as most purchasers will resist change and object to your initial effort. It is a normal reaction.

Not Interested in a Visit

You can provide or send some information for them to look at, and then move on. Follow up at a future time to see if you sparked some interest.

Goal Met

If you can establish a need, show the benefits and create a willingness to listen further; you have completed the initial qualifying of your prospect.

The qualifying questions or small mini-closes you use while establishing needs, should not be intimidating, because they show the client that you are working with them to meet their requirements or solve a problem.

Before you can build confidence and trust, you must become a comrade in arms with your prospect.

You must take whatever time and effort is required to provide them with the right answers and proper solutions.

Keep on Track

During the entire presentation or closing process, you should be constantly reaffirming that your prospect is happy with your progress and that you are on the right track.

These are the qualifying closes or questions; and if done correctly, they will seem like part of finding the perfect solution for the prospect.

At the end of your presentations when you have put in all the effort to satisfy your prospects requirements; and have shown the benefits of your offerings, you should still be asking for the order not waiting for it to arrive.

The Final Close is where you will find out if you have covered all the bases and met or solved all their requirements.

ABOUT CLOSING

Closing questions are used everywhere in life; but in sales, they are very important tools that you will use to succeed.

They are not wrong because they will help you achieve the results that the company wanted when they hired you.

Or the Results You Wanted

When you Started your Business

The closes will help you reach all your sales targets and achieve your personal financial goals as well. Why spend all the time and money to reach the end of the selling process, if you do not ask for the sale.

Most prospects expect you to close because it gives them the chance to say no, ask a question or a chance to say yes.

Without Closing

You Have No Destination

The final close or request for a purchase order is where every presentation is headed and everyone, especially your prospect, knows it.

Do not Disappoint them!

If you do not ask, you may not get the sale. You could deprive the prospect from saying yes to the close which you have omitted from your presentation.

The fatal mistake that is most often made by many sales people, is that they know only one close or will make only one attempt to close.

When the prospect says no, the sales person may be faced with an objection or question and will try and handle it. If that does not work; they are defeated and can only go but back to the office or home.

How Many Times do you Need to Close?

The reality is that most sales are made on the fourth or fifth closing attempt; so, if you only know two or three closes, you have already limited your chances for success.

Like a Person Fishing

If one starts fishing and they have only one lure to use, the fish may not find it persuasive enough to go after, or it could get snagged on the bottom and the fishing is over.

The Day is Lost

The Secret

The secret to successful closing is to learn as many different closes as you can find. Once learned, practice them until the wording is you; and does not sound like someone else's words, that you are reciting.

Each close will suit a different set of circumstances and you will eventually see the signs of when and where to use the right close.

Most Important

In learning the closes; understand how and why they work so you can put them into your own words. They will then become as natural as breathing.

They will then not be intimidating or appear to be pressure tactics to your prospects. The entire prospecting and presentation process is a close. As we said earlier, the minute you open your mouth, you start the close.

The Best way to Learn

"When it's time" To Make your Final Close

Is by Closing Too Soon and Too Often

By asking closing questions or qualifying your prospect frequently, you will rarely appear to be applying pressure. You are simply doing things correctly to look after your prospects best interests.

Closes Generate Objections

Expect Objections as they are part of the process. You will soon learn in the next part of the training, that Objections are good things. They are clues that can show a prospects weakness or their reason to buy.

If you are not getting objections you are probably not asking enough qualifying or closing questions.

Many prospects (purchasers) will have several pet objections that they know will stop most sales people in their tracks when they start to ask for the order.

Arm yourself with as many closes and answers to objections as you can. All you need is one more closing question or answer to their objection; than the prospect can present, and you win the prize.

Closes and Answering Objections are a Team

They are the dynamic duo of successful selling. When you have mastered the closes and learned how to answer objections (which we also call questions) you will be in control of your own sales destiny.

We will be providing eleven main closing methods plus many smaller closing questions for you to get started with. *(Overcoming Objections will be Part 3)*

There are many more closing methods than the ones we will outline here in this part of our training. If you are serious about sales, you will keep reading, listening and learning new closes.

You will Never know too many

The more closes and answers to objections that you learn and commit to memory, that become part of your tool kit in sales; the higher will be your closing ratio and earnings.

Make sure you have covered everything necessary in your presentation and you feel that there is nothing left for you to say or add. Then you ask the Final Closing Question to Purchase your products or services.

THE GREATEST CLOSING TIP EVER!

THE MOST IMPORTANT PART TO CLOSING

IS

Whenever you Ask a Closing Question

SHUT UP!!

SHUT UP AND LISTEN!!

After you have Asked a Closing Question

The First Person that Speaks

LOSES!!

I do not know what happens to sales people. They ask a closing question and they wait a few seconds, they get excited and they panic.

They then start babbling on and try to add more to their presentation.

WHAT HAPPENS?

They let their Prospect "Off the Hook."

AND YOU KNOW WHAT ELSE HAPPENS?

THE SALES PERSON LOSES!!!

There is no Greater Pressure to a Closing Question Than

"THE SILENCE"

That comes after it…. So

SHUT UP AND LISTEN!

The Prospect will either give you

An Important Answer - An Order...Or - They will have an Objection (question)

After the next part of our training, you will be able to handle the objections as well.

An Objection is a reason for hesitation or a question that needs to be answered before you can complete the sale.

Without Qualifying and Closing Questions

You will Never reach this point

Where you will get an Objection.

What Closes Accomplish

- Mini closes provide you with answers and confirmations along the way.
- Knowing your Closes provides you with a place to go, after you have completed your presentation.
- Your Main Closes will either get the order or raise an objection.
- Raising the Objection provides the means to confirm the sale is yours.

Closes are the means to achieve your goals in this entire process of sales. They are not called closes without reason as they provide closure to all the events leading up to and including getting the sale.

There is no better feeling of confidence or control, then knowing how to get the sale when you are at the end of your journey.

Closing Creates the Prospects Deciding Moment

Answering Objections is the Other Half

Of the Dynamic Duo Team

To Solidify the Order

CLOSING QUESTIONS

What are Closing Questions

As we have already said, one way of making your closing ratios higher, is to ask small closing questions throughout all your meetings with your clients. These questions are also indicators to show if you still have a real prospect and continue to have their interest.

If you do not have a real prospect or their interest, you will not only need to know it; but, you will need to dig deeper, try harder or look elsewhere.

There is nothing worse than allowing someone to listen to your entire presentation without finding out if they are a real candidate for your offerings. Closing Questions will help you to prevent wasting time when no sale is there.

They are Your Directional Tools

They are the

1. What?
2. When?
3. Where?
4. Why?
5. How?
6. Which?

Methods for you to get an order, or the way to eliminate a no need or no desire. Closing Questions are the shortest forms of closing that will cause your prospects to purchase from you.

Ways to Ask Closing Questions

The Indicators

Whenever you ask a question that begins with a verb, the answer is always either a yes or a no indication revealing a person's preference. The person who is asking the question(s) has control.

1. Do you prefer the red or the yellow enclosure?
2. Will you be happy with fewer rejects?
3. Is your main goal to increase productivity?

There are also two types of questions

1. Open ended Questions
2. Closing Questions

1) The Open-Ended Question

Open ended questions are used to get the prospect to explain their thoughts or concerns in more detail. These questions will be used in your exploration of where or why they might need your offerings.

You may also want to have more information to solve a problem, meet a need or show a benefit.

Sample Open-ended Questions

- What quality problems are you having?
- How much time are you trying to save?
- Where are your production bottlenecks?
- Why are you changing the plant location of your packaging?

2) Closing Questions

The closing question directs the client to a yes or no and moves them in the direction of a sale.

When you ask these types of questions, you already have the information you need and are in the process of securing the order.

There are two types of Closing Questions

1. Positive.
2. Negative.

1) Positive Closing Questions

If the positive question gets a YES; (which is what you are after in this approach). It moves you towards a sale. If you get a no from these questions, change directions to get them back into the "Yes" mode.

Examples:

- Are you using this type of product in your production?
- Is this what you are looking for?
- Will you be deciding this week?

If the positive closing question gets a NO, it can be considered as directional or an elimination process and you need to keep going until you start getting yes answers again.

2) Negative Closing Questions

If the negative question gets a NO which is what you are hoping for, it moves you towards a sale.

Here a NO response Is

A Positive Directional Indicator for you

Getting a yes to a negative close is **NOT** a good response and **NOT** what you are after.

Examples of Negative Closing Questions:

- Are you happy with your present supplier?
- Is their product providing all the benefits you need?
- Are you happy with the delivery times of your present supplier?
- Are you happy with the quality of your present supplier's product?

If the negative question gets a YES, you need to continue until you start getting NO answers.

Final Closing Questions

When we use Final Closing Questions we are looking for confirmation of the order. Many times, all we need to use is this simple form of closing to get the sale.

The client has shown all the buying signals and the time is right for a simple question, the answer to which, confirms they have bought.

Closing Question Tips

Many times, you need only to ask for the order in a simple question.

- It could be at the end of your presentation.

- It could be after using one or more of your closing methods and you need a simple confirmation that they have bought.

- It could be after answering an objection or many objections (questions); you also need clarification and confirmation.

- You need to know if you have met their concerns and if they are now ready to proceed.

Often it is all that you Need

To get the order

Twelve Sample Final Closing Questions

1. Can we consider this is a yes for our product/service/project?
2. Shall we start by initialing the changes on the proposal?
3. Do you have a Purchase Order number?
4. Will you be proceeding with the order now that we agree?
5. Are you ready to get started with the project/service?
6. IF we have completely answered all your concerns, shall we get started with the order?
7. Does this mean that we are now your supplier of this product/service?
8. Have we now met all your needs to supply our offerings?
9. Shall we now consider that we are proceeding with the project?

10. When can we schedule the first shipment?

11. When would you like us to start the service?

12. When would you like the drawings for approval?

There are many more that you will be able to create for your offerings. Start a list of simple questions and keep adding to it. It is often these simple closing questions that will unlock the stalled ordering process and clarify that they have bought.

These Smaller Closing Questions can:

- Eliminate the need for a larger closing method
- Assist you when clarification of an order is needed

INTRODUCTION TO THE CLOSES

YOUR FIRST ELEVEN CLOSES

These should become some of the closes that you will use in many areas along the way to get the order. They can be used anywhere and not just at the end when you are asking for final confirmation of the purchase.

Each one will have a distinct time when its use will become obvious to you. With experience, you will clearly recognize when, where and why to use a specific close.

Your Destinations

These closes are the ports where you are headed on your sales journey. Some will be used part way through the journey and others will become closes that you will use when you reach your destination.

By knowing them you can also create many new variations and shorter or longer ones to suit a situation. They are all simply the conceptual ways to reach your goal, which is the order.

Knowing these closes will provide confidence and power. You will know that your journey is not without the means of closure. You will know that when you get to the end of your final presentation that you have control over the outcome to get an order.

Do not Stop at these 11 closes

As we have said earlier these are just eleven of the basic closes that are available to help you reach your goal. They will give you the opportunity to handle most situations that you will encounter.

It will take the use of four or five of these closes in many selling situations to get the order. Do not be afraid to use as many as it takes.

Closes are the vehicles you will use to provide a positive outcome during your journey; and obtain the success you desire, at the end of your journey.

Close # 1 - Alternate of Choice

This alternative of choice close is one that is used everywhere.

It is used:

- When making appointments - choosing the time, day or week
- As minor closes in the presentation
- In the final closing of the sale itself

How and Why it works

If you give your prospect only one choice; the answer will more often be a NO, than a yes. People like choices and when you ask which do you prefer, they feel that they are in control.

They may not choose either; but, they will probably tell you what they prefer as an alternative.

Examples:

Setting the Week and Day of an Appointment

1. *"Would you prefer next week or the following week?"*
2. *"Is Monday good or is Wednesday a better day next week?"*

Setting the time of day is next

1. *"Which is best for you, mornings or afternoons?"*
2. *Afternoons great*
3. *"Would 1:30 PM be OK or would 3:00 PM be a better time for you?"*

Confirm the appointment when you are done: *"OK we will see you next week on Wednesday at 1:30.*

It is a comfortable way of controlling and directing the time that you will see your client.

In most cases the prospect is not intimidated by these types of questions as they are normal and used by most, when setting appointments.

Sample Alternate of Choice Qualifying/Closing

a) General Questioning

- *Which is most important for you - price or quality?*
- *Do you have a preference of – North American made products or will off shore be acceptable?*
- *Do you prefer - Contractual services or do you order on an "as required" basis?*

b) During your Information Gathering

- *Was it less space or less noise that was most important?*
- *Which model do you prefer, the C100 model or the C150 with extra outlets?*
- *What is the maximum part length, six feet or ten feet?*
- *Do you prefer the mounted unit, or the portable type?*

During Final Presentation

- *Which layout do you prefer, number one, or number two?*
- *Which color would you like, the yellow or the blue?*
- *Would May 1st be a good start date, or would you prefer May 15th?*

As a final close, make sure the client has enough information, as this is a simple question and requires only a simple answer.

Close # 2 - Order Blank

This is perhaps the most basic close of them all and will consist of a simple request to obtain your prospect's signature of approval.

Before presenting any document for approval, one must be sure they are showing exactly what the customer wants or has verbally agreed to, or it will not work.

You mast review its contents with your client completely and ask your mini-closes during this process. When you are finished and there are no issues, ask them to - *OK it or approve it.*

NEVER ASK THEM TO SIGN IT!!

For Your First Order

It could come after introducing and testing your offerings and you have made an initial list of requirements to start the delivery of your products.

Note: This will not work as an easy close if you have not dealt with all their requirements or if they still have unanswered concerns.

Move Slowly

If you rush this close before it makes sense to use it, you may be starting over from the beginning. You should have already obtained several yes responses or indications that they agree.

You might need to use more than one of these to get the final go ahead.

- *Is there any reason why we cannot proceed?*
- *Do you have any concerns to prevent us from getting started?*
- *Shall we get things underway?*
- *What Purchase Order Number shall I use for reference?*

At the appropriate time, you can turn the paperwork around and hand the prospect your pen and ask them to approve it or OK it.

Repeat Business

This is often used after you have established a working relationship with a prospect, and you are there to get an order.

You will use this when you have just completed a final review of their inventory or presented a list of your recommendations. You simply show them your list and ask them to OK it?

A Larger Order

It could also be used at the end of a 20-page presentation that has been given by you.

You have several hard copies that outline all the criteria that the customer has asked for, and you have answered all the questions.

If required; you should have made the changes to the proposal as you have gone through it, you have initialed each change and each page as you proceeded through the document.

You should wait until the entire proposal has been reviewed and you have made all the changes and placed your initials beside the changes.

You now place your signature in the appropriate location on the final page of the proposal and date it.

You then turn the proposal toward the client and you ask the following:
"Let's review the changes we have made and if you agree with the wording of the change, just place your initials beside mine."

When all changes have been initialed they may automatically put their signature on the document and date it as you have done.

If they hesitate, you simply say: "All that's left is for you to approve the document, date it and we can get started."

If Requested

At this point the customer may not like the idea of the initialed document. You can indicate that after they have initialed the changes; and approved and dated all the copies; you will prepare a new clean document.

By initialing and approving this one, you can use your copy to create a clean copy for each of you. They will retain their copy of the initialed one until the new one is completed and can verify all the changes have been made correctly.

Note: The new clean copy may be a necessary step, but it should not prevent you from getting an order with the initialed one.

If there have been several changes, additional descriptive wording has been added and initialed and the document is cluttered, it may simply be a comfort thing.

By initialing and approving the altered document before you leave, you have achieved a sale.

The Right Way to Ask

- Do not - ask them to Sign it.
- To sign you need a lawyer.
- Ask them to Initial the changes or OK it or APPROVE it.
- Do not refer to it as a Contract!
- The same situation exists regarding needing a lawyer.
- Refer to it as a document or an Agreement.
- People will OK or Approve a document or an Agreement.
- They just won't Sign a Contract.

Always provide the new clean copy signed. Provide several copies of your signed clean document with the client, placing removable tabs where each change was made.

Ask if they want to review it now or shall you come back tomorrow or the next day to pick up your copy. Do not panic if they want to look it over. You have the original hand written one and it is a legal commitment.

Close # 3 - Question/Question

The question/question situation is one of the most obvious of all the buying signals that exists, yet sales people are almost always missing this opportunity to close.

The client's question usually comes from a position of real interest in the product or service. The prospect is ready to buy and has a simple question.

This is where many sales people miss their chance to close.

Without thinking or recognizing the opportunity or the buying signal, the sales person simply answers the question and misses the opportunity to get the order.

YOU MUST!

Answer their Question

With Your Question

1. Sample question by Prospect – Start Date

The prospect asks: *"Can you start in two weeks?"*

Here is the Wrong way to Answer

The Unprepared sales person says: *"Yes we can"*.

> Why was this just answered the wrong way?
>
> Yes! It is a correct answer,
>
> But the wrong one for closing
>
> They just lost an opportunity to close.

This simple response has just left the closing process open ended and will require more closing attempts.

Answered the right way

Reply to it with a Question in this way: *"If we can start in two weeks, shall I schedule it for then?"*

> Now – when the client says YES
>
> They have made the purchase
>
> It is so simple, that it is often not recognized.

2. Sample question by Prospect - Colour

The prospect asks: *"Can I get it in Blue?"*

The sales person replies: *"Yes you can get it in Blue."*

The Wrong way to answer again!

> Why have they just answered the wrong way?
>
> Again, it is a correct answer
>
> But the wrong one for closing
>
> And they missed the sale.

Answered the right way

Answer the Question with a Question: *"Do you want it in Blue?"*

If they say YES!

The prospect has bought.

3. Sample question by Prospect - Model Type

The prospect asks: *"Does it come as a portable unit?*

Another Wrong Answer

The sales person says: *"Yes!"*

Again, answered the wrong way

Again, a correct answer,

But the wrong one for closing

It is not going to get the sale.

Answered the right way

Answer the question with a question: *"Do you want the portable unit?"*

When the prospect says YES,

They have bought.

Do not just answer yes!

Turn their Question into your Closing Question

And

GET THE ORDER!

Close #4 – Free Trials

We will outline two approaches for **Free Trials** - A, and B. We will show the trial parameters of each.

We will summarize and provide the closing method which will be similar for approaches A and B, because they are trials using tangible offerings.

Approach A) Free Trial - No Up-Front Close

The Trial Parameters

- This approach is often used with offerings that will involve a larger cost for equipment or services.

- It could also involve a significant change in the present way of how the client is doing things.

- The product or service may be a new concept or just new to the client.

- The prospect is uncertain of the benefits or its dependability or Return on Investment. They are reluctant to try something different or new.

- The prospect is probably satisfied with their existing equipment, products or services and needs a nudge to consider something else.

What better way than a "Free Trial"

This is a soft sell approach that gives the sales person the opportunity to get a foot in the door. (as the saying goes)

Their prospect can try something at no cost or up-front commitment, which often eliminates any objections.

It is an extremely good way to introduce products or services that perform better, increase productivity, are easier to use, reduce cost of materials, increase quality or improve appearance.

In the end

The Product or Service Sells Itself

Note: In the following two examples, you will see how the trial is presented. You will change the wording to suit your own offerings.

There will be many versions because of the wide range of products or services that can be offered. The two examples are conceptual.

Example 1 – Try the Offering for a set time for Free

This is great for equipment or services that can be easily integrated into present activity. It can be used in both office or plant environments.

This approach was used a lot when *Color TV* first appeared. It is often referred to as the "Puppy Dog Close." The TV appliance dealer would approach the prospect in the store, who was looking at the color TV.

The dealer would say: *"I bet you are wondering if you could live with one of those things in your home."*

The customer was expecting the owner to try and sell it, and they did not. The sales person just asked an opening question. The relieved prospect probably breathed a sigh of relief.

The prospect might say something like: *"Yea I was sort of thinking that way."*

The prospect is still expecting an attempt to sell.

Instead the store clerk would say something like this: *"Why don't you try it out for a week?"*

"We will deliver it and you can try it at no charge."

"If you find you cannot live with it, we will also come and pick it up at "no charge?"

The store owner knew the color TV would sell itself.

On the next day after delivery, the store owner would simply call the prospect.

They would ask: *"Do you have any questions on how to adjust the color or picture?"*

If there were questions, the owner answered them and then simply said "Enjoy" and would hang up.

Again, there was no close, no pressure

After having it for 4 – 5 days – the prospects wife loved it, his kids loved it, and all the neighbor's kids have been in to watch. Can he now say I do not want it?

Most of the time the prospect would call the store and ask: "How do I go about getting one of these things anyway?"

Example 2

It's the same close that car dealers have been using for years. The presentation has gone reasonably well but there is still some hesitation.

The dealer says: *"Why don't you take it for a test drive and see what it feels like behind the wheel."*

When the prospect gets back

The Free Trial close has won again.

Some Examples of Free Trial Equipment

a) Photocopy Equipment

b) Accounting Software

c) Material handling equipment: lift trucks, hand trucks

d) Process equipment: Paint Spraying systems, hand tools

Approach B) Free Samples – Free to use (no return required)

Often a company will allow their sales people to leave their prospects with free product samples for testing to see if they will meet the client's needs.

No return or purchase is required

This will usually be for consumables that are used in larger quantities.

There is not a lot of cost involved in the sampling process, when considering the size of the order at hand. Usually the volumes are large enough to easily write off the samples or products that are consumed.

Setting the Parameters

If you can use this method; be sure you have explained or demonstrated the use of your offerings, so they can be tested properly.

You Say: *"There is one way that you will know if our offerings:*

Will do what I say"

Will increase office efficiency"

Will work in your plant"

Will improve production"

Will improve quality"

Will improve appearance:

If they do not live up to the requirements, we have our answer and I will be on my way. If they do what I am saying, then you will have an alternative source for your needs.

Some Examples of Free Trial Consumables

- Office supplies: copy paper, toner, coffee, floor mats
- Process Consumables: Sandpaper, cleaning chemicals, gloves
- Packaging supplies: sealing tape, boxes, plastic wrap

These items will usually be used in high enough volumes to justify a free trial.

Trial Process for Approaches A and B

Start the Trial

Make sure you have provided complete instructions for use and where required provided an actual demonstration. Before leaving, confirm that you have answered all their immediate questions.

Tell them you will call the next day to see if they have any further questions or need more instructions. You will then make or confirm your next appointment for after the trial, while you are there

You now say: *"When the trial is over, I will be looking for your comments on the outcome of the trial."*

Your opinions are very important and are very much appreciated because I get to learn firsthand how people feel about the product." especially if they did not work out."

Feedback Statement

If you do not set this review and feedback requirement in place, they may feel that they have no need to see you.

You might find your equipment or any leftover products waiting for you at reception, when the trial is over.

Call the next day after the Trial Start

Call to see if they have any questions about the use of the product or service. Do not leave it longer than one day to call in case there are questions, or your offerings may end up not being tested at all.

If they do have any questions, answer them and hang up. At this point, do not even ask if they like it so far!

If they did not say: *"Your offerings did not work out, come and get your equipment or samples we have left"*

Consider the telephone call

A preliminary close and a positive response

Re-Start of a Trial

If the prospect asks a question or two, answer them. If there are too many questions about the equipment or service or they have used your samples and are asking for more, suggest getting together.

When you visit, they might expect an attempt to get an order even though you are just there to answer questions provide further instructions of use or provide more samples for testing.

This will allow you to get the trial re-started on a positive note and if appropriate, you can do a few trial-qualifying mini closes while you are there. It is however, not the right time to ask for the order.

The Appointment after the Trial

The Normal Outcome

When you arrive, ask the person doing the assessment how it went. Answer any questions. They know why you offered the free trial and why you are there.

If the trial was successful, the prospect will either order immediately, or they will expect you to ask for the order.

Now, you might use any of your closing options. The prospect will either come up with an objection or purchase it.

Possible Roadblocks

You could arrive for your appointment and your equipment or leftover samples are at reception for you to pick up. They may be trying to just return your offerings without seeing you.

If this is the case, ask to see them when you are there so you can learn why things did not work out. If that is not possible, try to make a follow up appointment. For some people, this *"no access"* is their easy way out and saying no. They will not be faced with your request to purchase and you do have their answer.

If this is the case

Leave it for a Future call back

and Move On

Close # 5. - The Comparative List (Ben Franklin)

When to Use This Close

You have made your presentation and the customer's needs have been met. Quotes have been presented and price is not an issue. The customer is interested and has said they want your product or service but cannot decide whether it is the right time to proceed or not.

At this point; for the prospect, there appears to be no urgency and there is no indication that they wish to move forward with an order now. The prospect is hesitating, unable to decide, and you may have already made one or two other closing attempts, without success.

They may be saying: *"I just don't know if it's the right time."*

It is now your job to move them from this position of indecision, to one of moving forward by placing the order.

Yes - They Are Procrastinating!

They have said that you will be the supplier. It appears that it is not a question of who will be getting the order when it is placed.

Their Question is When

Or a little bit If

They should Purchase it?

The Obstacles

- Using this with an experienced purchasing agent is not easy
- It has been around a long time
- Few buyers will allow you to do it
- Still try it if the situation fits

Most often it is used in a situation where the client is not a professional purchaser and is not used to making these types of buying decisions.

It could be a small business owner purchasing software, advertising or new office equipment. It could be a homeowner purchasing a car, a new home, home renovations, life insurance or a cottage.

This close is a tough one but it works very well in the right circumstances. Experience will tell you if it is right.

If you Proceed, do not just jump right into this close. Prepare the client slowly and sympathize with them.

You can say: *"You know that you are not alone. Many people have found themselves in a similar position as you find yourself today."*

"It is not often that you are making this kind of decision. It's not easy and I understand."

Pause for a second - And as if an afterthought

You say: *"As a matter of fact there is a way that many people use to handle such a situation."*

Optional *"It is a method that many people including a former US President Ben Franklin used when he needed to handle tough decisions."*

"Let's see if it might work for you? It is called the Ben Franklin Decision Process"

You add – *"We will stop at any point if you wish."*

If they agree, you take out a piece of paper and draw a vertical line down the middle from top to bottom.

Then draw a horizontal line a little down from the top crossing the other line and creating a "t"

Continue - *" Here is what we will do. On one side of this page we will list the reasons why you should do it today, and on the other side we will list the reasons why you should not."*

"Does that seem OK?"

If you get a Yes

You say: *"I will start writing all of the reasons why it makes sense to move in a Positive direction today?"*

Make sure you come up with a lot of reasons

You now ask:

- "How about this?" - Provide the reason and write it down.

- "Is this a good reason?" - Write it down.

- "Does this make sense?" - Write it down.

- Keep asking and keep writing.

Make the YES list - as long as you can.

Finish the YES list first before you start the NO side.

Your Sample List

The YES Side	The NO Side
Reason 1 – write it down	* Reason 1 help them
Reason 2 - write it down	* Reason 2 help them
Reason 3 - write it down	* Reason 3 stop here and let them do it
Reason 4 - write it down	
Reason 5 – write it down	
Reason 6 – write it down	
Reason 7 - write it down	

We used the word POSITIVE when asking them to proceed.

We used the word NEGATIVE when we talk about not proceeding.

When you are done, the Yes Side

You say: *"Let's think of all the Negative reasons why you should NOT move forward today."*

The words "Negative and Not" create a subtle way of indicating a wrong direction.

If the prospect has already mentioned several reasons why not to move forward with a purchase during your presentation, you write them down first and read them out loud as you write them.

You then ask the question: *"What else can we think of?"*

YOU HAND THEM THE PEN AND PAPER

You say: "It's your turn"

YOU THEN SHUT UP!

Your prospect will either start giving reasons and write them down, or they will give up.

They might just say: *"OK let's go ahead with the purchase."*

They might try to come up with more reasons not to do it today or they will end up presenting an objection. An Objection you will soon be able to handle.

If they come up with more reasons why not, you might be in trouble.

A Usual Result

Very often you get started with the YES reasons and they will feel foolish and say let's do it and you do not need to finish. This is very often the outcome to this close and why it is used successfully.

The prospect feels uncomfortable. It is almost like they are being treated as one might treat a child or pupil. The positive reasons are so obvious that it becomes almost embarrassing and seems pointless not to proceed with the order.

Summary of this Close

We have referred to this close using Ben Franklin as the example. You may wish to ignore the reference to Ben Franklin altogether and that is your choice and OK.

It's Origin

It is what Ben Franklin used to do and it is where the name of the decision-making process came from. It has obviously been around for a long time.

Note: Never refer to it as a close when talking to the prospect. It is a "Decision Making Process" or "The Ben Franklin Decision Process"

The Obvious Concept

List the reasons for making a purchase (with a lot of help from you) and then leave them on their own to come up with the reasons why not to make the purchase.

Yes, it can backfire and make the client angry

So, explain and ask permission first.

They could also come up with more reasons not to go ahead. That is why you need to present a lot of reasons why they should buy today. It is entirely up to you if you wish to use it; so, find the most comfortable and professional way for you to present it.

The Concept is There

And it Works!

SIMILAR SITUATIONS

Overview

This close is very like the Ben Franklin Close and could often be used in its place for the same reasons. The main difference is that while the Ben Franklin close involves writing; this one is verbal.

The Circumstances

You have already asked for the order and there seems to be uncertainty or just procrastination that is causing the client's hesitation.

Depending on your offerings the subject matter will differ; but, the concept of the close will be the same.

We will outline two Alternative Closes

In which this can be Presented.

The prospect has reacted favorably to your presentation and your offerings; but, they are reluctant to do something today. Again, they are uncertain if it is the right time or thing to do.

Many people will put off deciding even if it is the right thing to do.

You begin this close by saying: *"I can understand how you feel."*

(Short pause)

Continue *"You know several (months, years) ago, our company called on a client who found themselves in a situation very like yours."*

"They had the same questions and concerns that you are having right now, and this is what happened."

Right here – You can go in one of two directions

- **Close #6 - The Positive Direction and Outcome**
- **Close #7 - The Negative Direction and Outcome**

Close 6 - The Positive Direction and Outcome

Many people will put off deciding even if it is the right one.

You begin this close by saying: *"I can understand how you feel."*

(Short pause)

Continue *"You know several (months, years) ago, our company called on a client who found themselves in a situation very like yours."*

"They had the same questions and concerns that you are having right now, and this is what happened."

The Positive Direction

You can say: *"After we resolved their major concerns and ironed out all the details; like what we are doing here, they went ahead with the project."*

Continue: *"You know today they are enjoying higher profits, less rejects, higher quality, increased sales and happier clients"*

You can make the list the length you want. It helps if you can have a name or testimonial letter available to show them.

Unless they are competitors in the same marketplace, you could even offer to let them talk to your client.

Make sure Your Previous Client will allow this first

And, that they are Still Happy with the Results

You continue and say: *"You know I feel good because we were able to show our client why they should move forward at that time, and now they are enjoying all of the benefits we have just talked about with you."*

"I feel happy that we were able to help that company to become more profitable, more successful. That is what I would like to be able to do for you today.

The Preliminary Close:

You ask: *"Would you be excited if the same results happened to your company in the next (six months, year)?"*

If they say: *"YES"*

You Say: – *"So why don't we get started today?"*

If they say no

or

If there is still hesitation

It is time for a recap

Your Recap

You Say: *"We have reviewed your production methods, material costs, manpower and energy costs and you have already expressed your desire to:*

- *Expand your company*
- *Increase your profits*
- *Increase production*
- *Increase quality"*
- *(Whatever it is)*

"Is there any reason why you should stop your company from enjoying the benefits we have just outlined?

You are now at a Crossroads

If they say:

"No"

This is Good - You can now use a short closing question.

You Ask: *"What was the delivery date you wanted, April or early May?"*

Keep going in this positive direction. Ask for a purchase order number or ask them to OK, APPROVE the document.

If they say: "YES, there is a reason

Not to get started."

Find out why and answer the objection and then try another close.

Close #7 - Negative Direction and Outcome

It could be added after the Positive approach has failed. This is often referred to as the negative sales approach. Be careful!

This one Could make a Prospect

VERY ANGRY!!

You say: *"I can understand how you feel,"*

(Short pause)

You Continue: *"You know, several (months, years) ago our company called on a potential client who found themselves in a situation very much like yours."*

"They had the same concerns that you are having right now."

"Unfortunately, we were not successful in showing them why it was the right thing to do at that time."

"Thus, they were unable to improve production, and could not improve the quality or profitability.

Their sales continued to drop, and customers continued to leave, and now they……..

You Continue the close by using Result 1 or 2

Result 1 – They are in very bad shape, struggling to survive and can no longer afford to take full advantage of what we offered back then."

This could be difficult to provide a referral without breaching a trust.

Result 2 – They are out of business"

Do not use this unless it is true

You Say: *"You know I feel bad because we were unable to show that client why it was right to move forward at that time. Had we done so, their position could have been so different than it is today."*

"They would be enjoying the benefits the changes would have brought and now be a thriving business."

You Continue with *"We have reviewed your production, material costs, manpower and energy costs and what this project will do for your company."*

"Is there any reason why you should stop your company from enjoying the benefits we have outlined in our proposal?"

If their answer is a "NO"

Continue with: *"Let's get you started in that direction.*

If it is a "YES"

It's on to more closes and Answers to Objections

Summary

There are unlimited ways to use this similar situation close. It means putting your client in someone else's shoes to visualize either a happy ending or bad one.

Each type of offering whether it is a product or service can be used to illustrate the outcome of making or not deciding to purchase.

It is powerful, and it works

Close # 8 - Secondary Question

This close involves asking two questions in succession, with the second one being the easiest to answer. When the second question is answered, they also will have answered the first, and confirmed that they have bought.

This one has also been around a long time and the approach must be very subtle. You will need to perfect this one before you try it as it may have the reverse affect as it may appear to be trickery.

You will Know when this one is Right to use

When it is Used Incorrectly

It will be Called Trickery

It is right when you have given and reviewed your entire proposal and they have agreed with the benefits and like the product or service you have offered.

Pricing has been reviewed and finalized and the terms and conditions have also been discussed and settled; but, they have not yet said the order is yours officially.

You are Almost There

You need to tip the scales just a little, and it needs just a little nudge to push them over the edge.

This happens Sometimes

And it is Normal Occurrence

Right now, the client is in a safe zone and is not committed and you need to get confirmation of the order.

Make it Easier for them

It makes it easier for them; because, when they say yes to a minor question, which is much easier to handle, it also means they have said yes to the major question.

It works

It sounds a little crazy, but some purchasers do not want to appear to be too easy to sell. This sort of gets them off the hook. Make sure the secondary question is an easy one and you know what they will answer to start with.

Do not Pause Between the Two Questions

1. A Correct Secondary Question Close

FIRST QUESTION – *"It looks like we have reviewed everything and have answered all of your concerns. Have we reached an agreeable position for the project to be a go?"*

DO NOT PAUSE!

SECONDARY QUESTION – *"By the way would you want the delivery to be scheduled for June 15th or June 28th?"*

When they Provide a Date

They have Bought

2. Another Correct Secondary Question Close

FIRST QUESTION – *"We have outlined everything, and it appears that we have what you need, so shall we proceed now with the approvals of these documents?"*

DO NOT PAUSE!

SECONDARY QUESTION – *"By the way was that two copies you wanted for your records or three?"*

When they say the number of copies, they have bought

Even if they laugh at your closing method, it probably means they have bought. After their answer, use one of your short closing questions to confirm the order.

The worst thing that can happen is that you will get an objection.

ANSWER THE OBJECTION
THEN TRY ANOTHER CLOSING QUESTION!

There will be many secondary closes that relate to your product or service. Make a list of possible secondary question combinations and make the list as large as you can.

Memorize them and Use them

Close # 9 - Summary Question

This approach can be used to re-start stalled decisions and move the Prospect to a YES. It is also used after several failed attempts to close have occurred or maybe even more closing attempts were made.

The client has not yet presented a clear objection

Perhaps the prospect is confused, and does not want to decide, because something seems to be not-quite-right. At this point, they do not feel comfortable in moving forward until all doubt is removed.

Perhaps the prospect is not confused, and they are purposely avoiding making a final commitment.

They have not said no but they also have not said yes. You are stalled and need to get things moving again.

This is not Uncommon

You are there because at some point earlier, whether it was on your initial call, or during your fact-finding interview; that the prospect indicated they had a real interest in your product or service or demonstrated a definite need or problem to solve.

It has been re-affirmed during the final presentation, but something is still holding them back, and we need to find out what it is.

The summary question close is usually presented this way, because the prospect is stalled, and you cannot quite find out what they may be objecting to.

You have already made your entire presentation and they now act confused, or maybe even you are now confused.

You now say: *"Just to clarify my thinking,*

Look Baffled or Confused

You Continue: *"What part of our service/product/project is it that you find unclear and is causing you concern about moving forward today? "IS IT?"*

DO NOT STOP!!!

You immediately start going through the main points of your presentation and continue until you find the reason for their hesitation.

You begin by asking:

> Is it this? (provide example)
>
> Is it this? (provide example)
>
> Is it this? (provide example)

Continue asking until
They provide an Answer

If you stop after asking: *"What part is unclear and keeping you from moving forward today?"*

They will probably jump in and say: *"The whole thing, I am just not sure.*

If that happens you are finished, or must start all over again, or find a way to get back to the Summary questions. The important part here is to keep going and follow with several questions of various things covered in your presentation.

1. *Is it the way we do this?*
2. *Is it this feature you are unsure of?*
3. *Is it this clause?*
4. *Is it that option?*

Use as many "is it's" as you can.

Keep going and cover the entire presentation if necessary OR until something is presented as the reason why they are hesitating.

To Get to That Point

Summarize the key points of your presentation. Make sure you cover the areas that you know may cause many people to hesitate.

At some point the prospect will probably identify the problem area:

They may Say: *"That's it! I feel uncomfortable about having so much down time during the project"*

Then you say: *"OH! - IS THAT IT?"* – (Look apologetic) *"I AM SORRY!! - Did I not cover that part well enough?*

The following is Part of Overcoming Objections

Step1. QUESTION IT

Step 2. SHUT UP AND LISTEN to their entire explanation!

Step 3. CONFIRM THEIR ANSWER BACK TO THEM

Step 4. ANSWER IT

Step 5. CONFIRM YOUR ANSWER

Step 1. You Ask! "Just what is it about the down time that has you concerned, or confused?"

Step 2. Hear them out! Shut up and Listen

Step 3. You now say: *"So this is the area" (outline it) that was holding you back from moving forward today. Is, that right?"*

Look relieved that you have discovered the reason. Your client has now told you why they are hesitating.

Continue with: "*If you were more comfortable with the amount of down time, it would provide you with the confidence you need to get started?" "Is, that right?"*

Or

"If you understood how this part worked and saw that it did not interrupt your production time, and we could make the changes in non-production hours....

Would you feel more confident about getting started with the project?

At this point the prospect has indicated that this is something that is holding them back from deciding today. In the prospect's explanation, you have now learned why they are concerned.

Step 4. Answer how you will overcome this concern. If you answer all their concerns fully you should be able to ask for the order again.

Step 5. When you have fully covered the solution to the objection,

You say: *"So that completely answers that – Is, that right?"*

If your prospect says: "YES"

Use an appropriate short close to get the order.

———————————

If your prospect says: *"NO"*

You can try another closing approach

PERHAPS TRY THE NEXT CLOSE

THE LOST SALE CLOSE

Close # 10 – The Lost Sale

The lost sale close will use the very same ending as the Summary Close but it will start differently.

That is why it is called the LOST SALE.

BE CAREFUL! If you have already used the summary question close, and your presentation of the Lost Sale is too much like what you have already used, you might not get the order.

Or

You could even be escorted the rest of the way out of the building.

The Approach

When you have NOT been successful in any of your other closing attempts, you stop, close your books and look totally defeated. You then stand up, thank them for their time and start moving towards the door so the prospect is convinced you are defeated and leaving.

Here Comes the Switch.

You then stop. You turn and say: *"I am sorry, that I was not good enough to show you that you should be proceeding today. Your response seemed to indicate you liked what you saw"* *(whatever has been presented)*

You continue: *"You know if I had been good enough, you could be looking forward to increased profits, increasing your quality, and improving your delivery service".*

Use the things you talked about with them

Act very Upset and Concerned.

You continue on with the switch: *"I am sure it was my poor explanation of our products/services that led to this moment?*

"Just for my future presentations, and my own information, so that I do not make the same mistakes again; would you mind explaining just where I failed in my presentation.

Pause long enough for them to answer

If there is no help forthcoming

Start asking questions

Note: Use completely different questions if you have already done a summary close.

> *"Did I fail to show you enough benefits?"*

> *"Did I fail show the complete versatility of our product?"*

Keep going until you get a reaction from your prospect.

They might say: *"I just do not see how your product will help us the way you say it will."*

You ask: *"Could you maybe explain why you feel this way?"*

Shut up and listen to their Whole Answer

Repeat their Answer back to them

You say: *"So that's it. I did not cover that well enough?"*

"Before I leave, just so you have the right information, let's do a very quick re-cap and see if I can answer those areas for you."

Answer Their Concerns

Start a review saying: *"You may remember this - you may remember this – we said this and keep going. Did I cover this? Did I tell you about this?"*

When you are sure you have covered their concerns completely,

Confirm Your Answer

You can say: *"That should answer your immediate concerns, have I missed anything?"*

> **If they say:** *"Yes,"*

> **Ask:** *"What did I miss?"*

Carry on until they have nothing left

Whenever they say: *"You have covered everything"*

Finish with *"Thank you for taking the time to explain where I went wrong (in not explaining the benefits well enough.")*

"From your reaction, I can see you have more confidence in what we can do for you – Is that right?

"And it looks like we have hopefully answered all your concerns – Is that, right?

USE ANOTHER CLOSE

Probably a Short one will do

Close # 11 - Closing on a Final Objection

The client has raised several questions (objections) and you have addressed and answered them all.

You feel that your answers have created another chance to close the sale.

The prospect appears to have nothing left to throw at you, and you are still in their office; so, you should consider they are still interested, or still want your product or service.

But, you are not Quite Sure

The whole exercise has been somewhat confusing, and you are not sure if the last discussion was their final objection or not.

You say: *"You will admit that we have covered a lot of ground today, and it appears that we have answered all of your concerns. Is, that right?"*

Your purpose here, as a sales person, is to confirm that there are no more questions or objections.

You continue*: "Can you now think of any FINAL REASON(S) that would prevent us from moving forward with the order today?"*

If they say: *"NO"*

You say: *"That's great then I would say that means we have a go."*

Or

You say: *"I would take that as a yes to our proposal."*

When they now say: *"YES"*

It's time to finalize the order with a short closing question. You can ask them to approve the documents you have prepared or ask if they have a Purchase Order Number.

CLOSE IT!

Time to Re-Group

The Reason to Stop

The closes are designed to get orders or objections. Sometimes, despite everything you try, you cannot get an order.

It is very important to know when it is time to finally stop, and step back, before you push the client too far.

> It is often a very difficult call to make
>
> Sometimes you may not catch it in time
>
> There is a thin line between Persistence and Annoyance

This may seem like it is giving up, but if you have made 7, 8 or even 10 closing attempts, and answered all the prospects objections, and you find them no longer receptive.

- Maybe they are even getting agitated.
- They may even be showing their anger.
- This is not how you want to finish all your efforts.
- If you wear out your welcome completely you will not get back in.

Stop Before it is too late, if you can!

We know that often pushing the client to the annoyance level gets an order.

But this time it's Different

You can see you will not get the order today. It's time to step back and salvage the situation, so you can possibly have a chance to come back again.

You might say: *"I respect your position and I see you are not ready to make a decision today."*

You Continue: *"I AM LEAVING because the most important thing here is for you to feel comfortable about placing the order when you are ready." It is apparent that today, right now is not the right time. - Am I, right?"*

They will probably say: *"Yes that is definitely Right"*

You Continue: *"You know I have been trying very hard to get an order here, and that's my job."*

"I believe our product/service will provide everything you are looking for and I am truly sorry if I have pushed so hard. I hope we can see you again when you are ready?"

If they say yes, you ask: *"When do you think that you might be ready to make that decision?" or "When might that be?"*

Wait for the answer

And ask: *"How do you see our chances?"*

Wait for the answer and you finish by saying: *"I will check back with you (name the date mentioned).*

Perhaps Add the Following

"May I ask if you have any concerns with me, our company, our product or offerings now?"

"Are there any changes that you would like to see or additional information you would like to have?"

Write down everything indicated and repeat the list back to them.

You then say: *"Thank you for your time today and the information just provided.*

You Continue: *"I will do a total review of our proposal including the areas of concern that we just discussed. I will also see what other benefits I can add as well."*

"I understand and respect your reasons for hesitation and will use this new information to provide something that you will be much happier with."

If a time to call was given, confirm it again, before you leave.

You Say: *"I will call next Wednesday to arrange a time that is suitable for our revised proposal presentation."*

If this new opportunity happens to you

Get Prepared

- Review of all the events from your first contact until the end of your unsuccessful presentation.

- Find something that you can change or add; because, something new provides an additional reason to present your offerings again with these value-added items.

- Make sure you cover all the details and areas of interest discussed and provided solutions to all the concerns that were expressed on your last visit.

- Get any additional information that they have requested.

- Make all the changes they have requested.

- There will be answers somewhere in your failed attempt that will improve your future efforts.

- Look for them! Find all of them!

Call back at the discussed time to arrange a meeting.

Do not ask for an Answer when you call as that is often a Disaster

If you ask "*Have you had enough time to think about it?*

Their reply could very well be "Yes we have, and the answer is No!

And it is over

You should start by saying: "*On my last visit there were several things that were not quite right. We have made those changes and added some additional items and reviewed our pricing.*

"*What time is suitable for us to come in for a final review?*" (*Use your alternate of choice to arrange the meeting*)

When you get the appointment, you will be doing a

"CALL BACK"

SUMMARY OF CLOSING THE SALE

Some people put off qualifying or asking for the order because:

- They are afraid the customer will say no, or they are not interested

- They do not know enough closes.

- They do not know any or enough answers to objections.

It could be fear that they have not done a good enough job of presenting.

Because of these fears, they stall, and they dance around waiting for the prospect to say that they want to place an order. While they play this waiting game, they end up not even asking for the order.

If this happens all their time and effort to date, could be totally lost.

The Best approach

1. Learn these closes and more.
2. Memorize them and rehearse them with Enthusiasm.
3. Learn your Answers to Objections. (Next)
4. Do not change the overall concept or intent of the closes.
5. Do make them part of your own personality and find your unique way of presenting them.
6. If the timing is not right to get the order, the next best thing is to find out where you stand and request the opportunity to come back.
7. If you know your closes and the answers to objections, you will be in control and will never need to fear a no or an objection.
8. Do not be Afraid to use your own Personality to Close
9. Never Avoid Making the actual Attempt to Close

WHEN YOU ASK, THE CLOSING QUESTION

SHUT UP

AND LISTEN!!!

The first person to speak

LOSES!

Do not be afraid to use more than one close. Most sales occur on the fourth of fifth closing attempt. If you know only two or three you will miss many potential sales.

The Benefits of this Skill Set

- Qualifying and Closing gives you the opportunity to make sure you are working with a qualified prospect.

- You are also able to show them that your main objective is to help meet all their needs and provide solutions to any problem.

- This process will keep you on track and provide the feedback you need to confirm whether your efforts are successful.

- You know where you are headed with any meeting or presentation.

- You will know what to do when you finish your final presentation.

- You will know how to ask for the order.

So

CLOSE IT!

END OF PART TWO

DIRECT SALES 101

PART THREE

OVERCOMING OBJECTIONS

AND CONDITIONS

"Answering Your Prospects Questions"

Why are Objections really buying signals?

Why are Objections Important in the Selling Process?

When, Where, Why and How to Use Your Answers

Written by

Wayne E Shillum

INTRODUCTION

The process of "Overcoming an Objection" is really answering a question or concern that a prospect has, that is preventing you from continuing with the selling process.

Many people new-to-sales consider Overcoming Objections to be trickery, and they could not be farther from reality.

Knowing the fundamentals of answering an objection is a sales person's way of eliminating the obstacles that are continuously being placed in their pathway to the order.

Knowing how to handle objections will clarify one's message and allow them to continue with a presentation.

If left unanswered the client will build resistance to the sales effort and they may end the process, before the full message can be delivered.

Conditions

There are also obstacles known as conditions. A Condition is a real reason for the customer not purchasing a product or service.

They can be either permanent obstacles or temporary.

Many times, objections are presented as conditions. One will need to know how to establish if it is a real reason why the prospect cannot buy, or if it is information they need before they will proceed.

Misunderstood

The greatest misunderstanding of objections in the sales process is that they are often viewed as bad things, a prospects final answer, a final rejection, or the loss of opportunity; when they are only questions that need answers.

All prospects resist being sold something; but most will buy something they want or need. They will invest in those benefits or solutions, if the roadblocks are removed by answering their concerns.

Defense

Objections are defense mechanisms that are often used spontaneously by the client, to resist an unsolicited approach or the attempt by the sales person for them to make a decision to purchase something.

They can also just be indicating a need for clarification or a request for more information. The greatest mistake is to treat objections as bad things and something to be afraid of.

Objections are often buying signals that provide the seller with the keys to what will make the prospect purchase their offerings.

Once the sales person treats objections in this manner they will no longer fear an objection. They will look for the hidden message and get excited when an objection occurs.

Vulnerability

Objections often indicate a prospect's vulnerability when they are presented with an idea, asked a question or asked to purchase one's offerings.

They are indeed roadblocks when this happens; and they are used to slow down the momentum of the sales effort, to avoid drifting into a commitment that the prospect may not want to make, at that time.

There are five steps to answering an objection. These steps will allow one to clarify the objection (question) and provide a way to find the right answer for the prospects hesitation.

It is impossible for us to provide examples of every objection that might occur; but, we have separated and provided common groupings that objections will fall into.

Answering Objections is a necessary skillset to find out what is holding the Prospect back from going any further. Your job will be to hear them out and answer their concerns.

When Objections Occur

Knowing how to handle objections is very important in the selling process because objections can come at anytime and anywhere in your discussions.

You do not even need to be asking for an order to find the need to handle an objection.

First Contact

An objection can come from a first contact in your prospecting efforts simply because many people dislike the intrusion or interruption of their daily routine.

Often as soon as you start talking about your offerings and ask some questions you will be met with objections. Objections are rejections of what is being presented, how something is presented or when it is presented. They can also give the prospect time to think.

Their First Reaction Often

Is simply to *Object to the Intrusion*

Knowing how to respond to their objection can give you a second chance to be heard.

Objections are the roadblocks that stand between, where you are in the selling process; and your goal to find a need, make an appointment, qualify a prospect, or make a sale.

Objections can come during a first meeting, fact finding meetings, when you are making your final presentations and when you ask for the order.

When Closing the Sale

Overcoming or Answering Objections is the other half of the Dynamic Duo in the Closing Process. It is also the completion of the Closing Process.

Once you have mastered *"Closing the Sale" and" Overcoming Objections" (the Dynamic Duo),* you will be ready to fully appreciate and use your Prospecting skills and Sales Presentation skills.

Prospecting and Sales Presentations appear to come before this "dynamic duo" in the selling process.

And yes, the first thing you may be doing is prospecting; but, you will need both dynamic duo skills to achieve any kind of success in Prospecting or making Sales Presentations.

"Overcoming Objections," will be required from the moment you start your selling efforts, and it will be used right to the very end when you are securing the order.

Wrong Concept

The time for answering objections is often viewed by many as something only required at the very end of a selling presentation, where the sales person has asked for the order.

This is indeed a moment when one will surely get objections, but it is not the only time that they will be presented and need to be addressed. You can expect to be met with objections the minute you begin talking to your prospects.

If you want to be successful in your sales efforts, you must be ready to answer these earlier objections the moment that you start your conversations.

The Five Steps

There is a proper way to answer objections and you will need to know the five main steps to do it properly.

Our Approach to Answering Objections

- We show these five steps and how to use them.
- We show you how to change a condition into an objection and then how to solve it for the sale.
- We show you the bad words you should not use
- We show you the right words to replace them.
- We provide examples for the different types of objections and the ways to answer them

The examples we provide might not be the type of sales that you find yourself in; but, the concept for solving them, is what we are showing.

The expertise of overcoming objections is not trickery but an absolutely required skill in your professional sales tool kit, to be successful in selling.

The ability to answer objections will provide you with the confidence to be able to say (when you get and objection):

Great - an Objection

This will be one of the items

They will base their Buying Decision on

This Sale can be mine if I answer it right

OBJECTIONS OR CONDITIONS

The Definitions

The Dictionary Defines OBJECTION as follows:

- A comment or reason offered in opposition,
- A refusal or disapproval
- A feeling of dislike or disagreement
- A protest, a feeling of hostility or Doubt

Our Definition of OBJECTION

An Objection is a Question that is based on a customer's lack of understanding or insufficient information. It is a legitimate reason for not moving forward or buying at that time.

The Dictionary Defines a CONDITION as follows

- A state of a person or thing
- A modifying circumstance
- A prerequisite

Our Definition of a CONDITION

A Condition is an actual reason for not buying that exists.

Conditions can be temporary or permanent. They are legitimate reasons that will prevent prospects from being able to purchase your product or service.

Why Objections Happen

The Prospects Right to Object

It is the prospects right to object to an untimely or poorly presented prospecting call, a badly presented idea, a misleading comment or any excessive pressure for an answer or commitment to buy.

It is the right of the prospect to "Object" to making a purchase" or "Question it," if someone is trying to close, and the prospect is still not happy with all of the facts at hand.

It is their Right to Object

To any Information that is Not Clear

Where do Objections Occur?

As previously mentioned, they occur everywhere along the way from first contact to the end.

Many attempts to approach a client in the beginning and throughout one's dealings with them; right up to the end, may be met with conditions, objections or questions.

They become extremely critical items to solve; for the sales person, in the final stages of obtaining the sale.

Unless you know how to handle these objections correctly, you will stumble and fall before you reach the finish line. Knowing how to answer objections is like putting the icing on the *"Sales Cake."*

This part of the selling process will provide closure to each part of your mission.

By learning the reasoning (the why) behind our answers to objections, you will acquire a key component of your closing tool kit. Understanding the "why" gives you flexibility and depth in your ability to handle the many different situations that will arise.

Different Groups for Objections

Our "Answers to Objections" will fall into distinctive groups. Recognizing a group, will allow you to use a similar response for each group.

In each group, you will need to change the ingredients to suit the situation, but you will always find a common ingredient in that group that allows you to select your answer.

Our Six Main Groups

1) Preventable Objections
2) Price Objections
3) Competition
4) Change of Base
5) What Would You Do
6) Conditional Objections

The Importance of Understanding the Why

In the beginning one might think there are just too many ways to answer objections and they get frustrated and confused. Fortunately, after learning our methods and examples, a pattern should emerge, and our groupings will make sense.

It is not our intent to present the following examples as a script in a play to be learned and recited verbatim.

The memorizing of our example responses is intended to embed the concepts in one's subconscious. The final wording and presentation should become that of the individual and not the teacher.

Once the conceptual part of the process is learned and understood the presenter (sales person) will have unlimited scope in the ability to overcome objections. It is our intent to leave you with an understanding of what is behind these groups and different responses.

What We Want to Happen

Learning the WHY is important, because it gives one the ability to handle almost everything that will be thrown at them in the selling process.

CONDITIONS

What are Conditions?

Conditions exist because of circumstance. They are different from objections because the prospect has a legitimate reason for not buying and it exists.

Objections are often Presented as Conditions

Sales people will often believe what has been presented is an actual reason that is preventing the Prospect from making a purchase.

Whether Condition or Objection, it is a roadblock created by the prospect that is presented to avoid deciding.

A Condition Always Needs to be Challenged

Conditions do exist and once they are discovered to be an actual condition, they become a justifiable reason for not making a purchase.

It may be time to move on to the next lead or find out if it is temporary, long term or permanent.

Examples of Conditions:

- No money, no credit, too sick to carry on
- Price is totally over our budget (for real)
- Need to talk to Someone who is not there
- I am waiting for all the prices to come in
- Product is too big for the space available
- No need. No possible use for it

Handling Conditions and Objections

Treat Everything as an Objection

It is important to understand the difference between a condition and an objection. It will also be your responsibility to challenge what has been presented as a condition.

As already mentioned, many reasons presented as conditions are really an excuse for not buying. They are not conditions but perhaps procrastination hidden behind a condition.

The First Time you Hear a Condition:

- Acknowledge the condition that they have presented.
- Then continue (by pass it).

If it is a real condition, they will bring it up again and it may be a real condition.

- If it isn't a condition; but an objection, and the condition doesn't exist, and you have accepted it as a condition, **you lose.**
- If you do not challenge it and fail to continue to qualify and use your skill set for handling objections, **the prospect has won**.
- If it is only an objection; and you do not get a potential order, it's your fault and **you have failed in your mission.**

When you have listened to the reason (condition) presented the second time by the prospect outlining why they cannot proceed, you must always challenge it.

The Situation

A customer's condition, objection or question is what we refer to as a request to get further information, or solve an issue, before they (the prospect) will proceed.

The Mission

You will need to find out exactly what the condition or objection is, answer if fully to their satisfaction, before you can expect the client to proceed. Very few sales occur without having to answer an Objection.

Their Right to Say No

The prospect has every reason to expect and get everything they need to make them comfortable with what you are asking them to do.

Your answers to the prospect should give them the information they are asking for. This knowledge is what they need to solve their concerns. Your answer should remove the concern and the objection.

If the information or answer is not sufficient, then you will need to continue the process until you have fully answered all their questions and removed all their concerns.

Your Right to Continue

Once you have answered their objections, it is then your right to expect an okay to continue, or the right to ask for an order from them.

When closing a sale, you should always finish your answers to an objection with the request to proceed or for an order.

At the very least, expect a confirmation that you have answered their question and they are satisfied with the answer.

Continue this process throughout your prospecting, your fact-finding meetings, sales presentation, and your closing attempts until the customer says yes to your final request for an order.

Asking a Prospect to Purchase

Before you have Provided all their Answers

Is like

Expecting a Campfire to give you More Heat

Before you put Wood on it

Objections are Good!

Look for objections or questions, for they are the things that are important to your client, and they are ultimately the reasons that will cause them to go ahead or reject the possibility of an order.

When you hear an objection, get excited because often they are positive signs and show interest. Say to yourself this is great because this may be a reason why, they will buy

Mastering the skill set of *"overcoming objections"* will help you unravel what the prospect is really thinking and show you the way to get the order.

A right answer puts things into a proper prospective for everyone.

Changing Conditions to Objections

Often you will be presented with objections in the form of conditions and below are some examples of conditions that are really objections, that we will cover in more detail later.

1. Alternative viewpoint - Change of Base – *Time not Distance*
2. What would You Do – *That's what we did*
3. Need to Talk to Someone – *Let's call them or go see them*
4. Call back Objection – *Just leave the information*

The Customer is Always Right!

When you are presented with a condition or an objection:

- Do not disagree
- Do not argue
- You are not there to prove them wrong
- You are there to prove them right.

Proving them right is what will make them want to work with you and purchase your products or services.

Proving them wrong will prove why they should not be talking to you, and they should give the order to someone else!

First Part to Handling Objections

If someone throws a punch, do you normally step into it?

NO! – I hope not!

Not unless you want to be knocked out before you get started, or you wish to experience some damage or pain.

So why; when most sales people hear an objection, the first thing they do, is to jump right in and fight it? They throw themselves right into the line of fire and challenge it.

Is that ever a BIG Mistake!

What is the best way to avoid the damage of a punch?

- You step back,
- Or step aside
- And you roll with it.

Every time you hear an objection for the first time.

Step Back

> **You Say:** *"I understand your point of view"*
>
>> Or
>
> *You Say:* *"I understand"*
>
>> Or
>
> *You Say:* *"I can see why you feel this way"*
>
> **Step aside**
>
> **You say:** *"By the way"* and carry on with the presentation
>
> **You Roll with it**

By continuing with your presentation; if the objection is real, it will come up again.

If it is a real Objection

If the SAME objection comes up again, it probably is a legitimate Objection or maybe even be a Condition. This time you do not by-pass it. The next five steps are critical to Determining Conditions or Overcoming Objections.

If you skip any of them, you will usually not finish this part of the process successfully.

THE RIGHT WAY TO HANDLE OBJECTIONS

We have already mentioned there are five steps to handle an objection or condition. Most new-to-sales people and many experienced sales people do not know the proper way to handle objections.

They fear these roadblocks because they do not understand that if an objection or condition occurs, it can be and usually is, a good thing. When an objection occurs, you have just been issued a warning by your prospect, that you need to explain something further or correct it.

If you know how to approach either an objection or a condition, there is no reason to panic. In fact, these warnings can often be a buying signal; the solution to which, is their reason to buy.

The following five steps are a tried and proven way to remove the roadblocks, so you can continue your journey.

Use These Five Steps

Clarification Part

> **Step 1 – Question it**
>
> **Step 2 – Shut up and Listen!**
>
> **Step 3 – Confirm their Answer!**

Solution Part

> **Step 4 – Answer their Concerns!**
>
> **Step 5 – Confirm your Answer!**

Steps 1, 2 and 3 usually follow the same approach. The Changes occur in the solution part Steps 4 & 5.

> **Once you Confirm your Answer - Carry on with the process**
>
> **Or Ask for the Order**

Clarification Part

Step 1) Question It

- Ask them to explain what they are Objecting to
- They will either start to explain and realize it is a stupid reason, or in explaining it, you find out their real objection or if it is a condition.

Step 2) Shut up and Listen

- Here them out
- Even if you think you know where they are going with the objection
  SHUT UP AND LISTEN.

Even if you guess right, you will probably upset them

And you could guess wrong!

Step 3) Confirm Their Answer

You Say: *"Just to confirm my understanding of why you feel this way?"*

Outline your understanding of the Objection / Condition as they have explained it.

Solution Part

Step 4) Answer Their Concerns

- When you know what, they are objecting to
- Provide your solution or answer to it - completely and thoroughly.

Step 5) Confirm Your Answer

You Say: *"Now that should answer your concern, am I, right?"*

By following this proven format, you will have the greatest chance of discovering the real objections and answering the prospects concerns or you will learn that it is a condition. This format is used in all our methods to answer objections and conditions.

When combined with your closing questions and main closes you will take control of your prospecting and your sales presentations. You will know where you are headed always, how to get there and what to do when you get there.

When the Objection is fully Answered; Continue, or Ask for the Order

PREVENTABLE OBJECTIONS

There are ways that sales people often create their own objections and allow objections to occur that are not necessary to endure. There is often no formal training to cover the following two examples of preventable objections.

Many sales people both new and experienced make these unnecessary mistakes day after day, when they talk to new prospects and their existing customers as well.

Many presentations are not successful because the prospect is turned off by these preventable reasons for objections. The worst part, is that the sales person is totally unaware that it is happening.

The following two areas will point out what many sales people do that prevents them from getting a sale.

The Two Areas

1 – Bad Words

2 – Built in Objections

1 - Bad Words

Overview

The time to avoid the use of bad words is when you are asking the prospect to do something, or you are telling them something about your offerings.

Bad words Create Negative Feelings

The only good time to use these bad words is when you are referring to your competition. This is a very subtle way of creating a subconscious negative reaction when a competitor is mentioned.

For your Offerings

The first way you can eliminate many of your prospects objections before they occur, is by stopping the use of these bad words when referring to your offerings. It is the use of these words that will create much of the negativity that prevents you from making the sale.

"Objection" - Our Inherited Bad Word

Objection is the term that, we as sales people use when talking to others in our profession.

Never call it that to a prospect! It is always a QUESTION or a CONCERN when you are talking about it with the prospect.

It really is Misnamed

It is universally used by sales people and is truly a bad word. It is the prospects right to object or question us, if they are not sure, or do not have enough information.

It is our responsibility to answer that question correctly and completely, before expecting to proceed on our journey to an order. If you say this word OBJECTION to a prospect it could possibly turn into a REJECTION for the sale, or even from their office or home.

IT IS A QUESTION or IT IS A CONCERN, when discussing it with the prospect and you should try to look at it in this way even when you just think about it!

Other Bad Words

How often do you use the following words?

When you say these words, you create resistance, because they present the negative side to a sale.

Do not ask them to:

BUY – They have bought enough already.

PAY – They are already paying too much.

These words imply hardship or an obligation.

Ask them to:

INVEST! – They are getting something back from an investment.

OWN – When you own something it implies pride of ownership.

Do not ask for a DOWN PAYMENT – That sounds like a bad thing.

Ask for an INITIAL INVESTMENT: They are starting something good.

Do not Say: MONTHLY PAYMENT – They hurt. People hate monthly payments.   They have too many already.

Call it – A MONTHLY INVESTMENT - They are much easier to deal with and this implies good things are happening.

Do not Refer to it as a: PURCHASE – They do not want to make purchases

Call it: AN INVESTMENT - They do not mind making investments

SOLD - They do not want to be sold.

SOLD is only good if you are selling their house.

SELL - They do not want you to sell them something.

SELLING PRICE – Selling & Price are negative and obstacles.

Use the amount to OWN – People like owning things.

Use - When you OWN – Something to look forward to

The Strangest Thing People DO NOT like to:

BUY

PURCHASE

PAY

Be SOLD SOMETHING

BUT, THEY WILL *ACT*

***TO OWN* SOMETHING!**

Bad Phrases

This occurs a lot in retail sales and it is very annoying. You are checking out with your selected items at the cashier.

They Say: *"Is that all?"* or *"Is that it?"*

Your mental reaction: *"Are you not happy with my business. Do you think it is not enough? Are you expecting More?"*

How many times have you experienced this?

The right way

One should ask: *"Is there anything else I can help you with"*

Or

"Did you find everything you were after?"

How many people fail to show their appreciations for your purchase with these bad phrases Maybe you are upset to the extent of going elsewhere in the future.

Sales Pitch, Spiel

Have you ever heard a sales person use these words? After I am finished my sales pitch/spiel, we will discuss that question.

- Pitches are what people with trench coats on the street corners make.
- They are what the criminal element of our business does.
- Spiel – that sounds like a con job to me.
- Your clients do not want to listen to pitches or spiels, but, they will listen to a Presentation

Sign Something

- Do not ask people to sign something.
- How many times are we told not to sign anything?

Don't sign anything until your lawyer looks at it. **Sign** is a bad word - yet it is used all the time.

OK or Approve

- Ask them to OK something or APPROVE it.
- It's strange, they will OK it or APPROVE it,
- BUT they will not SIGN it!

They do not need a Lawyer to - OK it or APPROVE it.

Contract

- How many times have you been asked to sign a contract?
- What have you been told about a contract?

The Warnings about the word Contract

- ◦ Watch out, be careful, and beware.
- ◦ Read it very carefully.
- ◦ Take it to a Lawyer or you will end up in court

They will not SIGN a CONTRACT

BUT

They will OK an AGREEMENT

Trade Terms

Every Industry has them, and too many people use them when they are talking to their customers. Often, they do it to show off.

Trade terms are OK, if you are talking to someone in your industry, because they are used by all the people in your trade or company. People in your trade or your industry understand what you are talking about.

Have you ever heard of radio sales people who are selling spots?

- My lawn has bare spots. I have enough of them.
- When my carpet gets a spot, I need to get it cleaned. I do not want any more spots.

It could be, when we finish your pro-forma.

- Maybe the client knows what you mean,
- Maybe, they are not quite sure.

If they do not understand, or are not quite sure, they will doubt you, and they will not buy from you.

Forget the Trade Terms - Use People Language

2 – Built-In Objections

Overview

If you know that your company, product or service has a built-in objection or even several of them; do not live in fear during your entire presentation, waiting for it/them to surface.

Most Companies Have them.

They are there just waiting to knock you off your feet. You feel that your client is waiting to hit you with one or all of them, so you begin to concentrate on how you will fight them off when they finally come.

You Lose your Focus

And the Impact of your Presentation.

How to Overcome it

Do not wait for it. Do not waste all your time waiting for it to happen; because, *"IT WILL HAPPEN."* It will usually happen just when you are describing your biggest selling feature, or you are about to close.

BANG! It hits you right between the eyes.

Brag about it. Make it a Feature

You will know what these things are, because they are part of the things that will drag your presentation down, and start you defending yourself, instead of selling your product or company

1. Terms and Conditions - Example

Let's say it is your ten pages of the clauses in your terms and conditions, that every one of your competitors is telling your clients about.

It is not a secret that most people hate a lot of *"small print"* when dealing with an important undertaking.

If your terms and Conditions are at all lengthy, you can expect this to be used against you.

You must turn this seemingly negative condition into a positive one.

Do not avoid talking about it because your competition almost certainly is. Even if they are saying nothing, your prospect is having a negative reaction, just looking at your 10 pages.

Your Competition may be saying: *"You should see their terms and conditions section."*

"Talk about fine print. It is 10 pages long. Our terms and conditions section is only one page and is simple and straight to the point."

Or

Your Client is mentally comparing it with your competitor's simple terms and conditions and starting to feel very uncomfortable.

Before your Prospect Hits you with any Criticism:

You say: *"You know our company has discovered that most people want to be comfortable in their working arrangement with another person or company."*

"We have recognized that this feeling is very much a concern with most of the people we talk to about using our service or our product."

"We are proud of what we have done about it."

Continue:

"We have put together a detailed list of the things, which we will do for our clients."

"We provide a complete description of our product and service."

"There is no second guessing about what is… or is not there."

"We show and explains everything that we can possibly think of, that our customer wants to see and needs to know."

Emphasize this one: *"We do not Hide things"*

And then Continue:

"People do not like surprises especially ones that end up costing extra dollars at the end."

"We are proud that our company has taken the time to outline full product descriptions and show a complete list of terms and conditions and explained them in detail."

Continue: "We fully Explain:"

1. *"What we do, and what the customer needs to do"*

2. *"They are totally spelled out; so, there is very little chance of a misunderstanding during, or at the end of the project."*

3. *"If there is an issue, it is visible and can be addressed in advance, and solved before the order is placed."*

4. *"We know that when we present our proposal to our clients, they have all of the facts right up front."*

5. *"There is no reason to be afraid of what has not been said or not been written."*

6. *"COMPETITION often leaves things out or hides them; which can result in many grey areas or questionable items in their quotations."*

7. *"They are often able to show a considerably lower price because these things have not been said or shown."*

8. *"Their **not included items** go unnoticed, and it is often too late when the EXTRA COSTS OCCUR."*

The Reasons

"We have found that what we show is the kind of information that all good managers today feel they need to be well informed in their decision-making process."

"That is why we have done this."

The Close

"Do you not agree that what we have done is a real benefit in your decision-making process?"

What Have You Just Done?

Can they now object to your 10 pages of terms and conditions? If they do, then they are saying that they are not a good manager.

Make this an entire up-front presentation of your terms and conditions.

Write your own version, memorize it, and rehearse it until you can deliver it with emphasis and enthusiasm. Choose how and when you introduce your explanation to suit the circumstances.

Continue with your Presentation or Your Close

Your company may not have a Terms and Conditions issue, and many do not. This is just an example of a built-in objection just waiting to happen.

2. Product is too Small - Example

Very often people relate size with ability to get something accomplished faster or better. It is therefore not surprising that competitors will use this idea to discredit your product if it happens to be smaller than theirs.

You know your competition will probably say that your product is too small and maybe they will infer that the smaller size will negatively affect performance.

Your prospect may be thinking this very same thing when they look at it and compare it to the size of others.

That is Why

You must Immediately Turn the Size

Into a Benefit

You Say:

"Before I start; may I say that as a company, we are proud of the fact that we have a product that is smaller than most.

"Not only can it still provide everything that is expected of it, it can provide even more benefits than some of our competitor's larger products."

"They may imply otherwise because of size."

Continue:

"We offer something that will reduce the foot print required by normal equipment while providing the same, or even slightly better performance."

"It is our belief that size should not the issue!"

"One should be asking instead - can this product achieve what I need it to do in my (manufacturing or work environment?")

Finish by saying:

"I am sure you will agree that it is performance, not size that you are looking for. Am I, right?"

Continue with your Presentation or Your Close

3. Company is too Young or too New – example

Every company has a beginning. Very often a new company will have a younger management team than their established competitors.

This is a very easy target; and something that many salespeople highlight when speaking about your company, if you are new or management is young.

There is no benefit in trying to outrun the inevitable road block because it will surface eventually.

If you let it happen on its own; it will then be a negative situation, because you will be defending the accusations of newness and lack of experience.

The best approach is to turn it into a positive situation by bringing it up first.

Before the client can say it

You say: *"Many people might think that our company is too new, or our management is too young; but, we are proud of our wealth of knowledge, and the vibrant energy that our young company has."*

Continue:

"As a company, we are not hampered by bad habits, or ruts that time can often create. We are excited about what we bring to the table, and the benefits that our company has to offer a company such as yours."

"Our management team is proud of their leading-edge technology, and their energy and ability to get the job done, quickly and properly."

"Is that not what really counts?"

If this is your company, write your version of this and memorize it. Practice it to perfection, so you can deliver it with enthusiasm.

Continue with your Presentation or Your Close

Note: This approach can be altered to suit *"too old"* as well and many other situations. "Too old becomes experienced"

4.Better Product or Service – Creates a Higher Price

If your company has higher quality offerings with more benefits and features, it will often mean higher prices.

If your design or engineering department does not cut corners to achieve a better Price; while competition does....

Make this a Feature and Benefit

Brag about it

Establish early that you may not have the lowest price at the end, but your clients do not unknowingly suffer with:

- Offerings that do not meet performance expectations
- Premature failures
- Improper Service or back up
- Warranties that are not honored

Qualify right up front and ask if they are willing to sacrifice the above for the lowest Price.

Summary of Built in Objections

These are only four examples of built in objections.

Every company has them and your competition is almost guaranteed to present them to your potential customer. They might even be referred to as skeletons in your closet, mistakes, shortcoming's or failures.

It is essential that you review everything about your company and its offerings; that can be presented by your competition *negatively*, in their efforts to create negative reactions or doubts with your client.

Do not Run from Them

Because they will Always Be There.

You Must

1) Face them

2) Make them benefits

3) Brag about them

4) Explain why your company is proud of these facts

5) Use them in your introduction meeting and in your presentations and when you are closing.

If you're that proud of them - How can they be bad?

The Biggest Mistake you can Make

You Start Thinking:

- Why should I even bring these items out into the open?

- Maybe my competition is not even saying anything.

- Maybe my prospect is not thinking this way.

- By bringing these things out into the open, I might be harming my own chances.

Wrong! – In this kind of Reasoning

- You will still live in fear that prospect will present them

- You will lose your focus and control of your presentation.

- If your competition is aggressively after the order, they will very often do whatever it takes to get it.

- Built in Objections are real.

- Your Prospect can also see them, without help from others.

Take Control

Present Things Your Way

The Best Defense is Always a Good Offense!

PRICE OBJECTIONS

Overview

Pricing is the largest area where objections occur. There are many reasons for the variance in prices offered.

Companies will position themselves based on either 1 or 2

1. Providing quality offerings and proper servicing of client needs
2. Providing the lowest price and sacrificing quality and service

Some Reasons for Higher Prices

Bad Reasons for a Higher Price

1. Product Sourcing – too many middlemen, inefficient suppliers
2. Their Company Overhead – extravagant facilities and expenses
3. Company Profit Margins – too high to meet 1 and 2
4. Operating/manufacturing methods – inefficient, outdated
5. Delivery – their own is inefficient or they use outside sourcing where costs are too high

If you are the owner, you will always be faced with the problem of being too high for the "Bad Reasons" unless these items are resolved.

If you are the Sales Representative and these problems are not resolved, you will always be faced with this pricing issue. Perhaps you should look for a different employer.

Some Good Reasons for Being Higher

1. Your Product – Offers more features and Benefits, saves energy, provides lower operating costs or is more operator friendly and easier to use.
2. Service – Better equipped, more trucks, 24/7 availability, quicker response times, proven track record of dependability.

As the sales person or owner, you will need to show why your prices are higher for the **"Good Reasons"**

Prices can be lower because of the following reasons.

Bad Reasons for a Lower Price

1. Product Design or Quality – Poor design, corners cut for price
2. Product Service Quality – Poor to meet price, not dependable
3. Warranty – No ability or intention of providing it

If this is your Competition, you need to know about it. You need to find ways to effectively overcome prices that are lower for these bad reasons.

Good Reasons for Lower Prices

1. Company Sourcing – Excellent and cost effective
2. Company Overhead – Efficient and cost effective
3. Company Profit Margins – Effectively priced to sell
4. Company Manufacturing – Efficient and cost effective
5. Company Shipping – Good sourcing or have their own trucks with cost efficient delivery controls.

These reasons should become selling features of your company. There is nothing wrong with being lower for these reasons.

Make the above features part of every presentation

In working with your Prospect, you can:

1. Establish quality and performance as the clients most important criteria and continue your journey and use your benefits and features to out-sell your competition.
2. Maintain your pricing. Emphasize what problems the prospect may be inviting or what they will be giving up, if they choose only based on the lowest price.
3. Emphasis your benefits and quality and try to come close enough to your competition's price to get the order.
4. Recognize that price is all the prospect wants and move on.

Prices can Also Appear Unnecessarily High because of:

a) Your Incorrect Qualification of Clients Needs

In this case, you must improve your process of qualifying and establishing your client's needs.

b) A Poor Presentation, where Value of your Offerings is not Seen

In this case, you must improve your presentation to show value of product or service (or both). You might need to add more enthusiasm or add better content and examples.

Point out features like

- Extended life of products (cost reduction)
- Lower Energy or Process Costs
- Space Savings, time savings
- Environmentally Friendly, less noise
- Much easier to operate, happier employees
- There are many more which will relate to one's offerings

If this seems difficult, you probably do not know your competition's offerings well enough (or even your own) to show the value-added features of your offerings.

There will almost always be objections to price as it is every purchaser's quest to get the best price possible.

Even when they are looking at what they know is the best value for their investment, the client will often still object to price.

As a company or the sales representative for a company one should always make allowance for this normal behavior of a purchaser.

Be Prepared

This is an Inherent "Price Trait" of a Buyer

General Trends

- Emphasis on price seems to follow the state of the economy.

- When times are good, and the economy is strong, price seems to be second to quality, performance, benefits and service.

- When times get tough; purchasers still want the same quality, service and other amenities, but more emphasis is placed on price.

- Outwardly price will always take a prime considered position regardless of economy status.

All companies want products or services that have added value; and they often say price is most important, even though performance, service and quality is what they are mostly after.

If there appears to be little difference in quality, benefits, service or performance, price most often wins.

There is always more Loyalty in a Strong Economy

Those who service the prospect well and give the best advice, are often given the advantage position in consideration of any order.

Often the profitability of the prospects company itself; and the type of offerings it brings to the marketplace, will influence their decision.

Wherever a prospects own quality, price and performance level is; will often determine how they view the importance of these areas in a supplier.

How can they Focus on the Lowest Price?
If they Sell *"Value Added"*

This reference can also be a good example to use in answering any price objections.

No matter how strong or weak the economy is, or how profitable the company is; most purchases will still stress price, as being high on the requirement side of things.

To do otherwise; would be a big mistake and invite higher costs for the products or services they are considering.

Price will Often Determine Quality

Price often determines the quality of the offerings and it will be up to the sales people to show this and justify a higher price.

Every purchaser wants the best that their money can buy, without paying an unjustified premium to get it. They do not want to become victims of *"supplier greed."*

The purchaser also knows that price is often an indicator of what they will get, and it is up to the sales person to justify a higher price by showing:

- More benefits,
- Better quality
- Better performance
- Better warranty and service back up

Competition and Branding

You will be competing against companies that have achieved a better image due to their advertising, branding and past performances.

Often this can Justify their Higher Prices

You may have equaled their offerings in all the areas we have mentioned but may have a difficult time getting the order without offering a lower price to tip the scales.

This is when your own Good Marketing

And company's Past Performances can pay off

Make your company stand out in an area such as service, quality or performance to make the difference. Show that you do have more to offer.

Provide testimonials and references to show that your company is reliable and provides everything you say it does.

Lower Prices Achieved by Cutting Corners

You will compete against companies who use price as their greatest selling feature. They cut corners in quality and performance to achieve the best price.

Often purchasers are unable to see where or when this is happening, and you must find a discrete way in your qualification questions and presentations to show why the competitor's prices are lower.

Learn everything you can about your competition. Where are, they positioned as far as quality, benefits, service, performance and price?

Find out how and where they cut these corners

Prepare Yourself

Build an Inventory of rebuttals for price comments. You can subtly place them in all your presentations from your first meeting and along the way.

Do not just place them at the end when you are trying to get the order, or it may be viewed as mudslinging and unethical.

Along the way, they become fact

At the end, they will seem like Excuses

Use your mini-closes and answers for objections to find out where the prospect is placing the importance of price in their requirements.

Part of the selling process is conditioning your client for what you are going to ultimately present to them. You must show why it is their best choice and why it is better than what your competition will offer.

If they can visibly see all the benefits and features of your offerings, then price often will not become the main criteria for their decision. It will also not be a big surprise to them at the end.

The Inventory of Price Rebuttals

Use Phrases such as:

- A fair price allows the seller to provide the benefits, quality and performance, warranty and service back up that their clients are usually looking for.

- When price is the main or only criteria for measurement, then quality, service and performance will certainly suffer.

- The excitement of the lowest price ends when the offerings fail to provide what the purchaser expected and needed.

- Many sellers hide behind price to avoid providing quality and performance and eventually service.

- The lowest price often can only be achieved by cutting corners and providing inferior products or services.

- The lowest price is not always the best choice when it comes to benefits and performance or honoring a warranty.

- We ask for a fair price; because it allows us to deliver what the customer needs in performance, benefits and quality - while still providing excellent service and full warranty.

- What are you ultimately after; the lowest price, or products and services that provide what you want and need at a competitive price.

- It is easier for a company to offer the lowest price if they have no intention of standing behind their offerings for service or warranty.

REMEMER the good reasons for offering a lower price. It is why you have it. Always stress these reasons for being able to offer it.

How to Handle Price Objections

First Encounter with a Price Objection

This will usually happen when you have finished your presentation and you have just provided your price.

You may not have even tried to make your final close and the client is already objecting to price. Often it is just their normal way of treating all prices.

They say: *"Wow! your price is too high!"*

When This Happens

The first time you hear it, acknowledge it and by pass it.

You say: *"I understand how you feel*

Bypass it and Start or Continue your Close

If the objection or condition is real, they will repeat their earlier comment that the price is too high

Second Encounter with a Price Objection

The prospect might Say *"This all sounds great so far, but that's a lot of money and as I said earlier, it's too high for me to consider."*

You must now take them seriously because it has been said twice. If you ignore it this second time you may be out of the game.

You will now try to find out what their reason was for saying your price is too high.

Steps 1 to 3 for Overcoming a Price Objection

The initial Clarification part of the approach for a Pricing Objection will involve **STEPS 1 to 3** of the answering objections process.

In most cases these first three steps will almost always be the same for any price objection.

Clarification

Step 1 - Questioning of the Objection

Step 2 - Listening to Their Answer

Step 3 - Repeating your Understanding of the Objection back to them.

Clarification Steps of a Price Objection

STEP 1 - QUESTION IT

You ask: "Could you explain why you feel our price is too high.

Do not fear what they will say, because it is the only way that you will be able to see why it is too much money, and if it is a real condition or just an objection.

After you have asked this question

STEP 2 - SHUT UP AND LISTEN!

Listen to their entire explanation.

Do not interrupt until they are finished unless it is clarification of a comment. We have already explained why it is important to hear them out.

Write down their Reasons

STEP 3 – CONFIRM THEIR ANSWER

Tell them your understanding of why they feel the price is too high.

You say: "Thank you for explaining. If I understand correctly, your main reason(s) for saying the price is too high is……

After telling them your understanding of why they feel the price is too high; if they agree, you will be dealing with their stated reason for the objection.

Solution Steps of a Price Objection

STEP 4 – ANSWER THEIR CONCERNS!

You will now take the appropriate steps to overcome the condition or objection and find the solution for them.

This is where your responses will differ. We have separated the main kinds of pricing objections into four types.

STEP 5 – CONFIRM YOUR ANSWER

Once you have provided your solution, you need to confirm that you have answered their concerns. If you have answered them, it is time to close.

The Four Types of Normal Price Objections

The following examples are the four main types or reasons for saying the price is too high.

We will outline the final approach that should be taken for the solution of each of them, separately.

Normal Price Objections

1. Over our Budget
2. We found Used for Less
3. We do not see the Value.
4. Higher than Competition

Normal Price Objections

Overview

The first three steps of the PRICE OBJECTION

Have been completed per our previous example

The Clarification Answer for "Over our Budget"

This is usually the result of not enough qualifying questions and you have been assuming everything is on track.

Your Present Position

You now need to determine if you can solve the situation dealing with price alone while you are there, or will you need to return to your office for a complete review.

This could also be a condition; but, we will treat it as an objection until proven otherwise.

Most purchasers will complain about price to get the best price they can for their company, as that is their job. If they are insisting that your price is over their budgeted amount this possibly makes it a condition.

Before you go further, you will need to ask approximately how much you would need to lower the price, to achieve their budgeted amount.

The Solution Process

STEP 4 – ANSWER THEIR CONCERNS!

You ask: *"If we are able to resolve this price issue, will you be placing the business with our company?*

If they say YES keep going

If they say NO, you need to ask more questions until you get YES

Or find out why their answer was No

When you do get a Yes

Continue with: *"To deal with this properly I will need to know approximately how much over your budget we are talking about here."*

"Based on the figure that you give me, we will have two possible directions to take.

1. *If we are close, I will call the office for our best price."*

2. *If the price difference is too great, we will probably need to do a total review back at the office.*

Based on the Figure they give you

You will Know Which Direction you are Taking

Direction 1) Price is Close

You Say: *"I will now call the office and see what the best price is that we can offer, based on you making a decision today."*

Note: You should always leave some room to lower your price for any presentation to be prepared for this part.

You have now turned this into a close when you offered to call your office for your best price if the prospect places the business with you that day.

This way you can get the sale while you are there.

You have now called your manager (office) and asked them to do a quick review while you are in the prospects office.

Note: This part should be only for show. You should already have made this review before you left your office for your final presentation. This way you already have your best Price available.

Make it for your offerings *"as-is"*

With No Changes.

This is a good procedure to follow on all reasonably sized orders and maybe leave some room to move in all the smaller ones as well.

Leaving room to move in any final presentation; to get an order, is a very good procedure to follow. The reason why you never go in with your best price to start; is that, most purchasers feel you have room to move anyway, so do not let them down.

Play their game

The Set Up for the Close

Before you called your manager, you explained to your prospect what you are about to do.

You said: *"What I will do is call my manager and ask what our best price will be if we proceed with the order today. Does that sound fair?"*

The Key Phrase here is *"if we proceed with the order today"*

It justifies the Call while you are there

When they said "OK" you make the call

When you called your manager, you explained the situation even though you had pre-arranged the possible call. You stated the price that you are trying to get down to. (if available)

You said: *"If we can meet this price they will be placing the order with us today."*

You asked if they would do a quick review and you will call back in about 10 minutes to get their answer.

Note: Make this offer to call, even if you know you can probably meet the price. Do it in front of your prospect.

Even if you cannot meet the price stated, you have shown that you made the attempt and can now make a counter offer, without changing anything in your proposal.

Call your office back after the 10 – 15 minutes are up and pretend you are discussing the results of your request.

Say things like:

- "Yes, I know
- *We covered that*
- *They want to keep those benefits"*

Carry on and finish with: *"OK I will call you back before I leave."*

STEP 5 – CONFIRM YOUR ANSWER

You may be presenting what they want or making a counter offer. Whichever it is you will be confirming the results of the call you made to your office.

You Say: *"My manager has agreed to offer you everything with no changes for (state the price)*

SHUT UP!

Wait for an answer

This is a close

If they accept the price you say: *"Great Let's get started by changing the price on the proposal and initialing it."*

You have just presented a closing statement and have an order if they say "Yes"

NOTE: We have just covered the approach for reviewing price only. This approach will work for any situation where the price is close.

Direction 2) Price Difference Too Great

We will deal with two types of proposals here

a) An offering with Accessories and/or Installation
b) An Offering without Accessories or Installation

STEP 4 – ANSWER THEIR CONCERNS

They have provided information that clearly shows that the price difference is too great and is beyond a simple price reduction.

We will outline your approach for two types of Large Projects.

    a) A large system with many accessories or Installation.

    b) A large System with no accessories or installation.

a) Large System with Many Accessories or Installation

It will be necessary to separate as many items from the main price and show them as options. You will then need to go back and review everything and prepare a new proposal.

You Say: *"It appears the difference is too great. You and I will need to review the proposal to remove as many items as possible to price separately as options, to see if we can get the price down."*

"We might even find some things that we are doing that you were planning to do, or our competition is not doing, and we will show them separately as well"

"We will then need to review our pricing to see if we can improve any areas and show these items priced separately as options for both of us to review on my next visit."

You Continue: *"That way you decide what stays and what goes once you see the numbers."*

"Is this an acceptable way for us to proceed?"

Wait for the Responses of your Client

If it is not a condition but an objection, and just an attempt to lower price, they may hesitate in eliminating features and benefits to get there.

Either way you will find out if it is a condition or objection by the time you finish this process.

- If it is a condition the next steps could solve the issue.
- If it is an objection the next steps will certainly test the waters and allow you to close.

If the Prospect Agrees

You Say: *" Let's see what we can separate to lower the price."*

You will now suggest eliminating items from the main price to show as optional items.

Explain that you will show separate prices for each option for them to pick and choose so they can get the cost down.

It will be like a summary question close; but here, you will separate items to show them as options. This approach will mean gathering information and going back to the office for a review and some number crunching.

Begin a summary of components and features. If an installation is part of your proposal responsibilities, review responsibilities and the items that could become options.

Often items such as electrical, plumbing or other civil work could be done by their own maintenance department instead of your crew and covered by their own overhead infrastructure.

You ask:

- *How about this item?*
- *How about this item?*

Continue through the entire list of items you know can be eliminated without affecting the overall integrity of what is needed.

When you are finished, your goal is to have a substantial list of items to be eliminated or shown as options. If this happens, you will go back and review everything with your manager.

Say you will try to separate as many additional items as you can come up with, to price separately. Ask them to also think of what else they might want to see as an option.

This exercise will be similar for any larger type of product or service where the price difference is too great to adjust on the spot. The concept behind it is to provide as may optional items as possible to allow your prospect to feel they have a say in the final price.

In the process, you may hopefully discover things you are doing that your competition is not. This restructuring of pricing exercise will be substantial, and you cannot resolve the matter when you are there.

Before you go back to begin your Review

- First you need to re-confirm how much too much you are. Even approximately will do at this point. You must have a target.
- In most cases, what they say will be lower than what they can live with.
- Secondly you must confirm that they will wait until you have time to review and can present a new offer with options for consideration.
- If they agree, arrange a new day and time for your next meeting before you leave.

Return to your office

- Remove the items to be shown as options
- Begin your price adjustments.
- Part of this review may involve your installation (what you do, and they do) and maybe pricing or other terms and conditions.
- You will call your client the next morning following your meeting to see if they have thought of any more areas to be shown as options.
- Add their items (if any) and continue preparing your new proposal with as many options with separate prices.

Do not stop with what was discussed at the first meeting and the results of the call the next day. Give the prospect as many options as you can.

b) An offering with no Accessories or Installation

We have just covered the approach for a large project that involves many items and Installation. A similar approach will be taken for any *over-our-budget* situation where the price difference is too great to review while you are there.

The main difference here is that you will only be re-working your numbers for your best offer possible.

It will be the type of offering where there is no installation or there is nothing tangible in the way of accessories to remove. Here the only thing you can do is offer to go back and review everything.

If you did this, the prospect would possibly get angry as it would appear that you were overpriced to start. Too much to review for an immediate answer regarding Price is not unusual.

STEP 5 – CONFIRM YOUR ANSWER

In both cases a and b; when you are finished the review, and adjusted your pricing, return and present your new proposal.

Ask for the Order

CLOSE IT!

WITH THE APPROPRIATE CLOSE

2 - Used for Less

Overview

We will take the position that the Clarification STEPS 1 to 3 in your Answers to Objections procedure have been done.

The prospect has said they have found a "Used item for less". Therefore, they feel the price is too high. This means you possibly faced with a condition. You will now try to change it to a simple objection.

You will continue

Your client has shown interest and is saying the price is still over an amount they want to pay.

They say that you are the only one left offering new equipment that they are talking to, and they would like to have your product or service, but, they just cannot afford it.

Yes! It could be a Condition

But Initially treat it as an Objection.

If it is a condition, and you cannot overcome it; you can offer a leasing plan.

But, first

- ◦ Doubt it as a Condition
- ◦ Acknowledge it as an Objection
- ◦ Begin Step 4 – Answer their Concerns

If it is an objection, it might turn out to be just more than they feel they want to pay for the product or your services.

The Solution Process

Option 1 - Call Your Office for the Best Price.

You can call your office for a price reduction and proceed the same as we did for the previous example Reason 1 - *"It is over our Budget."*

Make your Closing Attempt with your best Price

If not Successful Proceed to Option 2

Option 2 - Price Features Separately

Very often when comparing New and Used there will be value added features that the new equipment offers.

Offer to remove features that the other equipment does not have and show them as options, the same as we did for Reason 1 - *"It is over our Budget."*

If the Prospect Agrees

Start the Separating Process

Follow the same procedure and come back with your revised offer. Make your Closing attempt to get the order.

If at this point they still feel the revised price is high and do not want to give up any of the options. The client is now being a little stubborn or ridiculous.

Ridiculous or stubborn or both, you need to become a little ridiculous back.

We will now Treat it as an Objection

Our Example Situation:

Let's say the prospect needs a new lift truck to handle larger loads and their significantly increased material handling volumes. They are now on a two-shift basis, and the one truck they have is just not enough to handle the increased requirements.

Your truck is perfect because it is NEW and has everything the prospect wants.

- It has the extra load capacity they need.

- It can lift the height required in the new storage area.

- It also has a reach option for the maneuverability in their narrow aisles.

You are the last supplier of new trucks they are talking to. They like your truck

But they say: *"Your truck is just too expensive.*

A friend of theirs has a used truck they no longer need

Its Qualifications

- It is five years old; it has a greater load-lifting capacity than yours, and far more than they need.

- The higher load-lifting capacity makes the used lift truck larger in size and more difficult to maneuver in the small isles.

- This means they will need to widen the Isles for turning; thus, they will end up with less storage capacity.

- It does not have the full height capability or the reach feature that your truck has which means they will be limited to the existing truck to reach the upper storage shelves.

- Your lowest price is now $5,000 more than their friend is asking for used, and you know you have now given your prospect your best price.

The items just listed emphasize your value-added selling features as well as the used truck's limitations. If this is not enough to convince your prospect, continue the process.

The Solution Process for our Example Situation

STEP 4 – ANSWER THEIR CONCERNS

You now say: *"I can understand how you feel; I agree that $ 5,000 is a lot of money."*

Have your Calculator Ready

Start the Process

Do this Exercise

Reduce the amount the client is objecting to, down to the absurd, and throw it back to them. It may be your only way left to get the order. Money can usually be reduced to the lowest common denominator. The approach may change depending on what is too much, but this method can be very effective.

You already know that you are now $5,000 higher in price, so you state that as a known fact and go from there.

You say: *"You have said that we are $ 5,000 high, is that right.*

Once you have established this as your base you start the questions.

Ask the Questions and Know the answers already

You can also eliminate the questions and just keep going with just suppling the answers or **some of both**.

The question/answer process will involve them more and this is better; but, it could also annoy your client.

Choose the right Mixture to Suit the Situation

Begin the Questions

Question 1 - "How long do you want this truck to last?"

Answer 1) – They have already said ten years.

Question 2 - "How much is that per year averaged over ten years?"

Answer 2) their answer is $500.00 per year.

Question 3 - "How many days in a year are you in production?"

Answer 3) their answer is 240 days, or you provide it.

Question 4 - "How much is that a day?" Help them if they start to hesitate

Answer 4) you say: "I have my calculator. It is $ 2.08/day."

Question 5 - "How many hours do you work per day?"

Answer 5) the answer is 15 hours on an average day.

Question 6 - "That's how much an hour?"

Answer 6) the answer is 13.9 CENTS round it up to 14 cents

You have just taken your client on a journey that has shown them how little they are talking about when it comes to the actual ***time-of-use*** cost.

STEP 5 – CONFIRM YOUR ANSWER

You now say: *"We have already established that:*

- *You have a ten-year life requirement*
- *You really need the lift height on the second truck as well, for the top row storage.*
- *You also need the reach to enjoy the narrow aisles and extra storage capability.*
- *You really do not need the higher load-lifting capacity because of the load limits on your storage racks.*
- *Our smaller truck size will make maneuverability possible in your narrow aisles giving you more storage."*

Ask: *"How much business might you lose in a year by sacrificing your needs for this lower price?"*

Wait for an Answer but you do not really need one

You just want them to think about it.

You now Say: *"We know our truck is new and will last ten years and it has everything you want and need for just 14 cents per working hour more."*

Ask: *"How long do you think the used truck will last before you experience repairs and extra maintenance costs?"*

Pause but - Once again no answer is needed

If they are still Hesitating

Continue: *"How often could you experience an employee pay raise for such a low amount as 14 cents per hour?"*

"Would you not agree to it, if it meant keeping one of your key employees?

Pause - Once again no answer is needed

Continue: *"By giving up height and reach you could also lose considerable time and storage capacity by choosing used. As we stated earlier this will cause you to lose potential income and lower your profits. Do you really want this?"*

Pause - Once again no answer is needed

Finish with: "Is it not worth 14 cents an hour to have what you want and need, instead of settling for something that cannot do the total job?"

Without looking extremely ridiculous

How can they now say that 14 cents an hour is too much to pay?

Leasing rates will make the hourly costs even more ridiculous.

Ask for the Order

CLOSE IT!

PRICE AND POOR PRESENTATIONS

Often you will have objections because you just did not make a good enough presentation to show your prospect the value-added features.

You may Not have asked enough qualifying questions

You may have failed in your presentation to show how your products or services provide benefits that will offer things like:

1. Additional savings, easier to operate, happier employees
2. Provide better quality of their finished product
3. Save time and energy and increase productivity.

Often companies have products that are far superior to some of their competition and this will probably be reflected in the price.

The biggest mistake that is often made; is that the sales person will assume that these features are self-evident, and they do not need to be fully explained.

The prospect is viewing other suppliers and if there appears to be no additional benefits because of your higher price….

Their Choice Will Probably Be Price

Avoid this objection by improving your presentation and emphasize every benefit and feature; to the point where, there is no question in the prospects mind that the extra value is there.

Often you will need to make this review of value added benefits or features; because the prospect needs a little more convincing, to tip the scales in your favor.

Poor Presentation Price Objections

1. We do not see the Value
2. Higher than Competition

1 - Cannot See the Value

Overview

The STEPS 1 to 3 in your Answers to Objections procedure has been done and they have said Reason 3 *"They do not see the value"* is why they feel the price is too high.

This response is an indication that you have not done a good enough job in presenting your offerings.

You have Failed to Establish Value

For future situations, you will need to review all your presentations and find what you need to do, to show value.

Often discovering the true objection will simply provide a doorway to use one of your other closes.

In this case, it is probably an overall review type closing. You must now try to fix your mistakes, while you are there.

The Solution Process

STEP 4 - ANSWER IT!

Your answer can be to do a Summary Question Style Close or Lost Sale approach. (*Shown in Part 2- Qualifying and Closing*)

The Close

You would take the following approach and apologize to your prospect. You should also be very embarrassed with the presentation you have just made.

You say: "Obviously, I have done a very poor job in my presentation and for that I very much apologize."

"If I had done a proper job you would not have this question of Value."

"Even though I know the value is there, I have done a very bad job of explaining the benefits of our product and where the value is for you."

"So, that I do not make the same mistake again and perhaps discover what I did wrong here, do you have a quick few minutes to see where I went wrong?" I am sure you will also benefit if my previous presentation failed to show benefits you need and want."

If they say: **"Sure or Yes"**

You say: *"Let's just do a quick review of the features and benefits of our products and services to see if we can find out where I failed to show the value.*

If the prospect feels they have missed something, they will probably want the review as well. Do not panic.

Make your review as a *Summary Question Close* and cover your features and benefits step by step. This time do a better job of demonstrating value.

You review and explain each feature and ask after each: *"Do you see the added value in this feature?*

Review and Ask: *"Do you see the extra value in that feature*

Keep going...

Continue through the entire description of your offerings until your questions produce a *"NO, I do not see the value here."*

At this point you stop and say: *"So that is where you do not see the value, is that right?*

Wait for an answer and say: "I *am truly sorry if I did not explain this well enough. What is it about (the item) that you do not see the value?"*

1. **Let them answer completely**
2. **Review the benefits and features and where the value is**

When you are finished your Review

You say something like: *"Can you now see that this feature has*

> *Cut operating expenses,*
>
> *Increased production capabilities*
>
> *Will lower the rejection rates by considerable amounts*

Continue: *"Were these not three of your greatest concerns."*

STEP 5 - CONFIRM THE ANSWER!

You say to the prospect: *"From what we have explained, have we provided everything that you have asked for and need in this product/service?"*

You now ask: *" Does our review answer your concerns on value or shall we continue our review further?"*

Continue your review until they say there are no more questions of value or you finish everything possible in your review.

You now ask: *"Do you feel that we have shown the value-added benefits and features, that you were after?"*

Wait for a YES

Finish by saying: "I think you can you now see the value. Am I right?"

If it solves the issue and they say

"They can now, see the value"

CLOSE IT

2 - Higher Than Competition

Overview

The STEPS 1 to 3 in your Answers to Objections procedure have been done and they have said *"You are higher than your competition."*

Therefore, they are probably suggesting the price is too high. This means you are faced with an objection. Again, this is probably a presentation problem and a failure to show value over your competition.

You are possibly faced with someone who cuts corners or offers lower quality, poor service or does not meet all the prospects needs. This objection comes from the prospects lack of understanding and seeing where your value-added features will create a far superior return on their investment.

Again, improving your presentation will greatly reduce these kinds of objections. This is where you might need to use more of your price rebuttals earlier in the process.

You will continue with STEP 4 and answer their concerns and then ask for the order

The Solution Process

STEP 4 – ANSWER THEIR CONCERNS

Stage 1

You say to your client: *"You have indicated that we are higher than our competition and I am not surprised by this comment."*

"We hear this on many occasions and it causes us great concern because too many people just look at price."

You say: *"Do you not agree that any company that provides products or services today has two directions they can take.*

1. *"They can choose to provide a product or service that will give their customers everything that the client will possibly need and expects."*

2. *"Alternatively, they can do as little as possible and provide the least that they can get away with, so that their selling feature will be the best price?"*

"Would you agree with those directional options?"

Unless the prospect is being ridiculous

The answer will be a yes.

Ask them: *"May I ask approximately how much higher we are?"*

The prospect should tell you the approximate difference. If they do give you a figure, take whatever number they give you. Use it in your answer.

If they will not tell you; even approximately, and since they have said your competition is cheaper, you are now ***shadow boxing***.

It is not out of line to make the following statements about price vs. quality, benefits, performance etc.

- **Again, do not forget** the list of rebuttals you made to argue against price or the bad reasons for a lower price.
- It is alright to look a little concerned because they are about to waste your time with the shadow boxing.

If they do provide you with an answer regarding price carry on.

- Thank them.
- Acknowledge the price and continue.

The Turning Point

Of your Answer to this Objection

STEP 5 – CONFIRM YOUR ANSWER

Either way; with a price, or without a price, keep on the same pathway.

You say: *"Our Company does not cut corners to obtain the lowest price; but we are aware of others, who do."*

You continue: *"They will make their selling feature price, and not performance, or customer satisfaction because they know most purchasers are looking at price."*

Summary Questions you may ask

1. *"Would you not agree that doing as little as they can do for you, puts them in the best position to talk about price?"*

2. *"Which would you prefer Price or Performance?"*

3. *"What do you need this product or service to do for you?*
   - *Everything you want and need,*
   - *Or as little as the supplier you choose can get away with?"*

If they say *"Everything I need and want"*

Ask for the Order

CLOSE IT

WITH THE APPROPRIATE CLOSE

Continue to practice ways to improve the message of value. This is primarily a presentation problem and one that happens all too often for sales people.

COMPETITION OBJECTIONS

Overview

You will almost never be without competition. I will not say that you will *"never"* have competition because on rare occasions; if you have serviced a client well enough, they will not seek competitive bids.

You have gained their complete trust and they know you will be fair.

Having a very good reputation and service record can also often place you in a preferred category when submitting a proposal as well. Here price is not always the main consideration, but it is still important.

These privileges must be earned and not abused. It is great when you are in either of the above two positions. Most often you are not, but it does happen.

On many presentations, you will be on the other end of things and will be up against the competitor with the preferred position. When this happens, you will often see the signs. Do your research and look for a history that your competition might have with your prospect.

Most times you will have a relatively level playing field. We say relatively because often the person who makes the first "best impression" starts off with a slight advantage.

If it is you, then you must fight extra hard to stay there.

Marketing Advantage

The successful marketing of a company and its offerings will often make a big difference where one starts and can provide an initial advantage. That is why having a good marketing plan is essential when creating a company image.

Good Branding of a company or its offerings, creates a comfort zone with the prospect right from the beginning, even before they begin conversations with the sales representatives.

You will often find yourself competing against these types of companies. It is a challenge but not impossible to overcome.

A Starting position behind these companies can often be temporary if you present yourself, your company and offerings well enough. Many races are won by people coming from behind.

Become a Familiar Face

Companies will rarely buy from an unknown source or a stranger.

A very Important

Part of your job

Will be to become very Visible and Known by the client

If you make one call as a stranger and return with a quotation and have had little or no interaction with the prospect in-between these visits; you will most often, remain a stranger.

And find it difficult to get an Order

It is important to find ways to become a familiar face and well known. You need to become a comfortable source as a supplier. Find ways to accomplish this without becoming a pest.

Unethical Competition

You will often run into competition that does not play by any rules. They will undermine you, your company and its offerings, to gain a better position for consideration of an order.

They will cut corners, provide inferior products to be able to present a lower price.

It will always be a challenge when this happens because often these things will go undetected by the client and you. The below standard offerings are not seen by the prospect, and the mudslinging is not seen by you.

When you encounter an attitude change with a client, look for the cause and it will often be an unethical competitor.

Do not Become one of them

Defend yourself because it is your right to do so. Use your closes and answers to objections in an ethical way to outsmart them.

Three Competition Objection Types

In the following examples, we will deal with three most common types of competition objections that you will face.

1 – Your Competition is Better

2 – Happy with my Present Supplier

3 – Brand B is Better.

1 - Your Competition is Better

Overview

This is a common occurrence as branding, and a familiar visible image of a company or offerings will often be the cause.

There may be a history of business between the two companies or maybe a better presentation was made by them.

You must now challenge this statement and find a way to take over the primary position for the order.

The prospect says: *"Your competition has a better plan or a better product or service."*

- You should know your competition and what they offer, because that is your job.
- If your (product, service) has everything they have, or you are well positioned with other benefits or prices, you have a good chance.
- Do not argue.
- Do not challenge them with your knowledge at this point.

The Clarification Process

STEP 1) - QUESTION IT?

You say: *"Just to clarify what you are referring to, what is it that you feel our competition has, that we do not have?"*

"What makes them better?"

Your prospect might try and come up with something, draw a blank, or start providing you with some examples.

STEP 2) - SHUT UP AND LISTEN!

- o Listen to the complete list.
- o Write the complete list down

When the prospect is finished

Then you say: *"Is that everything that you can think of at this point?"*

STEP 3 - CONFIRM THEIR ANSWER

Look and act extremely concerned and interested – *because you should be!* The prospect has just told you where and why they feel your competition is better.

If you know your product or service is equal or even better in some areas; you should be very excited, but also embarrassed at the same time because you did not cover these points well enough.

You say: *"So these are where you feel our competition is better."*

Wait for their *"Yes"*

"Are these areas holding you back from making a decision in our favor?"

LOOK EMBARRASED

I MEAN REALLY EMBARASSED

Because you should be

If you failed to point out the features the first time

Now you say: *"You know I am truly embarrassed that I did not make things clear enough. I am upset that I missed those features when I made my presentation and I am very sorry that I did not do a better job."*

Start Repeating the list they gave you

And say: *"Let's take a quick look"*

The Solution Process

STEP 4 - ANSWER THEIR CONCERN

"You say to them: You have said -

- "They have THIS" **you reply** – *"We also have that feature."*
- "They have THIS" **you reply** – *"We also have that feature."*

o "They have THIS" you reply – *"Whoops that is new one for them. I did not know they had that. We also have it."*

o *Here our features are much better. (explain why)*

o *Here we have more benefits. (explain them)*

Build your list until you have totally overshadowed the competition with your features and benefits.

Answer the entire list

Then say: *"Can you think of anything else that you feel makes their product better, before I go on?"*

If they say: *"Yes"*

You ask: *"What is it?"*

Start making a list again if necessary. Carry on until they have nothing left.

STEP 5 - CONFIRM YOUR ANSWERS

You now say: *"So it looks like we have fully addressed your concerns about the competition being better. Am I correct?"*

Ask for the Order!

CLOSE IT!

2 - Happy with Present Supplier

Overview

This will usually occur during your first meeting.

The prospect says: *"You know I have been working with "Bill's Plumbing" for over six years now, and I am really happy with their services."*

You say: *"I can fully appreciate that, (*by pass it and ask*) by the way how long have you been in business?"*

They answer: *"15 years - but I am really happy with Bill as a supplier." (Second time mentioned)*

The Clarification Process

STEP 1 - QUESTION IT

You now continue: *"If you do not mind me asking, what brought you to start using Bill's services six years ago?"*

STEP 2 - SHUT UP AND LISTEN!

Hear your prospect out completely. Write any significant items down.

STEP 3 - CONFIRM THEIR ANSWER

Repeat their answers back

"So, what you are saying is that Bill had the best service, best prices and the most number of things that you wanted to see in a (plumbing service/supply company) at that time, six years ago."

They say: *"YES"*

CONFIRM IT! – *"So, that is why you started using them, Right?"*

The Solution Process

STEP 4 - ANSWER THEIR CONCERN

Wait for the answer and continue: *"I am sure that these things are still very important to you today - is, that right?*

Pause and continue with: *"I feel our products and service might be able to offer you equal and even have some additional benefits."*

"We have more service vehicles on the road, a much larger inventory to draw from, and we understand from our customers that we are extremely competitive in our prices."

5. CONFIRM YOUR ANSWER

Qualify his original reason for choosing Bill.

You say: *"Service, quality and price - Is that not what you are still looking for in a supplier?"*

Wait for the answer and it should be a "YES."

You continue: *"We can help you reconfirm that the same conditions still exist today with BILL as they did six years ago, by providing you with some pricing for products or services that you currently use?"*

"In this way, you will find out if the same situation holds true as it did 6 years ago?"

If the customer starts to object to the direction you are taking,

You say: *"I understand what you are thinking right now; but there is a real benefit in what I am proposing, and it is this."*

"If after doing this, we both find that the same circumstances still exist, and BILL still has the best of everything you need, your situation is reaffirmed, and we will have our answer and be on our way."

Continue with: *"If it **does not still exist,** I see two choices for you.*

The Choices

1) You can try to get better quality, better prices or services from BILL, (using us as someone wanting your business) and if you are successful then it's a win situation for you.

OR

2) You can give us a chance somewhere that does not mean switching over completely, and you get an opportunity to test us as a back-up to Bill, without damaging that relationship.

Does that sound like a fair approach?"

GET THE LIST - COME BACK

AND CLOSE IT.

3 - Brand B is Better

We will look at two possible times when this situation might occur.

1) Your first meeting
2) At the end of your final presentation

1) Your First Meeting

You have just introduced yourself and your company. You are just starting to explain your products and services.

You have not yet started to ask questions and the prospect decides to cut the meeting short and send you on your way. They may have changed their mind about seeing you.

It also could be that you did not Pre-Qualify the prospect well enough when introducing yourself and setting the appointment.

The prospect says: *"I did not realize what you were selling when we made the appointment and we use Brand "B". It's a great product and we are very happy with it."*

They continue: *"There is not much point in wasting your time because Brand "B" is better than anything I have previously looked at or used, so I am not really interested in looking at anything else!"*

Even though the prospect is trying to end the meeting; you did travel all the way to meet with them, and there may be a tiny bit of guilt feeling. If you get up and leave now, your trip is totally wasted.

The Clarification Process

STEP 1 - QUESTION IT

You now say: *"I apologize if I did not explain the reason for the meeting well enough"*

Pause for a second

192

Then continue: *"Could you take a quick few minutes to tell me, what it was that caused you to choose Brand B in the first place and what still makes it better?*

"This will really help my future knowledge if I run into Brand "B" again."

STEP 2 - SHUT UP AND LISTEN

At this point it looks like they have succeeded, and you are leaving. They will probably be more than happy to provide the reasons Brand B is better.

Their answer was that "Brand B" had more features and as they explain the features - you write them down. They had better service, better this, better that. They explain why, and you write them down.

Their prices were better. Their quality was better. Their service was better. Keep listening and writing until they are done.

STEP 3 - CONFIRM THEIR ANSWER

You respond by saying: *"Thank you for taking the time to explain"*

Continue: *"So the reason was that, at the time you did your original survey, "Brand "B" had more of the things that you needed in a product than anyone else that you had talked too? Is that, right?"*

Here is the Hook

A YES answer is almost guaranteed

They have just told you told you they were not interested because Brand "B" is the best. They have also just listed all the reasons why they like Brand "B" and are using it.

Can they now say NO?

When they say "YES they had all the benefits"

You say: *"May I ask? Does the same situation still not exist today?"*

Wait for a response – It should be a *"Yes or What do you mean?"*

Continue: *"Are you not still looking for the product (service) that can offer you the most benefits to help your company also provide excellent service and better quality to your customers?"*

Repeat the list of benefits they gave you

You Say: *"Would that not be something worth looking at again, even if it is just for reaffirmation that Brand B is still better?"*

If their previous answer indicated that these things are why they chose brand B. Can they now say that they are not as important today as they were when they selected "Brand B"?

When they Confirm these areas are Still Important.

The Solution Process

STEP 4 - ANSWER THEIR CONCERNS

You say: *"While I am here we could select a few items and we will provide you with some prices and some product samples to try.*

*You can see if our products are equal in performance or perhaps - **what we hope for** - is that they might even be better than brand "B"*

"Is that a fair request?"

Wait for a response

Continue: *"If after doing this, we find that the same situation still exists, and brand "B" still has the best of everything you need, your situation is reaffirmed, and we will be on our way.*

If they have responded to the questions this far, it will be very hard for them to say no without stating: *"they do not want what's best for their company."*

STEP 5 - CONFIRM YOUR ANSWER

You continue: *"If brand "B" does not still have all of the reasons why they are the best, I see two choices available.*

1)You can try to get better quality, better prices or services from brand "B" using our products and prices as an example and if you are successful you have benefited."

OR

2) *"You can give us a chance somewhere to act as a safety back up and supply a few of your needs as a secondary source."*

"Does that sound fair?"

Get your required information. Come back with the samples for them to try. At the end of the trial period visit them again.

CLOSE THE SALE

2) At End of Your Presentation

You have done all your homework and it is your second or third visit. You have put together a final presentation that is based on the answers you got earlier on your first, second or additional visits.

Nothing was said indicating a strong loyalty to Brand "B".

You feel that you addressed everything that was outlined and came up with answers to all their questions and showed features and benefits that were equal to or better than your known competition.

You have supplied samples and/or provided items for a trial of your products and you saw that they were successful.

You have now just completed your final presentation and you know that you are competitive, and you have now asked for an order.

Your prospect has now said: *"I have listened to your presentation and tried your products and we still feel Brand B is better."*

You now look, and act concerned and confused by their statement that "Brand B" is better. Your efforts have just demonstrated that you have equaled and, in some areas, surpassed the features they originally gave you for "Brand B". Your prices are also competitive.

It is time to get to the bottom of their feelings or you will leave without an order - so start your lost sale close approach.

The Clarification Process

STEP 1 - QUESTION IT

You say: *"It looks like we have not been able to convince you to use our product and I accept your decision and I am leaving."*

Close your briefcase or folder

And get up to leave and Stop.

And you say: *"I have obviously failed to show you all of the benefits of our products and where we offer some definite advantages".*

"Of course, I am disappointed."

Look disappointed and continue with: *"Just to help me understand why you still prefer Brand B; may I ask which area still makes you still feel that "Brand B" is still better."*

Stop and wait for an answer

If they do not give one

Do a summary Question Close!

You Ask:

- Was it their prices?
- Was it their service?
- Was it their features?
- Keep going until they indicate a reason

STEP 2 - SHUT UP AND LISTEN

Hear them out!   Your hope is that they will say something that will allow you to respond.

STEP 3 - CONFIRM THEIR ANSWER.

When they do make a response,

Repeat their answers back to them: *"So this (the reason) is why you still feel Brand B is better. Is that, right?*

The Solution Process

STEP 4 - ANSWER THEIR CONCERNS.

It is time to provide reasons why your product has met or even surpassed Brand B. You have now fully answered their concerns.

STEP 5 - CONFIRM YOUR ANSWER.

You now say: *"Now that should settle your concerns. Is that, right?"*

ASK FOR THE ORDER

If they are still not responsive

It's time for the Ben Franklin Close

Or time to leave as Promised

You have done everything now that you can to change their mind. Maybe they are buying from a friend or relative.

You cannot win them all, but it is your job to try – so thank them and leave the door open to come back and try again.

They are still a prospect and now they know you
TOMORROW IS ANOTHER DAY

CHANGE OF BASE

Overview

It is not unusual for a client to view things from a different perspective and miss an obvious situation.

They see one thing when they view your products or services and it prevents them realizing that you have already met all their needs.

Your job here is to show them the other way of looking at your proposal to realize that it really does fit their needs.

You simply change their way of thinking

You will

"CHANGE THE BASE!"

The Three examples:

1. Product is too Small

2. Product is too Big

3. You are too far away

1. Product is too Small

Overview

You have just made your presentation and you have met every requirement that you were given during your preparatory meetings. In some cases, you have gone beyond expectations.

The biggest mistake here is not making a smaller size a benefit or feature earlier in your presentation. It is now an issue possibly because your competition made it one or it is a normal reaction.

This is a "Change of Base Answer"

Size to Performance

The prospect has said: *"Your product is too small to do the job."*

The Clarification Process

STEP 1 - QUESTION IT

You ask: *"Why do you feel size will affect performance?*

STEP 2 - SHUT UP AND LISTEN

Listen to their answer.

STEP 3 - CONFIRM THEIR ANSWER

Repeat their answer back to them as you understand it.

You now reply: *"I understand how you could feel this way. Many other people have had this same reaction.*

The Solution Process

STEP 4 - ANSWER THEIR CONCERNS

May I ask; *is it not true that today, results are all measured by how well people or products do their respective jobs, not by their physical size?"*

Wait for their Answer

It should be: *"Yes that's true."*

You say: *"Yes, performance is the objective not size, and the modern manager of today gauges a person or a product's value by performance, not size.*

You continue: *"Is that not what we are talking about here? You are really interested in performance not size. Is that, right?"*

They will have nowhere to go but say yes

Unless they are being ridiculous

STEP 5 - CONFIRM YOUR ANSWER

You say: *"You have tested our product and we both have seen that the results were more than satisfactory."*

"You have acknowledged that our price was more than competitive and yet we are discussing size as being a problem.

Continue: "You have also agreed that your main concern is will this product do the job that you want it to do? - Not how big it is? Isn't that, right?

Wait for their answer which should be a Yes

Ask for the Order!

CLOSE IT!

2. Product is too Big

Overview

You are dealing with a large piece of equipment here, or a large processing system.

You have just made your presentation and you have met every requirement that you were given during your preparatory meetings.

Your engineering department has calculated all the required measurements to ensure performance and product size capabilities and you know that you are not in an overkill situation regarding design.

The prospect has just said: *"Your product (System) is too BIG!"*

You know that your choice of materials and design allows you to build a very efficient product to fit into the smallest footprint possible.

The Clarification Process

STEP 1 - QUESTION IT.

You say: *"I am sure there is a reason why you are saying this and as I can see there are three possibilities here as to why you are saying our equipment is TOO BIG."*

You ask: *"Which one(s) would be correct?"*

1. *"You have reduced your part sizes or your specifications?"*
2. *"You have lowered the amount of floor space you have available?"*
3. *"We are too big compared to someone else."*

STEP 2 - SHUT UP AND LISTEN

You know that to handle the product sizes and specifications they originally stated, the equipment or footprint cannot be made any smaller without affecting their needs.

If the equipment is made smaller than you have proposed; it will mean cutting corners on design, sacrificing the integrity of your clients stated performance requirements, restricting the product size they can handle.

It might not meet code requirements which is not always evident. You also know your competition will do these things to get an order.

If #1 or #2 has changed

You will then ask to re-quote to adjust your size and price to suit. If nothing has changed in the part sizes, performance requirements or floor space, the only possible answer is….

It is TOO BIG when Compared to the Competition.

You have given them three choices and they have eliminated two of them.

This requires a "CHANGE OF BASE" Answer

Size to Price

STEP 3 - CONFIRM THEIR ANSWER

You say: *"You have now indicated that your part design or performance specifications have not changed."*

"You have also confirmed that you have not reduced the floor space available."

"But; You still say that our equipment is too big."

Continue: *"We know our equipment is not too big to fit the available floor space. The size is also needed to handle all the product specifications you requested, which also have not changed. It is also required to meet the industry code requirements."*

Conclusion by Elimination

You Say: *"It appears that we are too big compared to someone else, am I correct?"*

It is the only conclusion that makes sense and the customer should admit if it is so.

The Solution Process

STEP 4 - ANSWER THEIR CONCERNS

You Say: *"May we conclude that it is not just the size at issue here but probably PRICE as well?" Size usually affects price!"*

They will probably concede: *"It is PRICE."*

You know that your competition will undersize equipment or cut corners to obtain a lower price advantage. It often is done at the expense of the client.

STEP 5 - CONFIRM YOUR ANSWER

You now say: *"You have stated our equipment is too big on the premise that our competitor's size which is smaller can handle your requirements.*

Pause as if thinking then say: *"I think we may have a dangerous design problem here that is the real issue."*

Continue: *"My further concern here is that if this assumption (size of the competitor offerings) is wrong, two things will happen:"*

1. *"WE WILL LOSE the order based on our own design integrity which is reflected in the increased dollar amount quoted."*

2. *"YOU WILL ALSO LOSE by not being able to handle all of your product sizes and meet the specifications that you have outlined in your performance criteria or satisfy the industry code requirements."*

You have now effectively changed the BASE

From Size to Price

You have also brought design integrity into the picture.

You now might say: *"We often lose to price and it hurts. We also see that it is the client that suffers the most."*

"The sting of poor design and equipment performance painfully lives on – long after the initial joy of a lower price. The reality of inferior goods becomes a huge problem."

"It may be very costly to fix or even worse – it is not possible to fix."

"Unfortunately for us we must stand on our design integrity rather than provide a flawed system to obtain a lower price to get the order."

The final Questions

It is now time to ask the closing question using the alternative of choice:

You Say: *"Which is most important to you - a lower price today or getting the product you expected that meets all of your needs from now on?"*

SHUT UP AND WAIT FOR

"MEET MY NEEDS."

Ask for the Order

FINISH THE CLOSE

3. Location - You are too far away

Example Overview

You have just quoted to supply equipment worth $2,465,000.00 and you are there to get the order.

The prospect says that they like your proposal and that it has everything that they want but they have decided that you are just too far away to provide the service they need.

If you were closer, they would be very interested and probably give you the order.

This is a "CHANGE OF BASE" Answer

Distance to Time

Sample Locations for our Discussion

The prospect is in Toronto, Ontario

Your business location is Chicago USA - 708K or 440 miles

Your competition is in Hamilton, Ontario – 73K or 45 miles

The Clarification Process

This is where you need to change the base of measurement from distance to time to show the prospect that you can provide the same service and possibly even quicker.

You have already done your research earlier and know who you are up against and where everyone is located distance and time.

STEP 1 - QUESTION IT

You say: *"Why do you feel that Distance is the problem?"*

STEP 2 - SHUT UP AND LISTEN

Here them out completely.

STEP 3 – CONFIRM THEIR ANSWER

You say: *"I can see why you might feel that we are too far away to service your account."*

You now say: *"May I just quickly review what you have said? "You like everything about our proposal except that you feel we are too far away?"*

"If wasn't for the "too far thing", we would be doing business with you today, is, that right?"

When they say: "YES" Begin...

The Solution Process

STEP 4 - ANSWER THEIR CONCERNS

You say, *"At first glance, I might also be just as concerned if I were in your position."*

You say: **"I see that you are comparing distances as your base for measuring service capabilities."** *"Am I correct in saying that distance and serviceability is your concern?"*

Your job now is to change the way they are measuring your company's ability to provide service. To do this, you need to change the basis of their thinking.

Wait for their acknowledgment and Continue.

You say: *"If you will allow me to provide a different viewpoint we might already have an answer to your concerns."*

You now Ask and Answer this way

You do not need to ask every question and wait for an answer. It might be better to just provide the answers yourself in certain areas.

Find the right balance and begin

You Ask: *"How far is Hamilton from here?"*

You know the Answer: *"73 k or about 45 miles"*

You Ask: *"How much is that in time?"*

You know the Answer*: "70-80 minutes by car on a good traffic day"*

You Ask. *"How far away is Chicago?"*

You know the Answer: *"708 k or about 440 miles"*

You Ask: *"How much is that in time?"*

You know the Answer:*" 65 minutes by plane plus 15 - 20 minutes by taxi - 80 – 85 minutes"*

You continue: *"Is it not true that in the global business world that exists today, that we no longer measure things by distance, we measure them by time?"*

"Is that, not right?"

Wait for their answer and it should be a "YES."

STEP 5 - CONFIRM YOUR ANSWER

You Say: *"So what you are really concerned about is the time that it takes to service your business not the distance involved."*

|Is that, Right?"

Wait for their answer again and it should be a "YES."

You continue: *"That is how we measure things today "Time – not Distance?"*

The only Reasonable Answer is "YES"

Then you say: *"So that should completely settle the service because of distance concern Is that, right?"*

They will probably agree in most cases

It's time to ask for the order

CLOSE IT

They might say: *"What about Flight Delays"*

You Answer: *"What about Traffic Tie-ups"*

This cat and mouse list could go on and usually there will be a rebuttal for every concern presented.

In the End

If they still are opposed to the distance thing there is another answer that is a great follow up.

It is called – What Would You Do?

It is Next!

WHAT WOULD YOU DO?

This answer usually deals with what has been presented by the client as a Condition and usually conditions cannot be solved.

However, not everything that is presented as a condition; is one or must remain as one. We have learned earlier that all conditions should be challenged.

We have here three examples

What would you do?" Conditions"

1. No Service Close by

2. Objectionable Employees

3. Reputation of Product

There will be others that fall into this group. We are providing these three examples to enable you to follow the same conceptual outline to reach your goal.

1. No Service Close by

Overview

You have just made your presentation and made several attempts to close. You have answered all their objections and they are splitting hairs over your last answer to their objection.

Time not Distance

They still feel that because you are in Chicago that you will not be able to service them properly.

They empathize with what you are saying about time not distance being the measurement but have presented a counter argument about satisfactory flight times and airport delays, and perhaps a few additional reasons.

It may be Stubbornness

Or a Legitimate Concern for their Hesitation.

If local servicing is an ongoing problem and your company wants to sell their products in distance related situations – no local service – is something that you will need to solve anyway.

Your company will need to find a local service company for emergency time sensitive service requirements.

You can still offer ongoing troubleshooting and training with your own people in Chicago.

Once you have corrected this situation

You should not lose orders because of this distance condition

The Clarification Process

STEP 1 - QUESTION THEM

You now say to them: *"Have you ever been in situations where you have missed opportunities time after time because you have not been able to satisfy your customers comfort zone?"*

"You have met everything that your prospect is looking for - except for this one area. "In this case, it is Distance"

STEP 2 - SHUT UP AND LISTEN

They can say either: *"Yes or No"*

How they answer does not really matter

STEP3 - CONFIRM THEIR ANSWER

You continue: *I understand your concerns about our ability to service even using time not distance as a measuring point."*

"It is a very legitimate concern when entering into a project of this size."

"It is our ability to look after you in a timely manner that is causing you to hesitate to place your business with our company – right?

"Servicing capability not product is we are talking about here. You feel that Chicago is just too far out of your comfort zone to be able to service equipment in the Toronto are. – Is that right?"

Pause

"May I ask what you would do if something like this distance thing kept reoccurring with you and preventing sales?"

They will probably respond by saying that they would find a way to provide the required service locally.

If they do not say it, you say it

The Solution Process

STEP 4 - ANSWER THEIR CONCERNS

You say: *"That's what we are doing."* OR *"That's what we have done".*

You then say: *"We have retained a quality service company in your city that is familiar with our products for just this reason."*

"They will be available on a 24 hour 7 days a week basis to respond to time sensitive emergency requirements."

Optional; but if True, use it

"We are strong believers in using local installers whenever we can. We are doing this here. Since they are involved and working with us in the installation of your system, they will already be familiar with everything."

"They are more than qualified and will be providing our 24/7 service."

STEP 5 - CONFIRM YOUR ANSWER

You now say: *"As you can see we will be able to resolve an emergency requirement locally with local people. They will be able to obtain our input by telephone or internet connection if required."*

"As well, we can still provide our normal in-house assistance and trouble shooting from Chicago on a 24/7 basis."

"We also will still provide in person service calls, when required. You will be very well taken care of for service. Would you agree that this is a correct statement?"

Wait for their answer

It will almost be a guaranteed YES

CLOSE IT!

2. People Problems

Overview

This objection can happen at any time. It can also happen to anyone. It could be during your first call, during or at the end of your presentation or anywhere in between.

Things are going smoothly

And Suddenly this Objection is Made

Your prospect says: *"I remember now, I had someone call on me from your firm two years ago, and they really upset me and several of my employees. Because of this, I will never do business with your firm again."*

The Clarification Process

STEP 1 - QUESTION IT

You reply: *"I understand how you feel." "Do you recall the name?"*

Pause briefly for a name but one is not required

Continue: *"I think I know who you are referring to." Tell me; have you ever had one of your employees upset a customer in their actions or words so badly that the customer stopped giving you their business?"*

"You also discovered that this was happening with other customers and they were starting to reduce their business or even end their business with your company as well?

STEP 2 - SHUT UP AND LISTEN

If the prospect says: *"YES"*

You ask: *"What did you do?"*

If it has not happened to your prospect,

You say: *"Tell me, what would you do if that happened to you?"*

Hear them out. There are only a couple of directions they can go, but do not assume. Listen to their entire answer.

STEP 3 - CONFIRM THEIR ANSWER

Their answer will most likely be something that most people would do. They could say we fired that person, removed them from customer contact or severely reprimanded them.

No matter what they say

Repeat their solution back to them

The Solution Process

STEP 4 - ANSWER THEIR CONCERNS

You have placed them in your shoes and made them vulnerable to experiencing the same problem that they are objecting to. You have asked for advice and they have provided an answer.

You say: *"That's what we did"*

You have shown them that you did exactly what they said they would do, to solve this issue. Can they now object to doing business with your company when you have taken a course of action endorsed by them?

STEP 5 - CONFIRM YOUR ANSWER

Make sure the person is gone or is far enough removed so they will not have any contact with your prospect, if they are still with you.

If they are still employed with your company, indicate what strong definitive action was taken to remove the problem.

It could be something like: *"You know we discovered this was happening and this person was just not good with handling customers.*

Continue: *"We discovered they were great in other areas of responsibility completely away from customer involvement. We moved them to that position."*

"They are completely out of the equation."

You say: *"It seems we think alike, and our company has done the right thing to remove this problem, would you not agree?"*

Ask for an Opportunity to Quote

Or

If you have already quoted

Ask for the Order

CLOSE IT!

3. Product Reputation

Overview

You have previously made your attempt to set up an appointment, and you were successful in getting one.

You are now there to do your first presentation and you are suddenly met with this objection.

Your prospect says: *"Now I remember your company. I tried your products three years ago, and they just did not work out for me."*

"The quality was just not there, we experienced failure after failure, and problem after problem."

"So, tell me, why should I even consider talking to you let alone taking another chance with your company?"

The Clarification Process

STEP 1 - QUESTION IT

This is the same type as the People objection.

You say: *"I definitely agree with your thinking and position?*

Pause for a second and continue: *"May I ask if you ever have a product that just did not do what you expected it to do?"*

"It was being returned and damaging your business and you were losing customers because of it?"

Like the first two examples you are not challenging the prospect. You are agreeing with them and engaging them in an empathetic dialogue.

You now say: *"What did you do?"* - Wait for the answer

If it has not happened to your prospect

You say: *"What would you do if this happened to you?"*

STEP 2 - SHUT UP AND LISTEN

They will either tell you what they did or what they would do.

STEP 3 - CONFIRM THEIR ANSWER

Whatever their answer is, you continue and repeat their answer back to them. If they have had the same experience or just told you what they would do continue with the next statement.

The Solution Process

STEP 4 - ANSWER THEIR CONCERNS

You say: *"That's what we did."*

"We discovered that we needed a better product line for our number one line and found a new one to replace the one we were having problems with as our main product line."

"The other older line has a place in certain areas and performs very well there. We also still needed to service customers who were using it successfully.

"We have it available for several very specific uses where it performs well."

"We will be offering our new product line to you. It has a proven track record."

Make sure you have the Alternative Offerings

STEP 5 - CONFIRM YOUR ANSWER

You Say: *"So it seems that we have taken your advice and I think you will see that the bad situation no longer exists."*

"Does that remove your concerns?"

You are now able to continue with your presentation. You have successfully removed the problems stated by them with the same advice they have provided.

Not only have you demonstrated that you fixed the problem; but you also did not abandon existing customers who were happy with the older product line.

Clarification

There are many ways to present your correction for this situation; but make sure you have replaced this product as your #1 offering totally with a better alternative or are not using the old product for this prospect.

If you have a product or service that has caused problems, this situation has probably come up many times.

Corrective Action is the only way to remove this ongoing objection and any responsible company who wishes to survive will take the steps as we have mentioned.

If corrective action has not been taken, then this approach is not appropriate.

If a new product has been introduced, then you can do the following at the end of the solution Process.

GET A REQUEST TO QUOTE

Or If You Have Already Quoted

Ask for the Order

CLOSE IT!

CONDITIONAL OBJECTIONS

Overview

The next three examples are very common occurrences in the selling process. Most often they are conditions that exist.

Sometimes you may be able to create an answer that will change it to a simple objection.

You will then take Steps

To Overcome the Objection

To Obtain the Sale

Often, they may be time sensitive or require changes, and you will be faced with a call back and final presentation when the condition has been met.

That means that when you hear one of these conditions you do not immediately pack your bags and leave.

You must try your best to resolve the condition while understanding it will probably remain a condition for a while longer.

Knowing how to remain in the game is essential when this type of situation occurs.

The THREE Condition Examples

1. I need to talk to someone
2. I am waiting for another Price
3. I want to Think It Over

1 - I Need to Talk to Someone

Condition 1 Overview

The prospect has participated throughout the entire presentation with you, with questions and objections, and you have answered all of them successfully.

You have made your Final Close

The prospect says out of the blue: *"You know I like everything I hear and see. You have answered all of my questions and objections to my satisfaction, but, there is one more thing I have to do."*

Here is the Condition

They Continue: *"You see (my Aunt Jenny) has been a longtime confidant and mentor for me, and before I make a decision like this, I like to discuss it with her and get her opinion."*

This one is a zinger that can really catch you off guard. Their mentor could also be the father, mother, spouse, son or daughter and they are almost always

Someplace Else

The Clarification Process

a) Change it to an Objection

STEP 1 - QUESTION IT

Stay calm and do not get upset.

Start by saying: *"From the results of our presentation, can I say that you are completely happy with everything that we have proposed here today?"*

STEP 2 - SHUT UP AND LISTEN

The prospect says: *"Yes that is correct."*

They explain that this is a procedure that has been ongoing for years.

The prospect has now created a roadblock that they feel has isolated them from any further attempts to close.

At this moment, they have created a condition and it is up to you to try to remove it or change it to a simple objection.

STEP 3 - CONFIRM THEIR ANSWER

You now say: *"So the main reason you cannot move forward today is that you want to talk to your Aunt Jenny about this, to get her input, her blessing, the rubber stamp, so to speak; before you move on with this project."*

"Is that right?"

The client is happy with this question because it reinforces the condition and they are confident that you cannot go any further.

The Solution Process

STEP 4 - ANSWER THEIR CONCERNS

At this point you have confirmed their reason for not continuing any further until they speak with Aunt Jenny.

You will now begin to break down that defense with the following approach.

You Ask: *"Where is Aunt Jenny at this moment?"*

Find out where the person is and how they usually communicate, and if they are in another town or country.

Once you have established where they are and how they communicate in these matters respond accordingly.

If they are in a time zone where you can call now

You say: *"Would it make sense to contact your Aunt Jenny right now?*

Continue with: *"You can speak to her and explain what you are about to do, and that you would like her input and her blessing."*

I can step out of your office to allow privacy.

Continue "*In this way, I will be present to answer any questions that might arise, and if she feels it is a good idea, we can then proceed without any loss of time?*"

"*If more discussion is needed then I can answer any immediate questions and make myself available if more should arrive later. Does that make any sense at all here?*"

STEP 5 - CONFIRM YOUR ANSWER

If they can be reached and your prospect will make the telephone call, answer any objections that might arise. If it turns out the mentor is close by offer to wait or even accompany them and visit Aunt Jenny.

If they agree, have the telephone call or meeting

THEN CLOSE IT!

b) The Condition Remains - Unable to Talk to Aunt Jenny

If the prospect does not agree with your suggestion, or if Aunt Jenny cannot be reached.

You are faced with a Condition

It is time to step back and plan a **CALL BACK.**

After your attempt to solve it; your immediate suggestion for the call back may also cause them to be a little angry, so do not apply too much pressure.

You say: "*I can see that this is very important to you, and part of your process in these matters, so we can take one of two directions*

Direction 1- *We can establish a time when this discussion with your aunt Jenny can take place and I can make myself available by telephone or in person, to answer her questions.*"

Or

Direction 2 - "*We could establish a time to get together after you have had a chance to discuss this with your Aunt Jenny.*"

Finish with: "*Again, whatever makes sense for you is fine with me.*"

At this point you have done everything possible that you can do. The need to talk to someone may be

- A legitimate reason

- A great objection

- A great opportunity for them to buy some thinking time

- An opportunity to talk to your competition

- A way to make it easier to say no when you make your next closing attempt.

The pressure is now off them and when you make the call back appointment - it will be DO or DIE!

You will now be doing

A CALL BACK PRESENTATION

2 - Waiting for Another Price

Condition 2 Overview

This is a very common occurrence because not everyone can be the last one in. On the first call or during information gathering calls are times when you need to start to worry about positioning yourself.

Try to make an initial presentation or a preliminary offering that is done before preparing your final quotation. It is your dress Rehearsal as we call it. This is when the final positioning starts to become an extremely important factor.

The closer you are to last one in, the more information you will be able to obtain, to see where you are positioned regarding client preference.

If you know there will be another round, this is when you will make your efforts to be the last one in to avoid this condition. Everyone is now maneuvering to achieve the same thing and there are many tactics used to be last in.

The prospects choice of final positioning can sometimes indicate the order of their preference (saving the best for last), but not always.

No matter what the circumstances are; you will often find yourself facing this condition, and it is a difficult one.

Your prospect says: *"I am waiting for another proposal to come in." Or I am waiting for several proposals to come in."*

Again, stay calm and do not get angry.

You say: *"That's fine I understand."*

The Clarification Process

STEP 1 - QUESTION IT

You Say: *"I am sure you know that being the final presenter is what every sales person wants."*

"Would you agree with that comment?"

Continue: *"Someone has to be first or second and it looks I have made my presentation earlier than others. The only questions that I might ask right now are these."*

"Do you have any concerns with our company?"

"Do you have any concerns with our product?"

"Our delivery or Our price?"

You continue: *"May I also ask that, once you have listened to all of the proposals, if I might have the opportunity to talk with you before you make your final decision?"*

STEP 2 - SHUT UP AND LISTEN

The prospect will usually respond to your questions and usually will explain the situation; but, the condition will remain.

STEP 3 - CONFIRM THEIR ANSWER

You say: *"I understand and appreciate why you are still waiting for other quotations to come in. Making any kind of decision is premature at this point."*

The Solution Process

STEP 4 - ANSWER THEIR CONCERNS

You Say: *"I am sure you would agree that our promptness has made it more difficult to keep ourselves current with any changes that might occur."*

Wait for an answer

You Say: *"Often new conditions or questions arise after listening to everyone, and our existing quotation could no longer be in compliance with your new parameters."*

"That is why being first or second is difficult, because one cannot react to these changes."

STEP 5 - CONFIRM YOUR ANSWER

You ask: *"I fully agree that you will need to see all of the quotations before you can make a proper evaluation.*

Establishing the Call Back

You Ask*: "When do you expect that you will have seen all of the proposals, and will have had sufficient time to review them?"*

Wait for the answer

Continue: "Can we establish a time to meet before I leave today?"

This will probably not be possible at this point and it may appear to be rushing your client. Try anyway. It may also be better for your chances; to arrange when to call, to arrange the appointment.

You ask: "May I call you to set up a meeting (whenever they have said), so that I can answer any new questions you may have or make any adjustments before having our meeting?"

If your prospect says: "YES"

Set the time for your meeting

YOU ARE NOW DOING

A CALL BACK PRESENTATION

3 - I'll Think It Over

This is the one that stops most sales people in their tracks. The sales person has just finished the final part of the presentation and has asked for the order. It can also happen just before they can ask for the order:

The prospect says: *"Thank you for a great presentation."*

"You know, I like what I see, you have done a great job of explaining everything; but you know I just really need to think it over. Give me a couple of days, and I'll call you."

This is often because of the natural habit of procrastination

Some people just resist doing things right away

They have indicated they like your product or service but need to think it over. Maybe there are some areas that are causing concern as well. If you leave now they will go unanswered.

The prospect may also be chuckling because **"I'll think it over"** usually stops most sales people from going any further.

The prospect knows that if they do not have to decide today, they are off the hook.

Their attitude is often: *"If they (meaning you) want the order let them work for it. They will come back. Who knows maybe I can get a better deal from them or someone else. Let them sweat a bit."*

Here is Where you can Change the Direction.

You say: *"Thank you for your kind words and appreciation of our presentation. I understand, and there is a lot to consider."*

"I can see that we have truly sparked your interest, or you would not be taking the time to think it over unless you were really interested. - Is that right?

They will almost certainly say: *"YES"*

They feel they have stopped your attempts to get an order and you are leaving.

By adding this next question, you change the entire game. You are now going to try and make them squirm a bit.

You continue and say: *"I can see that you are very interested and like what we have presented. I hope you are not just saying you want to think it over - just to get rid of me?"*

This question has a way of making the customer qualify their interest and tell you that they have not been wasting your time.

It has a way of turning things around and now they are on the spot.

In some cases, they could get angry

But it's part of the game

Wait for the: *"No that is not it!   I am very interested, and I am not just wasting your time. I really do want to think about it."*

You now have them trying to justify the delay and they will usually emphasize that they really do want to think it over.

You then continue: *"You know I have found when people want to think things over, it is usually because they have some concerns, or something is unclear."*

"Just to clarify my own thinking, what part is it that is unclear, and you want to think over?"

Here the Approach is Different

Pause and wait for an answer

If they do not have one –

Then

Do a Summary Close

THE CALL BACK OBJECTION

Overview

No one likes the idea of a call back especially if an appointment needs to be set.

If it comes out of a genuine reason why the prospect could not decide at the time you made your first presentation. You asked for a time to get together while you were there.

If they did not agree at that time, you must now call to set the date to do your presentation again.

We will offer four different reasons for the call back

1. You simply needed to review and revise your proposal
2. They needed to talk to someone who was not available.
3. They were waiting for other prices to come in.
4. They needed to think it over

If no appointment was scheduled and only an approximate date to call was made; follow the next steps.

Call to set the Appointment

We are giving Four examples for a Call Back

 # 1 - You say: *"When we last talked, we spoke about getting together this week once I finished my revised proposal; which I have now completed.*

 # 2 - You say: *"When we last talked, we spoke about getting together this week once; you had a chance to speak with your Aunt Jenny.*

 # 3 - You say: *"When we last talked, we spoke about getting together this week; once you had received and reviewed all of the proposals.*

 # 4 – You Say: *"When we last met you needed time to think things over.*

Continue: *"Have there been any new developments or changes that I might need to look at or consider before I come in?"*

Get the details if any, and make the changes needed to your proposal.

Very often, getting back in is a very difficult process; and this is when you will be met with the objection to the call back.

Do not ask "IF" you can come in

You ask, "WHEN" you can come in

You ask: *"Which day is best to come in - morning or afternoon. - 2:00PM or is 3:00 better.*

Wait for confirmation.

Make your Call

And Presentation

CLOSE IT

Objection to a Call Back

No Need at Customer's Request

Your prospect answers your question about new developments in this way.

They say *"No - I think we have all of the information we need to make our decision without the need for you to come in."*

This is usually an indication that you are not first in line for the order and maybe not even in the finals. It usually indicates that you need to get back in or it's probably over.

You will need to re-position yourself if you want a chance to get the order. It is time to dangle a carrot to see if they bite.

The Clarification Process

STEP 1 – QUESTION THEIR RESPONSE

You ask: *"Why have things changed about our coming in to*

o *"Present our revised proposal."*

o *"Discuss what your Ant Jenny had to say*

o *"Review our proposal and discuss any changes we might need to make now that you have all of your proposals.*

o *"Had a chance to think things over"*

STEP 2 - SHUT UP AND LISTEN

Listen to their explanation and ask any questions for clarification; but hear them out completely.

STEP 3 - CONFIRM THEIR ANSWER

Whatever their answer is repeat it back to them.

The Solution Process

STEP 4 – ANSWER THEIR REASON

You say: *"I understand what you have just told me, but in consideration of:*

- *Previous discussion when I was there*
- *The extra benefits and better price we now offer*
- *Or any other appropriate reason…*

We certainly would appreciate the opportunity to talk with you. Do you not have 15 – 20 minutes on the day we originally set aside to quickly review the changes in our proposal? I will then leave it with you"

Continue: *"During the last few days, last week (whatever it has been), we have made some significant improvements to our proposal. I think that it makes a big difference in how you would view our (products, system, equipment, or services)."*

The Chances

If you are in the top two or three being considered, the client will usually agree to see you to avoid eliminating a better offer resulting from your revisions.

STEP 5 - CONFIRM YOUR ANSWER

You Ask: *"Can we set a time to get together?"*

If they say: *"YES"*

Thank them, set and confirm the appointment time. Take the time to review and make your changes sizzle.

Make your Call and Presentation

Ask for the Order Again

CLOSE IT

No Appointment Possible

If they say *"NO"* to your request for an appointment - Do not get angry.

You simply say: *"Since I was already going to be in the area that day anyway, I would like to drop off the revisions so that you will have our latest proposal for consideration or at least have it on record?*

"I will just leave it at the front desk."

You say: *"Thank you for the opportunity. I will drop off the information* (name the day)."

The Follow up

Call the client the day you drop off your changes to see if they got them, if they have questions and where you now stand?

It is obvious that someone else has the advantage position. This happens.

Tell them you will call back in a couple of days to see if they have any questions. When the two days are up, it is time to make your call.

You ask again: *"Would you have time this week or next week to discuss our proposal?*

If they say yes, you are back in the game. Set your appointment time, make your presentation and ask for the order.

If they say No,

There is always Another Prospect

And another day

MUDSLINGING

We felt this topic was worthy of some discussion. Unfortunately, there will usually be competition engaged in this negative activity.

This is a tactic that many sales people use to try and position their company to get the order. It is not a good tactic to use as it can often backfire on the person doing it.

It is Bad Selling Tactics and Not Ethical

If your competition is bad mouthing you, think of it as being a good sign. Your competition has shown that they fear you and/or your company and cannot compete on a normal basis.

Do not respond with the same mudslinging methods. Just like Hockey; it is usually the last person into the fight, that is sure to get the penalty.

In this case the penalty might mean elimination from any kind of consideration.

If the customer starts saying that they have heard things about your company or product that concerns them, even; if they are wrong, do not get angry or argue.

Hear them out

In many cases the prospect will be testing your integrity; to see if you have any, so do not retaliate.

Another Sign to watch for

You could also notice a sudden or significant change in the prospects attitude or involvement with you. This could also be a result of mudslinging. Whether it is stated or suspected you need to defend yourself.

In either case

NEVER bad mouth a competitor or their product – just out-sell them.

The minute you lower yourself to the level of mudslinging, you have lost the right for the respect of your potential customer.

The prospect will now find it harder to buy from you, as negativity generates negativity.

Knowing which competitors engage in these negative mudslinging comments will give you the opportunity to use different approaches.

Make it part of your Presentations

You can say: *"We know that some of our competitors engage in mudslinging. We do not believe or get involved in this type of practice."*

"We also know that it is just their way of trying to level the playing field because they are intimidated by the higher quality and benefits of what we offer."

"They often try to remove us from quoting or a position of consideration this way."

> *"If you have some information about us that concerns you, all we ask is that we have the opportunity to respond."*

> *"We are not asking for names, just what has been said.*

> *"We do not want to do battle with them."*

> *"We do however wish to defend ourselves, which we have a right to do."*

If your prospect indicates that they have heard some negative comments

Treat it as an Objection

Handle it the Same Way

The Clarification Process

You should respond with this: *"Could we get your concerns on the table right now, so we can answer them?"*

Listen to the comments.

Repeat them back to the client.

The Solution Process

Respond to them and defend yourself and your company.

When you have finished ask: *"Does that settle your concerns?"*

If No Cooperation

If they will not tell you what it is that they have heard, it is not good.

All you can say now is: *"There are always two sides to every situation. And of course, our competition is not favoring our side"*

You Continue: *"It is hard to shadow box with the unknown, and it is almost impossible to defend accusations you cannot hear."*

"May I ask if these factors will have had any effect on our ability to get this order?"

If they say: *"NO"*

All you can say is: *"Are there any other areas that you need answers to, or have concerns about, in what we have proposed?"*

If they say they have no other concerns,

ASK FOR THE ORDER

Mudslinging Summary

Mudslinging is a poor way to win orders and if the customer is not forthcoming with information, there is little you can do. Just do the best you can and that is all you can do.

As shown it is possible to still get the order if you ask the right questions. Do not return the mudslinging!

Remember the – *"What would you do"* approach discussed earlier and perhaps use it now."

Put them in Your Shoes

And ask

What would you do?

SUMMARY

The Answers to objections that we have presented are not meant to trick your prospect. They are meant find out why they are hesitating.

Pressure without answering their concerns first, will only damage your reputation and that of your company.

Pressure after an unanswered objection, will only make clients angry.

The power of; how to find the cause for the objection, and being able to answer it, will give you all the ammunition that you will need from start to finish.

We have provided some basic ways to solve objections. In them, you will find the ability to combine different aspects from each to create new ways to answer objections and find solutions.

- Always treat objections as good things
- Do not fear them
- They are Buying signals that can lead you to the Order

From the first call to completion of the process and the final close; your efforts should be to build respect, trust and create a good relationship.

The best finish is getting the sale, the right way

- Avoid the Use of Bad words
- Do not become a Mudslinger

ALWAYS USE

THE FIVE STEP PROCESS

TO OVERCOME OBJECTIONS AND CONDITIONS

END OF PART THREE

DIRECT SALES 101

PART FOUR

MEETINGS AND PRESENTATIONS

THE FIRST INTRODUCTORY MEETING

THE INFORMATION GATHERING MEETINGS

FINAL PRESENTATIONS

THE CALL BACK

Written by

Wayne E Shillum

DEDICATION

This Part is Dedicated to Everyone

Who Insisted on having a Meeting

For Everything you could Possibly Think of

It often seemed Anything Could Trigger

These Words

"WE NEED TO HAVE A MEETING"

But they All were

Invaluable Training for Use in my Career

When it Became My Turn to hold and run Meetings

And make Presentations.

Thanks to All!

INTRODUCTION

Selling is all about Communicating

The need to communicate will take place before you even step outside of your office to visit your prospects, clients, or peers. The need starts within the walls of your own company and involves everyone you work with.

Without establishing a solid base of communication within your own company, you will not achieve the full potential of selling success outside of it. In sales; as in life, you are very much controlled by how well you convey the messages you want to deliver to those around you.

It is not only what you are thinking and can convey effectively to others; but also, how well you interpret what others are transmitting in their actions and words back to you.

In Sales

The learned ability part of communicating well with others is often overlooked. Many sales people take this skill for granted and never reach their full potential.

Often it will take a determined effort by sales people to improve their ability to communicate and make effective sales presentations. Learning and fine tuning their communication skills will greatly improve their selling ability and increase their closing percentages.

These skills are essential when meeting with prospects and associates.

Areas where you rely on being able to Communicate Effectively

- Your office co-workers
- Your Prospects who are yet to become Clients
- Your New and Existing clients,
- Your Suppliers
- Your peers in the industry

From the initial prospecting stages, right through all your meetings with your prospects, your presentations, closing the sale and answering objections; communication is an essential part of selling.

Today we have many ways to convey our thoughts.

- Land lines, mobile telephones and other mobile devices
- Faxes, emails, post office, videos, You Tube
- Conferencing, webinars, podcasts,
- Skype – the online face to face meetings,
- In person face to face meetings.

Most of your meetings and sales presentations will be greatly enhanced by perfecting your communication skills.

The Different Types of Meetings

- Your initial introductory meetings,
- Your fact-finding meetings
- Your dress rehearsal presentations
- The final meetings for sales presentations and quotations.
- The Call Back Meeting

Your Challenges

Before you venture into the actual world of selling you must learn how to put successful sales presentations together and deliver them.

Unless you develop communicating skills to their fullest potential, your sales presentations will have little or only mediocre successes.

Successful meetings do not just happen. They are planned and structured with all the essential elements. They are rehearsed over and over until they can be delivered with perfection.

COMMUNICATION

The Overview

As we said in our introduction, most people do not give the area of communication much thought in their day to day lives, so it is very understandable why its importance is often overlooked in the sales profession.

We have three levels of communicating available and studies show that 100% of successful communicating is made up of all three of these areas. (We will refer to them as Levels)

We will list them in order of how most people place their importance and use them when they convey their messages to one another. We will also indicate by percentage how these studies view their overall effectiveness.

Level One – Content

Content in the words we choose and use; mostly in our written words (advertising) but also the content of our spoken dialogue".

Studies say Level One accounts for only 7% of the potential for communication success.

Level Two – Voice Toning

Our Voice and the way we say it makes a difference. Studies say voice tones account for 38% of our potential ability in communicating.

Level Three – Body Language

Facial and Body Movement – Our eyes, mouth, head, arms and legs account for the greatest portion at 55% of our ability to communicate with others.

Above Figures from studies by: Dr. Albert Mehrabian Professor Emeritus at UCLA. "The Essence of Communication"

When we look at the results of the studies made by **Dr. Albert Mehrabian,** we begin to understand why most of the sales efforts fail in communicating with others.

What you can Expect (based on these studies)

- 7% is accessed - when Sales People send or drop off literature and hope for a call from the client.

  o 93% of their potential effectiveness which are (Levels 2 & 3) will still be unused.

- 38% additional potential can be accessed - If they can talk to the person by telephone.

  o Now a total of 45% has been accessed if they combine content with voice delivery.

  o 55% is still untouched in Level 3.

This does not mean that they will be 45% effective, as no effort is perfect. Their effectiveness will be determined by how well they can perform the skills of creating content and talking on the telephone.

Many sales are made using these two levels alone, without a face to face meeting. Telemarketing sales is a prime example.

Add a Face-to-Face Meeting

Seeing the prospect in person provides access to the final and largest part of communication. This is the 55% that one can add using *Body Language* to communicate.

This body language feature occurs in both presenting your offerings and in observing the client's reaction to your presentation.

In most prospecting efforts, our goal is to arrange a face to face meeting so that we can present our company and its offerings using all three levels of communication.

Here we will find out the full extent of their needs and interest for our products or services.

Telephone Sales

Some direct sales companies use just the telephone to make their sales. Here they are accessing only content and voice to get the sale.

The need to do these two areas well is very important, as a sale depends on achieving one's goal by accessing only 45%.

These telemarketing companies develop very effective methods in the use of these two levels. They are great places to learn and develop these first two levels of communication.

For the rest of the direct selling methods, we use these first two areas (content and voice tone), to qualify and arrange a meeting in person. At this meeting, we can make use of all three levels of communication when we make our first face-to-face presentation.

Again, this in-person meeting does not mean we can have 100% effective communications results but, we have access to 100 percent of the process. It only means the opportunity is there to use all three levels. The results are up to you and how well you develop these skills.

Rate your Present Communication Skills

CONTENT - or promotional material

      Rate your ability from 0 to 7% =?

VOICE - delivery of your message

      Rate your ability from 0 to 38% =?

BODY LANGUAGE - when talking

      Rate your ability from <u>0 to 55% =?</u>

      Total out of 100% =?

For the average person, it would optimistically be as follows:

1. Content -   2 – 4%   average – 3%
2. Voice -   10 – 15%   average – 12%
3. Body Language -   <u>19 – 23%</u>   <u>average – 21%</u>

   Normal Result is -   31 to 42%   average – 36%

If this is an optimistic level of communications for most people to reach without any type of training, why do sales people limit themselves to only a 31 to 42% (36% average) chance of success?

Without Training in Communication Skills

Just sending or dropping literature off to introduce yourself is only 7% of your Prospecting Job. One might reach 4%. If there is a real need, sometimes this will create interest in your product or service, but why not improve your chances.

A telephone call by you and a brief conversation gives you a much-improved opportunity and adds another 38% potential in your prospecting efforts. One might add up to another 15%

You need an in person meeting to access all your communication capabilities. Optimistically one might add 23%. This is where you will have employed all three parts of the communication capabilities.

Do you want to be limited to 31% or even 42%? I hope not.

Many sales people send or drop off literature and feel that they have done their prospecting job. They are just getting started. It is important to use all three areas to complete their full prospecting responsibilities.

The goal is to make the most out of each communicating area and get as close to the 100% level as you can.

Level One – The Words

Content

The words you use; both spoken and in your visual aids, is where it all begins. Selection of the right words to use should be a priority.

Unfortunately for many; little attention is given here, and thus the limits are pre-set on how much can be achieved in all three levels.

Using great content allows you to create interest and optimize all three levels of communicating when they take place. With your content and words, you can create a powerful format that delivers a clear focused message to your prospect.

You will have the foundation to add emphasis with your voice tones and body language to optimum levels.

Without great content, you have already limited your chances for success.

Key Points for Content

1. Have a great Opening.
2. Provide Key Points that will Create and Hold Interest.
3. Use words that allow optimum use of all three levels
4. Provide a compelling Closing or "Call-to-Action"

USE CONTENT - or words that provide optimum possibilities

- Use words that are POWERFULL and allow you to use your voice and body to emphasize them.

- Use words that are PRECISE and are not just fillers or close substitutes of what you should be using.

- Use words that will provide a CLEAR and FOCUSED message.

- **Use words** that will create the desire to act.

- Use words that will MOTIVATE.

- Use words that will allow you to convey ENTHUSIASM.

Add words that Convey Emotion.

Use words that will convey HAPPINESS, SUCCESS and PLEASURE in the use your products or services.

Use a Thesaurus to access synonyms that achieve all the above.

Content is the first part of the communication process and it is what will allow you to do the rest effectively. In the preparation of your written material you should use all the support areas available to you.

Most writing programs have a spell and grammar check so there should be no excuse for misspelled words or bad grammar.

- Misspelled words can seriously detract from what could be a great article or presentation.

- Omitting Punctuation can lead to loss of clarity and will result in confusion.

- **A thesaurus** can be found in most writing programs.

This allows you to select powerful and accurate words for your descriptions and explanations; while avoiding repetition of the same word.

This allows you to provide clear and focused messages that are not boring to read or listen to.

A dictionary should never be far from your reach. The use of the wrong word in your narrative efforts can have disastrous results. It will cause the loss of attention and credibility.

Other people's quotes may be used on various topics to get your point across. This is often more compelling than your own words and these quotes can often add validity and can say it exactly to suit the occasion.

Preparation

The time to get it right, is in the initial preparation process for your first contact with the prospect. It starts with the content for the spoken word.

You should always make use of this very valuable *"time of preparation"* at the beginning to get it right; so, you can say it right.

Accurate, powerful and descriptive messaging creates the ability for you to add emphasis with voice tones and body language.

The written word is a permanent record for all to see and re-visit

Having the right content allows you to leave the right message to be viewed over and over.

Your written words will also remind your prospect of the key points and benefits of your products or services after your presentation becomes history.

Take Time to Prepare

And

You will be on Your Way

To Becoming a Great Communicator

Level Two – Voice Tones

Making Voice Presentations

Your voice is your trademark. It is your main identifying feature when you are making presentations or just talking in general.

Your Voice Must Consistently Sound:

1. Upbeat and Positive

2. Warm and Friendly

3. Under Control

4. Authoritative

5. Clear

Smiling will automatically warm up the tone of your voice and your audience will notice the difference even if they cannot see you.

Research done by the department of Psychology at the University of Pittsburgh USA; indicated that people make distinctive judgments of others based on the tone of the speaker's voice.

Specifically, that a Deeper Voice Tone

Creates more Authority and Credibility

Everyone has a voice range, so it would be good to practice the lower end of your voice range, to deliver better presentations. Try speaking at different levels that are comfortable to use.

Your voice will influence people and can often imply the amount of knowledge that you have. This also increases your degree of professionalism and will increase your closing percentages.

If you want to be a credible authority on the subject matter of your presentation, voice tone is an important factor.

People Respond - Either Negatively or Positively

To *"Voice Tone"*

Practice by recording your voice at different levels and listen to the results. Keep trying until you reach the right level. Get feedback from your friends and peers.

Negative Reactions to Voice Tone

A shrill or high-pitched voice tends to have a negative impact on an audience. They will find the high pitch irritating. These presenters are often perceived to lack authority and knowledge of their topic.

They lose the Interest and Attention of the Audience.

A Monotone has little or no variance in energy levels emitted. It tends to become instantly boring to the audience and is very dysfunctional in presentations. People usually disengage quickly and very little; if anything, is accomplished by the speaker.

Speaking Fast - It is also normal for people to speak faster when delivering a presentation. This is very dangerous. Keep it slow enough for your client to easily follow your train of thought.

There is a definite need to speak slower to allow people to digest what you are saying. People who speak fast are felt to be confusing, and less intelligent.

Things that Create a Positive Reaction

A varied tone rising and falling allows you to emphasize your words and phrases.

Emotions like enthusiasm, humor, excitement, sorrow and concern are all conveyed by different tone levels as they inject different forms of energy into your words.

There is also a distinct difference between a person hearing what has been said, and a person understanding what has been said.

- Hearing is automatic. It takes very little or no effort.
- Understanding is not automatic. It takes a lot more effort and concentration.

Understanding is the act of focusing one's mind on what is being said to grasp its meaning. Not only is it good to speak slower but pausing between key points, will also allow information to sink in.

Slowing down and pausing will also give you more time to select your upcoming tone levels and gestures. People who speak slower are perceived to be more intelligent and thoughtful. The implication is that they are thinking about what they are saying.

Examples of Reactions

How we speak does influence others and the following *"situation questions"* indicate how we express ourselves in different circumstances.

Situation Questions

- How do you greet a friend that you have not seen for years?
- How do you speak to someone who has just experienced a death in the family?
- How do you speak when you are angry, excited or sad?
- If you are scolding someone or calling out because they are in harm's way, how are your voice deliveries at these times?

Everyone can Improve

The way they Deliver their Message

Listen to the announcers on the radio. Listen to politicians, as they are usually the masters of voice deliverance.

Record Yourself and Listen.

Adjust your delivery until you are happy and comfortable with the new and improved presenter.

When making your presentation, standing provides the greatest range of communication possibilities. It allows the full use of the entire body to express yourself. It also allows you to breathe deeply and add more power to your voice levels.

Often it is a sit-down meeting by client choice, but you will still have many options available. Sit erect, shoulders back, chest slightly out and breath from the diaphragm. Before your presentation, it is good to drink some water to lubricate your vocal cords. If it is a long presentation try to have a glass of water handy.

Level Three - Body Language

Our Information Sources

Charles Darwin was the first one to bring forth this information in his book titled *"The Expressions of the Emotions in Man and Animals"* Published in 1872.

Paul Ekman - a Californian psychiatrist in the 1960's; and an expert in facial expressions along with **Sorenson and Friesen,** conducted and published the results of extensive studies with a variety of peoples and world cultures.

Their Studies Also Confirmed

Darwin was Right

When people think of sales, often very little attention is given to using body language to improve the results. Even though it makes up 55% of the potential effective communicating skills, it is still given the least consideration when people are making presentations.

The Four Levels of Body Communication

We will examine Body Communication from four areas.

1. Face and Head
2. Hands Arms and Legs
3. Body Positioning
4. Personal Space

When these four areas are combined, their effectiveness is greater than the sum of the individual parts. We can create even more powerful messaging, when these areas work in harmony.

1. Face and Head

Facial Expressions

There are 6 universal Facial expressions that are used and recognized in their ability to convey certain human emotions.

The 6 Expressions are:

1) Happiness

2) Sadness

3) Fear

4) Disgust

5) Surprise

6) Anger

They are:

Universally recognized

Human evolved

Genetically inherited

Not dependent on social learning or one's environment

Studies worldwide indicate that these emotions are recognized regardless of culture and educational background.

By using these facial expressions, we can transcend cultures and language barriers and can get an emotional feeling understood without the utterance of a single word.

Facial expressions can play a very important role and can often create subtle reactions that improve your message when used in the proper way.

1. Eye Communication

Our eyes are a very important part of the non-verbal signals that we send to others. It is often said that you can see into a person's sole by looking into their eyes. It is also said that the eyes do not lie.

To a certain extent, we all tend to be able to read people's eyes without knowing how or why. It seems to be an ability that we are born with.

We can also see whether another person's eyes are focused on us or not. (often indicating if they are listening or interested)

We can Easily Detect the Difference of:

- A Glazed Over lost or Confused look

- A Blank stare suggesting their thoughts are somewhere else

- An awkward or secret glance - often done in an embarrassing situation

- The prelude to a teary eye warning us of things to come

Just look at our eyelids, and the ability to widen and close our eyes. We also can enlarge or contract our pupils and move our eyes about. It is no surprise of the extent at which our eyes can convey a wide variety of messages.

The importance in conveying a feeling or an emotion during the deliverance of your presentation is equally as important as getting a direct reading on what is being felt by your audience in return.

The following will show what is normally meant as it relates to the person who is giving the signals and making the movements.

What the Eyes Are Saying When

The designation of right or left pertains to the person who is giving the signal. When someone is speaking, and left eye is stated, it means their left eye.

Of course, when you are listening, watching or facing these people their left is on your right side.

The following left/right designations refer to the Speaker's left or right.

When the eyes look

RIGHT AND UP – The person is imagining, fabricating.

LEFT AND UP – They are recalling or remembering.

When the person looks sideways

RIGHT – They are imagining sounds.

RIGHT AND DOWN – They are assessing feelings.

LEFT – They are remembering sounds.

LEFT AND DOWN – They are usually rationalizing or self-talking.

When eyes make direct Contact

WHEN SPEAKING: – The person is showing honesty.

WHEN LISTENING: – The person is listening and attentive.

WIDENING OF EYES SHOWS – Interest, appeal

RUBBING OF EYES SHOWS – Disbelief upset or is bored

AN EYE SHRUG – Shows frustration.

EYEBROWS RISING – Greeting or recognition

EYEBROW FLASH SHOWS – Indicates acknowledgment.

2. Mouth Communication

The mouth acts independently and smiling is a big part of body language, as is frowning and pouting. The mouth can be open wide, closed tight or any position in between. Each provides a unique expression and meaning.

The mouth is associated with many body language signals. The mouth can be covered by one's hands or fingers, and it plays a central part in one's facial expressions. The mouth has more moving parts than any other sensory organ; therefore, it provides almost unlimited variables of expression.

What the Mouth is Saying When

TIGHT LIPPED – Withheld feelings

TWISTED SMILE – Mixed feelings or sarcasm

DROPPED JAW SMILE – Is considered a faked smile.

MOUTH OPEN HANDS AT SIDE - Shows surprise.

BOTTOM LIP JUTTING OUT - Upset, Flirting

BITING LIP – Shows tenseness.

SMILE HEAD TILTED UP – Playfulness, teasing, coy

GENUINE LAUGH – Indicates relaxation.

A FORCED LAUGH – Signals nervousness.

GRINDING TEETH – Shows anger.

HAND OVER MOUTH – Shows shock, suppression holding back.

Head Communication

The head tends to lead and determine general body direction and is used in directional likes and dislikes.

The head is very flexible it can turn, project forward, withdraw, tilt sideways, tilt forwards and tilt backwards.

All these Movements have Different Meanings

When our hands interact with our head we achieve very powerful body language.

What the Head is Saying When

HEAD NODDING – Shows agreement.

SLOW HEAD NODDING – Attentive listening

FAST HEAD NODDING – Impatient, hurry up

HEAD HELD UP – Alertness neutrality

HEAD HELD HIGH – Superiority, arrogant

HEAD IS FORWAND UPRIGHT – Interest, positive reaction

HEAD TILTED DOWN – Criticism, admonishment

HEAD TILTED TO ONE SIDE - Non-threatening, submissive, thoughtful

HEAD SHAKING SIDE TO SIDE – Disagreement

PROLONGED HEAD SHAKING – Strong disagreement

HEAD DOWN IN RESPONSE – Negative, discontented, unhappy

HEAD DOWN WHILE PERFORMING ACTIVITY – Defeated, tired

CHIN UP – Pride, defiant, confidence

2. Hands Arms and Legs

1. Hand Communication

Body language involving hands is extensive. They are expressive and flexible tools and convey a lot of conscious signaling. When the hands are combined with the other parts of the body, there is usually a signal.

What our Hands Are Saying When

BOTH PALMS HELD HIGH AND FACING OUT – Is Defensive

ONE PALM IN FRONT FACING OUT –This means to stop.

HAND ON HEART – Seeking to be believed, allegiance

When

PALMS LOWERED FACING UP OPEN – Truthful, honesty, appealing submissive. Asking for a response

PALMS DOWN MOVING UP AND DOWN FINGERS SPREAD – Asking to calm down in a group

PALMS DOWN – Shows authority, strength, or dominance.

PALMS UP, THEN DOWN, REPEATED – Striving for an answer

When

FINGERS POINTING - Aggression, threat, emphasis

FINGER POINT IN AIR – Creates Emphasis.

FINGER SIDE TO SIDE – Indicates a Warning, or a refusal.

FINGER UP AND DOWN – Admonishment, emphasis

FINGER POINTING AND NODDING WITH SMILE – Acknowledgment

CLENCHED FISTS – Resistance, aggression, determination

HAND CHOP – Strong emphasis

When

THUMBS POINTED DOWN – Shows disapproval or rejection.

INDEX FINGER AND THUMB TOUCHING AT TIPS SAME HAND – Indicates approval. It's OK.

THUMBS POINTED UP – Means approval, OK

THUMBS CLENCHED INSIDE FISTS – Self comforting, insecurity

RUBBING HANDS TOGETHER – Shows anticipation

PINCHING RUBBING NOSE WHEN LISTENING – Thoughtfulness, waiting

REMOVING GLASSES – Alerting, wishing to speak

When

HAND SUPPORTING CHIN OR SIDE of FACE - Evaluation, tired, sad, bored

TWO FINGERED V PALMS INWARD – Offensive or contempt

TWO FINGERED V PALMS OUTWARD – Victory or peace

INTERWOVEN CLENCHED FINGERS – Frustration, negativity or anxiousness

HAND CLASPING WRIST – Frustration

CHIN RESTING ON THUMB INDEX FINGER POINTING UP -Evaluation, I am thinking.

When

HANDS STROKING CHIN – Thoughtfulness

TOUCHING SCRATCHING NOSE WHEN SPEAKING – Lying, exaggerate

NECK SCRATCHING – Doubt, disbelief

HANDS IN POCKETS – Disinterest, boredom

HANDS CLASPING HEAD – Shows a calamity.

HANDS OVER EARS – Rejection, resistance

FINGER TIPS AND THUMBS TOUCHING EACH OTHER ON OPPOSITE HANDS PUSHING TOGETHER AND POINTING UPWARDS –Indicates thoughtfulness, looking for answers or Deep thinking.

The Handshake

The Hand shake evolved from ancient times as a gesture of trust by showing that no weapon was being held by the outstretched arm.

The handshake has developed into a social process of greeting or saying goodbye and showing friendship. It is often used in business to signify that a transaction has been agreed to.

It is sometimes used as a way of judging character; but here, it is not always accurate.

What the Handshake is Usually Saying

When handshakes are uncomfortably firm they can display disrespect or appear to be phony and are faking affection. When they are, weak and feel like a damp rag, the person is judged to be weak and uncertain.

Different interpretations will occur in cultures where hand shaking is not a normal greeting and may not follow the same interpretation.

What the Position says when

HANDSHAKE PALMS DOWN – Shows dominance

HANDSHAKE PALMS UP – Shows submission accommodating

EQUAL AND VERTICLE – Non-threatening

When

HANDSHAKE USES BOTH HANDS - Seeking to convey trustworthiness honesty - Seeking to control

IT IS PUMPUNG – Shows Enthusiasm

IT IS WEAK – Varies maybe shows weakness or submission

IT IS FIRM – Outward confident

CLASPING THE OTHER PERSONS ARM - Seeking control

There is much more significance to handshaking than most people realize. Politicians know this only too well and often go to great lengths to be on the appropriate side during a press conference or during meetings.

Positioning

If the person they are greeting is on their left during the handshake when facing the audience or camera, their hand is on top of a handshake demonstrating they are dominant.

Their hand will be facing down while the other person's hand will be on the bottom facing up.

The variables of using one or both arms and hands also will imply dominance or submission. The use of both arms and hands implies control.

Observe Politicians

As an interesting exercise, the next time you watch when politicians or dignitaries greet each other; observe their body language.

Watch especially heads of countries greeting each other on camera. See if they are maneuvering to be on the dominant side with their hand on top and palms facing down, as seen by their audience.

Also, watch to see who will Clasp the other persons Arm.

They all know the implications of this positioning and it can be quite humorous sometimes to watch the efforts made to be on the appropriate side.

2. Arms Communication

Arms act as defensive barriers when across the body. When they are open, they demonstrate openness. Arms clearly indicate moods and feelings especially when combined with other parts of the body.

What the Arms Are Saying

CROSSED ARMS – Shows a defensive position or uncertainty.

CROSSED ARMS AND CLENCHED FISTS – Hostile, defensive

CROSSED AND GRIPPING UPPER ARMS – Insecurity

ARMS BEHIND BODY HANDS CLASPED – Confidence, authority

ARMS OPEN – Openness "hello world"

PLAYING IMAGINARY VIOLIN – Shows mock sympathy or sadness.

3. Legs and Feet

The body language of legs and feet is more difficult to control consciously than are other body parts. Often it will provide good clues to one's true feelings, because of this fact.

There are also definite differences between men and women due to cultural orientation.

Leg signals are often supported by corresponding arm signals such as crossed arms and legs signifying detachment disinterest rejection or insecurity.

Legs and Feet Will Normally Point
In the Direction of Interest.

What the Legs and Feet Are Saying

UNCROSSED LEGS – Shows openness.

CROSSED WHEN SITTING – Indicates caution disinterest.

OPEN WHEN SITTING – Shows arrogance or is combative.

ANKLE LOCKED SITTING – Is defensive

PARALELL CLOSE TOGETHER WHEN SITTING – Shows a Proper position.

When Standing

STANDING LEGS WIDE APART – Aggressive ready for action

STANDING AT ATTENTION – Is Respectful

STANDING LEGS CROSSED – Shows insecurity or submission.

STANDING KNEES BUCKLING – Under pressure

FOOT FORWARD STANDING – Directed toward a dominant group Member

3. Body Positioning

1. The Confident Stance

Hands clasped in front – at hip level

Feet are slightly more than hip width apart.

Chest is slightly raised.

This is the best way to start your presentation as it immediately portrays confidence and assumes the authoritative position

It creates a very positive appearance and a person who is knowledgeable. You are now in **Control.**

2. The Jester Request for Answer Stance

Open out your hands just above waist height, on each side. The wider they are apart; the more emphatic is the message

Palms up

Eyebrows raised

Head turned slightly

For a yes or no question

It is used often when one wishes to emphasize the need for an answer or are asking the audience to simply think for themselves.

This position can be subtle or can be greatly exaggerated depending on the situation. The exaggeration of it, can also inject humor into your speech or presentation and ease tension or regain attention.

3. The Leveler – Authority

Stand Erect

Put arms with palms down in front of you

Fingers open

Move hands and finger tips up and down in a fanning motion

If the audience is getting restless or noisy or are applauding or laughing at something you have said or done, this is a good way to assume control again in a polite but authoritative way.

Usually no words are necessary to achieve the results you want, and it is all done with the effective use of body language.

4. The Thinker

Raise one hand to your face

Thumb under chin

Index finger on one side of your nose

Other fingers folded resting on chin other side of nose

Other hand under elbow of think arm

Elbows at mid-chest range

PAUSE briefly with hands in this position. Remove the hand and deliver your message with authority. This can be used subtly to indicate you really are thinking. It is often used when someone has asked you a question. You can pause to think about the question.

It can be exaggerated in a humorous way. Many comedians will use this stance to obtain laughs without even speaking a word. Once you use it for humor it will probably lose the effect of your serious think-mode, if you try to go back.

5. The Joker

One hand on hip

Other arm raised in air about head level, stretched out, with Palm up

Leaning slightly back

Stomach out

Smiling or laughing

This can really project humor and can generate a lot of fun into your presentation at the appropriate time. It can be used to express an outrageous response for humor.

It can be used simply as a spontaneous reaction or you can "of course" stage it which is the most common use.

6. Questions – Show of Hands Everyone

For audiences of 5 plus

You Ask – *"Are there any questions"?*

Raise one hand high above your head palm out

Other hand down at side

Stand on toes

Wait for audience hands to rise

With your raised arm, point to the person who will ask the question. Then put your arm down

Repeat until no more questions

At the end of your presentation when you ask for question it is often hard to get this Q & A part going.

This gesture will usually do the trick and get the ball rolling. Get into the habit of using this as it is an easy way to get a response.

4. Personal Space

Personal space requirements will depend on personality and culture and environmental conditioning and the relationship with the other person(s) involved.

Edward T Hall in 1914

Originally identified the five distinct space zones and that interpretation remains the same to present day.

Hall's study interprets the amount of space that people find comfortable between themselves and others as it relates to their social intimacy with that person.

The term asking for one's space is representative of asking for respect in what is comfortable for a person.

When someone moves within these boundaries they are said to be invading or violating one's personal space.

Such a move will often cause the person being intruded upon to step back or feel challenged, pressured or overpowered. This maneuver is often used when attempting to take control of a situation.

THE FIVE ZONES of Personal Space

Zone one - 0 to 6 inches - CLOSE INTIMATE – Physical contact intimacy

Zone two - 6 to 18 inches - INTIMATE – Close friends, sports

Zone three - 18 inches to 48 inches PERSONAL – Family and close friends

Zone four - 4 feet to 12 feet - SOCIAL – Consultative

Zone five - Over 12 feet - PUBLIC – No interaction

Summary to Communication

Once a person has mastered Communication, they have already set the agenda for Success in Selling.

Communication creates the framework for our sales efforts. Becoming a good or great communicator allows the sales person to deliver a focused, clear message to their prospect.

All our Skills Involve Communication

Having a successful meeting or sales presentation depends on how well one can deliver their message.

PRESENTATIONS

The Basics

There are different styles of presentations or meetings depending on the size of the order or the reason for the meeting. It is important to know the differences and how to prepare for each type to obtain optimum results.

Types of Meetings

1. Introductory – First Meetings
2. Fact Finding – additional Meetings
3. Dress Rehearsal
4. Final Presentations
5. The Call Back

We will outline all the above types of meetings separately, as each will have its own purpose and structure.

Delivering a Presentation

Starting the Presentation

1. Open with a very short story or a great comment can be good.
2. Do not overdo the short story.
3. Make sure the comment is relevant and in good taste.
4. Maybe use a bit of Humor.
    ◦ It loosens up an audience and enhances memory.
5. Too much humor can make it difficult to get serious again.

Throughout the Presentation

- Use Body Language and voice tones for affect.
- Be descriptive and paint a picture with your words.
- Use quotes from famous people, only if they fit the situation
- Often quotes will create Interest; but, make sure you know them and can deliver them accurately.

- Use statistics to add impact.

- Use power words.

- Share something to create emotion and involve them.

- Use opinions from experts.

Closing the Presentation

1. Have a Summary – Your call to Action

2. Promise Hope for the future.

3. End on a positive note.

4. Do not introduce new information after you have finished unless you are asked.

Presentation Things to Do

Do – Know your material.

Do – Tell it and do not read it

Do – Focus on your message.

Do – Show that you believe in what you are saying.

Do – Focus on their needs.

Do – Have a structure that they can follow.

Do – Talk with enthusiasm

Do - Demonstrate confidence in your voice tones

Do – Make eye contact with audience. Hold for count of 3 elephants for maximum effect.

Do – Use gestures that enhance your message. (body language)

Do – Dress up not down. They need to look up to you as authority.

Do – USE THE 3 T's

1. Tell them what you are going to tell them.

2. Tell them.

3. Tell them what you have just told them.

Do – Use the 3 P's – Practice, Practice, and Practice.

Do – Use the 10:20:30 rule

- 10 slides
- 20 minutes
- 30 font size

Presentation Mistakes

- There are many mistakes made when people make presentations. We have outlined a few most common ones that occur.
- Spelling errors – Break concentration and destroy credibility.
- Little or no preparation – You look disorganized or confused and unprofessional.
- Practice is a must! - You will look organized knowledgeable and professional.

Lack of Structure

Often people do not follow a logical sequence when creating their presentation.

If it is not organized, it becomes difficult to follow.

1. If your message is not clear and is not focused
   o The prospect becomes confused and loses interest.
2. If there is too much information
   o You wear out your welcome.

Messaging

- The Filler Words - Get rid of them! – The use of (Uum's, so's aaw's, and's) – will make your presentation weak and boring.
- If your Presentation is ME focused not CLIENT focused. - It is annoying to them.
- Remember their needs *WIIFM, - "What's in It for Me."*
- It's what THEY want. - This is not about you!
- Wrong mission statement – No one cares about your mission statement. It's their goals they want to reach.
- Your ideas appear too radical
- They do not solve the client's problems or meet their needs.

Afraid to Engage

Often people will avoid a Q & A period because they cannot rehearse. This will usually occur if they do not know their material well enough.

If one does this, the audience will feel left out

They may even be Angry

Mistakes with Support Materials

Visuals

- Too many slides or brochures

- Not enough or none

- Find the right balance

Reading information on slides or brochures to your audience is a *"Big Mistake"*

You can speak at 100 words per minute and your audience can read at 200 words per minute. - This can totally disrupt a presentation.

If you are going to use information on slides, keep it point form. People will not read long paragraphs of material on slides. If using brochures, do not provide too many or clients will lose focus and interest.

Mistakes Using Point Form.

- Too Much of one type of power point will lose its effectiveness

- Size is too small

- Too bright or too dull

- Bad color choice – Find out the best Colors to use for the purpose.

All the above mistakes are Irritating to the prospect and will cause them to disengage.

Delivery Mistakes

- Weak Openings – There is no attention getter.

- Weak Closings – There is no strong "Call to Action".

- Meeting is too long – Keep under 25 minutes or have breaks.

- Too Much of a Monotone

No indication when you are changing topics. - You lose their attention.

Too much movement – Upsets or irritates your audience.

Too little movement – It is boring and does not inspire.

Presentations - Not to Do

Do not - Be afraid of silence- It is often more powerful than noise

Do not – Have too much continuous content in your presentation.

Do not have long sessions over 25 minutes. Separate it and take short breathers. 17.5 minutes is the average attention span.

Do not – Abuse slides - Too fast, too slow and Especially not knowing what they are!

Do not – Make the presentation one-way traffic only – Engage the client.

Do not - Dwell on your company history etc.

Do not - Boast about your company profits!   They will think that they are next to be added to your list.

You May Laugh – But I have seen it Happen

Side Conversations

Often you may find that people in your audience will start having their own little discussions and this can be very disruptive.

Do not be rude or Ask them to Stop Talking

If you are interrupted by others having a conversation while you are speaking:

You can say:

"I see there may be a question. Can I help you with it?"

"I sense there is a question over here. Can I help you with it?"

Lastly - Do Not EVER!

- Try and bluff your way through an answer.

- If you do not have the answer just say that's a great question and I will get back to you on that.

- If you try to bluff it, you could discredit your entire presentation by providing the wrong information.

GET BACK TO THEM!

THE FIRST MEETING

Overview

Be Prepared

The very first meeting will provide your greatest opportunity to make the right first impression and to start building your relationship.

The Prospect's respect and trust of your company and its offerings; will start, with the first impression that you will make. You are there to create interest, find out if there are needs and gather the information that you will require for your quotation.

Dangerous

The greatest danger is to underestimate the importance of this part of the sales process. Some people will not prepare themselves properly. They just make the appointment and show up for the meeting with no agenda.

They "Wing it" as the Saying goes

There Could Be Nothing Worse

It is here that you will bring together all the good things and benefits of your company, its products and services, and present them to an important decision maker. It is here that your prospect will be the most receptive to hear what you have to say.

If you do a Good Job

They will provide you with an opportunity to quote your products or services. If it is done properly; it will also make it possible for you to obtain a purchase order, to supply their needs.

You are there to gather information on how you can help this customer. It represents the beginning of finding out what their needs are. It will enable you to offer the right products, services or solutions.

It is also the opportunity to overcome negative thoughts, or incorrect information, that the customer may have obtained about your company, its products or services. *(Often provided by competition)*

What You Need

Start with the suggestions that we are providing in these chapters and establish the initial outline for your introductory meetings.

It will take three or four first meetings with new prospects to adjust and create an acceptable outline that you will eventually follow for all first meetings.

Once Created

Do not Stop There – Build on It

Constantly strive for improvement and use your experience to expand and make the content and delivery better.

Once you have created this blueprint for first meetings you will be able to make the minor adjustments to suit each new prospect.

If you continue to strive for improvement of your content and delivery, your closing percentages will get better as well.

Prospect Knowledge

You are there to learn how you can help the prospect. You do this by discovering their needs and finding solutions to their problem areas.

- Research the company you are visiting before you go so that you are familiar with:
  - Its management team,
  - Their products,
  - Size of facilities, Number of employees etc.
- Check them out with your peers and on the internet and find out all the information that you can.
- You want to be able to speak with confidence and authority and can demonstrate that you have done your homework and are there to help them wherever possible.

Questions for Preparing your Agenda Outline

- Whom do you wish to see?

- What will be your opening statements?

- What questions will you ask?

- What do you want to achieve?

- What will be your Closing Statement?

- What will be your Summary - *"Call to Action?"*

Support Materials

- What support Information about your company will you need?

- What Information about your offerings will you need?

- What references or testimonials will you use?

Tips for the First Meeting

- Arrive on time and make sure your appearance is professional.

- Speak clearly, not too quickly and pause occasionally.

- Be Polite, Show Respect. Ask permission to use first names.

- Show Interest in what they are saying.

- Listen to their answers

- Write the answers down to any of your questions.

  o Do not try to remember the answers to write them down later.

  o You will usually forget something, and it could be a key item.

  o Writing the answers down also shows respect and that you are thorough in your job.

Ask if there are any questions or areas of concern about your company or offerings when you are done.

Most of all - Thank them for their Time and Attention

And for any Opportunity Given

The customer is always right until they find out; on their own, that they are wrong.

- NEVER tell them or imply they are wrong.
- You are there to prove them right by listening to you.

An Introductory Presentation

All first-time meetings with a customer will involve the same concept. They will be your introductory meeting where you present your company and its offerings.

It will also be where you will find out the true extent of the prospects needs and their desire to consider your offerings.

The Types of First Meeting Will Vary

1. Some will be for smaller products, offerings or volumes
2. Some may be larger orders for annual supply requiring secondary visits.
3. Some may be process equipment or projects that will require many additional visits to gather all the facts and specifications.

The need to prepare for this initial meeting will be equally important for small or large. The questions asked, and number of people involved will differ. The Preparation and final presentations will also change.

Requirements for Your Meeting

a) Initial Qualifying – Before arranging the meeting make sure the reason for it is clear to the prospect.

b) Agenda - Although optional, it is always best to have one.

c) Introduction - Introducing your company and your products or services. State the purpose of the meeting when you start.

Your Company Information

1. Have a brief written history of 1 or 2 pages showing your present management, special skills, testimonials or awards.
2. Have brochures or information on your products or services

3. Do not hand this information out at this point. If you do, they will start reading and you will lose their attention.

4. Deliver a verbal point-form summary of 1 & 2

5. Before you leave, hand out your information and brochures

They now have a Reminder

Of your Visit

d) Their Company Information

- **Needs** – Before you begin any in depth promotional efforts of your offerings, confirm their specific interests or needs.

- **Interest** – Confirm they will consider changing suppliers?

e) Product description - Clearly describe your product in terms your client will understand. Speak their language not yours. Tell your audience what you have for them. Remember the 3 T's.

- **Benefits** - Outline the normal product or service benefits as they relate to the client's needs. Give examples of where you feel that you can help them.

- **Successes** - To drive home a point, mention some of your successes and have names and/or written testimonials available to show the client.

f) Positioning - Mention your unique projects.

- Show why you are better or different from your competitors.

- Show how you have solved difficult customer requirements where others could not.

g) Closing Comments – Your comments here will set the stage for your final part on your agenda. - It is the introduction to your "- Call to Action"

h) Summary - *"Call to Action"* – Based on the reasons for your meeting, you will be asking for:

- A Request to Quote

- Further Action to be taken

- A Request for a Purchase Order.

NOTE: Never ever refer to this part on your agenda when showing it or speaking to the prospect as a **"Call-to-Action."** It is a **"Summary"**

I) Undertakings - Establish what they will be doing and what you will be doing for the next meeting.

Use this as your basic requirements for your first meeting. Most first meetings will have a common purpose and that is to introduce your company and establish needs.

What will vary will be the opportunity types, which we will discuss in the next chapters.

The Two Main Opportunity Types

Type One will be for normal day to day needs of your products or services. They may be purchased weekly, monthly or as annual blanket contracts for supplies or services

These Types of Opportunities Could Involve:

- A one-time meeting for very simple and straight forward purchases. Sometimes no repeat orders are involved.

- Several meetings for introduction, sampling and quoting of the customer's needs for daily, monthly or annual requirements

- It could involve several meetings to solve a problem

Type Two will be for special onetime purchases involving:

Larger pieces of office equipment or plant equipment

Large Systems or Projects

These meetings will usually involve many additional fact-finding meetings and many people on both sides.

There are usually different specifications and customer requirements that need to be met.

Type 1 – Day-to-Day Needs

The Purpose for the Meeting

1) It could be a single visit for a one-time sale.

2) You could be gathering information to quote on some of their weekly production consumables, production services, office supplies or shipping supplies or services.

3) You may be gathering information and providing samples for annual consumption of materials or for annual service contracts.

Examples

It could be their packaging materials, chemicals, paint, photocopy supplies, or any part of their daily, weekly or monthly needs.

Usually these types of orders are usually handled by:

- The Purchasing Department,
- Plant, Production or Office Manages
- Maintenance or Shipping Departments
- Or a combination of them.

Usually upper management is not involved in smaller daily, weekly or monthly ordering requirements.

For larger purchases, such as their monthly supply of steel, paint or components for their manufacturing process, you will usually become involved with upper management, quality control and/or engineering in addition to the above.

Sample Questions you might Ask

- What do they know about your company and offerings?
- Do they know anyone who is using your products or services?
- What have they heard from these people?
- What is important for them in a supplier?

- Are they happy with their present supplier's?
  - o Deliveries?
  - o Service?
  - o Price?
  - o Quality?
- Are they looking for improvement anywhere?
- Do they have any problem areas that need solving?
- Who is supplying their needs presently?
- Ask if you could provide them with samples or a quotation for comparison?
  - o Ask for quantities, specifications or technical data if required.
- Ask to see their operation "if possible".
- Ask for their business card and email address?
- Ask who else is involved in the decision making?

Allow space to write in answers and any undertakings.

Distribution of copies

Ask how many will attend the decision-making meetings and always make extra copies.

The 30 Minute Timeline

It is important that you have set your agenda to suit the time allowed for your first meeting.

The time we are suggesting for this type of customer needs is approximately 30 minutes in length.

It will be up to the prospect to choose if that time line is extended. If they do it is a good sign.

The Sample Timeline

Introduction and General Description -	3 to 4 minutes
General questions including authority -	1 to 2 minutes
Specific prepared questions -	14 to 15 minutes
Summary - (Call to Action)	4 to 6 minutes
Undertakings - Set time line to establish	2 to 3 minutes

Total time - 24 to 30 minutes

Note: If your outline is completed within the above time frame you will have shown respect for their time and demonstrated your organizational skills.

Summary (Call to Action)

Most of the time this is an introductory and information gathering meeting and you will do a quick summary of the main points.

Occasionally it might be a presentation for an item that needs no research or additional visit. Here your call to action will be to ask for the Order.

Undertakings

If additional information is required, it is proper to ask if the prospect has any additional time available to gather it while you are there or ask if you should come back.

This is also where you will establish the things to do for you next meeting. If there is further action to be provided by the prospect this will also be part of the Undertakings.

Set the time line for completion of any undertakings to take place. Make it as soon after as possible, so that the momentum is not lost, and your first meeting does not become a distant memory to either party.

Undertakings Follow-up

After your first meeting follow up by email when you are back in the office and thank them for their time and the opportunity. There will usually be some undertakings that your client will have and some that you will have.

Provide a Short Outline of:

- What they will be doing
- What you will be doing
- Show the time frame that is involved
- Send it to them.

The easier you make this part the better they will like it and they will be more likely to do it quickly.

Summary of Type 1 First Meeting

Once you have created and perfected your first one-on-one meeting or presentation, you have overcome one of the greatest failures of many people in sales.

How to Successfully Organize and Hold

A First Introductory Meeting

Experience demonstrates the necessity to be organized and deliver a great first meeting. Unfortunately, many will not see the significance.

Importance of Practice

Once you have put your first meeting presentation together, it is time to practice your delivery of it. Nothing is worse than going unprepared and looking like it. You have done all this work to get ready so rehearse by delivering it to someone at your office, a family member or in front of a mirror or all.

Get feedback on the way it comes across. Ask for suggestions for improvement. Once you have made your adjustments, it is time to practice, practice, and practice some more until you can deliver it with perfection.

Your first meetings will be very important not only to impress your client, but to observe how your client reacts to your information. You do not want to have to worry about remembering what to say and not be able to observe the reactions and amount of interest shown by your prospect.

Confidence Builder

Having this area perfected as a skill set; will give you control and confidence, when you are making your first appointments.

Type 2 – Larger Equipment and Projects

General Project Meeting

Reason for this General Project Meeting

Our starting point here is that you initially made contact and talked with the prospect's project manager by phone or in a meeting like the one just outlined. This is the result of that discussion.

This is your first General Meeting with the main people who are involved in the project. People from your company and your prospect's company will now take part so that everyone involved can become familiar with each other.

Basic Preparation for this Meeting

You should have previously established how many will attend this meeting for distribution of your introductory information. Always make extra copies

Introductions at Meeting

1. Introduce yourself, your company and anyone else attending with you.

2. Ask for a quick introduction of those attending the meeting from the prospects side. This is often a good time to exchange cards if it has not already been done.

3. Provide a brief verbal outline of your company's offerings, its history and accomplishments, (You will hand out your written copy at the end).

You might Ask

- What they know of your company, products or equipment?

- Do they know of anyone who has your systems or equipment?

- What have they heard about these installations?

Be Prepared

This is where you will be called upon for the types of knowledge that we have discussed earlier. The main purpose for you is to present the best picture of your company possible. It will be your first impression and perhaps determine if you will proceed further.

The Next Move is Really Theirs

For them it could simply have been a meeting to assess you and your company's capabilities of handling an order or project of this size and they will be the ones who are asking most of the questions.

They will be Controlling the Time and Direction

If You Qualify

If they feel you meet their initial requirements, they may immediately begin by getting more specific and allow more detailed questions.

So Be Prepared to Continue!

Our Model for Discussion

 "A Plant Processing System". will be the example project that we will use for outlining things that need to be done and the questions we will ask. The actual questions for different types of large orders or projects will vary depending on your company's offerings and the size of the potential order.

If you can ask these types of questions during this first meeting, that is a very positive sign. You should be prepared to undertake this part even if you think that the prospect may not be ready to get into the specifics during this meeting with them.

Types of Questions that you will ask.

These questions could be asked (all or in part) at any time that is suitable during this meeting or your future project kick-off meeting.

Much of the following information could be covered by the prospect and you may not use some or most of these sample questions. We are providing them as examples of what you should know.

About the Project

- What are the reasons for their new project?
- Do they have a project description or list of specifications?
- Who will be your main contact to gather information and present your final proposal to.

- What are their production requirements?
- What parts of the project do they want to handle – if any?
  - Do they want?
    - Turn-key?
    - Equipment only?
    - Install only?
- What is the time frame for delivery?
- When is the full quotation required by?
- Who else is quoting? (*they may not provide this*)
- When will they be selecting the supplier (placing the order)?

Find out the names of everyone that you will be working with on the project. Ask for their business cards and email addresses.

Get the names of anyone else who will be getting copies of your recommendations.

Final Questions

- Ask them how many copies of information or drawings they will normally require for presentations.
- What plant area have they set aside for the equipment and ask if it is possible to view the area while you are there?
- Find out what their safety requirements are for visiting the plant or manufacturing area. Make sure you always have safety shoes, safety glasses and a hard hat with you.

Summary – *"Your Call to action"*

This is where you will establish your undertakings for you next meeting. If there is further action to be provided by the prospect this will also be part of the call to action.

Set the time line for completion of any undertakings to take place as quickly as possible so that you do not lose any momentum and your first meeting does not become a distant memory to either party.

Undertakings

After your first meeting follow up by email when you are back in the office and thank them for their time and the opportunity.

There will usually be some undertakings that your client will have and some that you will have.

Provide a short outline of:

- What they will be doing
- What you will be doing
- Show the time frame that is involved
- Send it to them.

The easier you make this part the better they will like it and they will be more likely to do it quickly.

Summary of General Project Meeting

We have provided an example of a typical project meeting. It is meant as a general overview of what you can expect for meetings of this nature.

One of the main things to remember, is to make sure you have more than enough copies of information foe everyone in attendance.

The person who goes without might play a key role at some point in the project. Do not alienate them at the starting line.

This meeting timeline will normally be set and organized by your prospect. Because of this you will not have presented an agenda of your own.

Other than your introductions and questions outlined it will be almost an open forum and agenda.

Exception to a First One-on-One Meeting

Project Presentation to all Competition as a Group

You may have been invited because of your Company Branding and Marketing, or from your initial contact and first meeting.

Very often a company will invite all the people who will be bidding on a large order or project to a general Kick-Off meeting. Here the agenda will again be set by the prospect and here you will largely become a spectator.

Usually you will introduce yourself and your company representatives, at some point. The other people who are bidding will do the same.

If this happens, make sure you write down all the company names, so you will know who you are up against.

The prospect will usually provide a general outline of the project, when and where it will take place. There may be some general specifications, but this is more of an invitation to bid.

After this meeting you will have your one-on-one kick-off meeting. It will probably be as an additional fact-finding session, which will be very much like the first meeting we just described.

Project Kick-Off after Group Meeting

Reason for Meeting

This is the first One-on-One Project kick off meeting that will follow the Group style we just discussed.

The first presentation of your company was at the group meeting and very little opportunity was given to promote it. You are now there for the one-on-one kick off meeting for the project.

The general parameters were set at the group meeting, but you are here for more specific information regarding the project. It is the beginning of a more personal relationship with those involved in the project.

A similar list will be prepared to request the information that you still need to continue the preparation of your offerings.

It is important that you have set your agenda to suit the time allowed for your first one-on-one meeting.

The time we are suggesting is approximately 45 - 60 minutes in length. It will be up to the prospect to choose if that time line is extended. If they do it is a good sign.

The 45 – 60 Minute Time Line

Introductions	1 – 2 Minutes
Presentation of your Company -	6 to 8 minutes
Discussion of Project	15 to 20 minutes
Specific prepared questions -	14 to 15 minutes
Summary - (Your call to Action)	7 to 12 minutes
Undertakings - Set time line to establish	2 to 3 minutes

Total time - 45 to 60 minutes

If additional information is required; it is proper to ask if the prospect has any time available to gather it while you are there, or shall you come back.

Summary

Once you have created and perfected your first outline for this type of meeting, you have accomplished another blueprint for success.

Experience does teach the necessity to be organized and deliver a great first meeting. Do not delay. Get this important part of your selling tool kit ready for use.

Importance of Practice (Restated to Emphasize)

- Once you have put your first meeting presentation together, it is time to practice your delivery of it.

- Nothing is worse than going unprepared and looking like it.

- You have done all this work to get ready so rehearse by delivering it to someone at your office, a family member or in front of a mirror or all.

- Get feedback on the way it comes across. Ask for suggestions for improvement.

- Once you have made any adjustments, it is time to practice, practice, and practice some more until you can deliver it with perfection.

- Your first meetings will be very important not only to impress your client, but to observe how your client reacts to your information.

- You do not want to have to worry about remembering what to say and not be able to observe the reactions and amount of interest shown by your prospect.

Confidence Builder

Having this area perfected as a skill set will give you control and confidence when you are making your appointments.

FACT FINDING MEETINGS

1) Type 1 – Weekly, Monthly, Annual Needs

Reason for this Type

Sometimes there may be a second or even a third meeting to obtain additional information, depending on the size of order or technical information in question.

These meetings are usually quicker than the initial meeting and less structured. There may also be some sampling and testing before you arrive at your recommendations and prices.

Have a plan. Be totally organized and know what you wish to accomplish at or during these meeting. Have an agenda to hand out with your questions and list of things that you need to know.

The same fact-finding process will exist for services that are multi-faceted and may involve several departments and several visits.

Benefits of Additional Meetings

Having several meetings before you make your formal presentation should be considered as "very beneficial" in the sales process.

The client will get to know both you and your company better during these subsequent meetings. You can also monitor your progress.

When this Occurs

You will no longer be a stranger and if you have presented yourself well and listened well, you are doing what it takes to build TRUST.

Always remember to follow the same protocol as outlined earlier and remember to thank them each time for seeing you.

Once you have all the information you need from the client, you are ready to start putting your main presentation or quotation together for products and services.

2) Type 2 – Large Equipment or Projects

Reason for this Type

For large projects for systems or equipment, there are usually many subsequent meetings where you are gathering all the required information.

These are also less structured and usually quicker in and out type meetings. You may also be taking measurements in the plant or speaking to other plant employees involved as well.

There will often be group meetings with more people depending on the size or complexity of the project. These will be longer meetings. The same parameters apply. Have a plan and agenda outlining your objectives and things you need to know.

Benefits (restated)

Having many meetings before you make your formal presentation should be considered beneficial as the client and others involved will get to know both you and your company better.

You will no longer be a stranger and if you have presented yourself well and listened well, you are again doing what it takes to build TRUST.

In each of these subsequent meetings, always remember to follow the same protocol as outlined earlier and thank them each time for seeing you.

Also, use these meetings to monitor your progress.

If you can take pictures of the area to be occupied, they could possibly be used in your presentation.

Once you have all the information you need from the client, you are ready to start putting your main presentation or quotation together.

SALES PRESENTATIONS

General Guidelines

You have gathered all the information required and you will now be preparing the document for your presentation. We will outline your preparation for four types of sales presentation meetings.

Meeting Types

1. The 35 Minute meeting
2. The 60 Minute Dress Rehearsal
3. The Final Presentation
4. The Call Back

It is important to structure your presentations to enable you to make trial closes throughout your delivery. This will allow you to make sure you are on track.

Getting this confirmation in small steps is much more effective than waiting for the completion of your final presentation to see where you stand.

If they are in the habit of saying yes to the small closes, the order will come much easier at the end.

Discovery of Opposition

You also will get negative responses to some of your trial closes. It will be important to be able to uncover the reasons for their reactions and change them to a positive situation.

Knowing how to close and overcome objections is essential.

We mention using these two areas closing and overcoming objections because they are part of the reasoning behind how you will construct your presentations.

Your goal is to have the prospect on your side when you get to the final closing question and your presentation is how you get there.

We are outlining the ways to put your presentations together to be able to reach a positive outcome at the end.

There will be a big difference between the quoting of everyday requirements and major equipment or projects. These differences will be reflected in the size of quotations (number of pages) and the time it takes to deliver them.

Some Things You Must Do

- Identify and eliminate any of your own internal company jargon.
- Use specific words and phrases that your audience uses and understands.
- Simplify any of your complex technical terms and subject matter.
- Be prepared with short answers to questions that might occur.

During your presentation, you should move forward by building on your last point. Do not just begin a new area or topic without any warning.

Construct your presentation in a logical sequence that is easy to follow. Do not jump from topic to topic in a random order or you will surely lose their interest and comprehension.

People must understand and relate to what you have said, what you are saying and what you are about to say to fully grasp your message.

If there is any point in your presentation where people can become even slightly confused, you are at high risk of disconnecting with your entire audience.

You Must

- Follow a logical sequence.
- Items out of sequence will lose your audience.
- **Notify** your audience when you are about to switch to different subject matter.
- **Use:**
  - Audience Participation
  - Examples of Success
  - Stories, or Magic Moments, the "WOW" factor
  - Visuals and Props

The Presentation Basics

1. Establish the Framework first – the Story outline.
2. Carefully plan your Opening minute to grab their attention.
3. Outline your Main thoughts.
4. Spice it up. - Sometimes a picture is really worth 1000 words.

If your quotation is only 3 to 5 pages and there is no support material, then it makes more sense to hand them the document and give them time to read it.

- Do not read the 3 to 5 pages to them.
- Have a point form document for discussion once they are done reading the proposal.
- Then discuss your solutions and benefits point by point

For 6 – 12+ pages of information delivered to small groups, the use of your lap top or other mobile device can act as a great presentation delivery system.

- Use a summary-point-form delivery format
- Hand out the full hard copy document at the end.

For larger groups the use of a slide projection system and larger screen is very effective.

- Use a summary point form delivery format in your slides
- Again, tell it - do not read it.
- Hand out the full written document at the end.

General Notes

- o All quotations should contain a point form section that covers the key features and benefits of your offerings.
- o For smaller quotations, it could be one page or less.
- o For larger presentations, it could be two or three.
- o You will use this as a base outline in your presentation.

It is best to avoid providing too much written detail before you make your entire presentation as people naturally want to read on their own. Many will immediately search for the price page.

We Suggest the Following Procedure

The following format should best control the meeting. In this way, you will avoid everyone reading your entire quotation at their own pace. If you allow this to happen, you will lose control of the meeting.

Explain what you are doing before you start.

a) Have Three Sections

1) Your Features Page(s)
2) Your Pricing Page(s)
3) Your Full Detailed Quotation

1) First - Your Features Page.

- Hand out and make sure it is in point form

- Memorize its sequence; but, deliver a longer version verbally.

- Explain that this is a summary of everything they have asked for or require

- Do not just read the point form. Refer to it but use your own expanded explanation of the point form

- Explain you will hand out the detailed version when you are done and the reason for your method is for clarity.

Delivered the right way, your message will be condensed and clear and will be remembered more easily.

o They will use the point form to follow your progress

o They will retain it for a reference after the meeting

You Do Not want your Message to be Encumbered

With a lot of Descriptive Fluff

Where the Message can be Easily Lost

The Features part is made up of key points to explain and maintain attention.

These points will be based on the following

- You asked for this and we gave you this

- You needed this and that is what we gave you.

- You must be able to deliver this without reading it.

Writing your points on a white board works well. Keep it short!

Using a pointer where your points are on a screen is good. (again, very shortened points)

The Detailed part is Usually Saved for Later Discussions

The last thing that you want for your presentation is for all to open the detailed document and sit silently as each person reads at their own pace.

Personal experience has shown this will be a disaster

If you attempt to read it out loud to them, they are finished reading the page by the time you are only half done your verbal presentation.

You are on page 2 and they are on 4

If you continue reading, it is soon realized that everyone has become disconnected, you lose complete control and you will have very little chance of achieving your goal, call to action or getting an order.

You Must

> **Memorize it.**

> **Practice it** until it has reached perfection and you can cover the key points quickly.

During the first minute the audience is deciding if it is worth their time to listen. It may be your only chance to create their real desire to listen or if they will half-listen or just pretend that they are listening.

If their Eyes Are Glazed or Blank
You are in Trouble

2) Next - Pricing and Terms and Conditions Page(s)

> Hand out and show the base price

> If there are options show them as add on prices separately.

> If you have an ROI (Return on Investment) show it here.

> If there is a financing option show it here

> For a longer terms and conditions remember to make it a feature and brag about it. Let them read it and then discuss it.

3) Last - Detailed Description Section

Hand out your support documents

- ◦ Pictures
- ◦ References or Testimonials

Give them a minute to absorb the package and ask if they wish to review it in detail now.

By handling everything this way; management can stay long enough to hear your quick outline and the price, and then leave if they wish.

They will leave the details for others to review unless they are a hands-on type person.

If they stay for the Detailed Section

You know they are Interested.

Why Memorize?

One often spends most of their time putting the content together and little attention is paid to how it will be delivered. Practice and test your presentation because the prospect likes it when you are well prepared.

A practiced and polished delivery will make a big difference in your closing capability. It also provides the confidence to make a great presentation and allow you to observe their reaction to it.

To Take Them on an Emotional Journey

You Must Be Totally Prepared!

If you have not practiced and perfected the delivery of your presentation before you arrive, it will not be effective, and you will not build their confidence or trust.

Clarity is the Foundation for Persuasion

35 MINUTE FINAL PRESENTATION

Overview

In the 35-minute presentation we are usually providing a simple 2 to 7-page quotation for smaller items that do not have a lot of information attached to them.

We may be presenting it to only one to three people.

The total meeting time will be scheduled to take a maximum of 35 minutes in length including questions pricing and call to action (request for order).

Four Tips

1. The best way to ensure success is to cover the key points in your main presentation in 15 - 17 minutes.

2. It is said that the average uninterrupted attention span in a meeting is 17.5 minutes.

3. If the main delivery part of a meeting is 25 minutes or over, it can easily get out of control and become boring and monotonous, and finish on a negative note.

4. Have a mini break of 1 – 2 minutes' midpoint if it is much over 20 minutes.

How to Organize

When you have found out who will need personalized copies, prepare enough copies for everyone and have some extras. In most cases these meetings will be small in the number of people present.

You Must

- Have an agenda that includes your time-line allowed
- Prepare and provide a brief history of yourself and your company to deliver verbally and a hard copy to hand out.

The Main Delivery

- Provide a summarized copy of your presentation in point form hand it out; but, verbally deliver it from memory

Part 1 - The Outline: (Point Form)

- The purpose of your presentation (their requirements)
- Your recommendations to meet their needs (your offerings)
- The benefits, solutions they get by using your offerings

Part 2 - Pricing

- Provide your prices and their optional extras later after your key points. Keep it as a separate section.

Part 3 - Detailed Section (Support Materials)

For the detailed section, (which you will hand out at the end).

- Include support information that will show how your product/services will help your prospect to resolve any existing problems or concerns that you uncovered in your initial questions.

Use your Sales Aids

Use slides and power point, product data and technical information, testimonials and samples.

Detailed Information

Have very specific technical data only, for the main presentation.

- Avoid too much detail in your presentation. Keep it simple.
- You will usually hand out the additional detailed technical information separately at the end, or when required for discussion

Extra Copies

Make extras for them to hand out to others of their own choice. Do not guess at who gets them or who does not. Let them decide.

Questions

After the main presentation, open the meeting for a short discussion and questions.

Be prepared to answer questions

Close the Sale

1. Have your objectives or call to action clearly defined.

2. Have a well-rehearsed transition from your presentation to the Q&A and then to your call to action.

3. If the meeting is for the order - Have your closes ready.

4. Be prepared to answer any objections that may arise which should be considered reasons to buy.

Sample Meeting Time Line

Introduction –	1 to 3 minutes
Main Delivery	15 to 16 minutes
Have a Q&A session.	5 to 6 minutes
Discuss Pricing	3 to 4 minutes
Final Q & A	1 to 3 minutes
Summary (Call to action)	<u>2 to 3 minutes</u>

Total – **27 to 35 minutes**

Optional

A longer Q&A or pricing discussion should be by the client's choice.

Hand out the pricing information to management and let them decide who stays or gets a copy.

Other Items to consider

- The 17.5-minute attention span does not include introductions or handing out information but refers to the verbal delivery part of the main content of your message.

- It is best to arrive ahead of time to set up any equipment needed for your presentation.

- You keep your start time on time.

- Delays come from others not you.

- If more senior key personnel are present (which can be the case) along with your contact, it is polite to let them know your agenda and time line to cover the information.

- Provide them with a copy of everything. Explain how you handle pricing.
- Ask if they might need to get away so you can cover the important areas for them first
- It's a great excuse to speak with the senior decision makers.

Make your Agenda Time Line Scalable.

Show the times you have allowed for each part of your agenda. Now the prospect is aware of what will take palace and how long you have allowed for it.

If they decide to extend any part of the agenda, they will also realize what happens to the time line.

Tell them your plan and give them the option to expand any area that the feel needs more time to cover.

If you know they have allowed more time for your presentation in advance, make your adjustments and show the new times on your agenda to suit the new total time allowed.

60 MINUTE DRESS REHEARSAL

The Overview

Why Have a Dress Rehearsal?

We call it our dress rehearsal.

To the Customer it will be a **Final Review Meeting** to make sure you have all the facts right and no new things have changed the scope of the requirements or project details.

This type of meeting is for the larger offering packages, equipment or projects. This meeting should be considered essential by you as your dress rehearsal before any final presentation is made.

It is also your Trial Close

The Request

Insist on having this Final Review Meeting. It is your review platform to see if you have correctly assessed all their needs and have all the solutions they require.

It is also a chance to see where you are positioned before final recommendations and final prices are provided.

Your Own Reason for the Final Review Meeting

Your company has perhaps spent 150 to 250 hours or more of their time so far; for questions, research, and design, engineering and proposal and pricing assembly.

It should be normal procedure required by your company or you to see if the final presentation will be accurate and complete.

The Dress Rehearsal Benefits

The reason for this dress rehearsal is the same as a dress rehearsal for any play. It is to find out where your weak points are before you make your debut (your unveiling, final presentation).

It is a trial close that gives you a chance to see where any loyalties of the prospect's employees; that are involved, may be.

It is also your trial close regarding pricing. Final adjustments will be made after this meeting before you present your final quotation and ask for the order.

This is usually for a multi-page proposal for a larger order and there may be many your prospects employees' who will be present.

Inform them of the Reasons

It is best to discuss the reasons for this meeting with your main contact ahead of time for approval and to allow them to decide who should attend and when to have this meeting.

This should not be difficult to justify as you can present it as a beneficial meeting for them. It is to make sure you have everything they want. It is their own special preview.

- Explain that this is a final review before your actual proposal to make sure you have all the information correct.

- It also provides them with their final input before you finalize your design; product specifications and estimating *(say whatever makes sense).*

Explain that often at this point new information or requirements have surfaced and these facts can be discussed and incorporated before your final presentation is made.

This meeting allows them one last review to make sure nothing has been missed or there are not items included that should not be there.

Pricing

You should say that your price will be close; but it is still budgetary. There may be some changes and there is still some fine tuning to do.

For You - this will be your own testing of the waters for price.

There is also a possibility that your prospect's upper management will also be there if the size of order is significant, so they will need to know the type of meeting it will be.

This way it will not be a surprise and viewed as a waste of time by them.

You Do Not need to Upset anyone at this point

General Notes for the Meeting

It is often a good gesture to bring and provide coffee, other beverages and donuts for everyone as they arrive at the meeting; especially a morning one. Find out how many will attend.

Note: Check with your contact before arranging to bring the coffee and donuts, to make sure it is alright.

Correct Protocol

If you will be bringing people from your company to assist you, then it is important to establish that they follow the correct meeting protocol.

When doing your presentation, it is extremely important to have one person in control for the entire meeting!!

And that is YOU!

Not your Manager!

Not an Engineer or Supplier!

It is YOU!

Make sure all of those attending from your company understand the protocol. You decide who speaks and when. You can even provide a brief outline limiting what they are to say.

Do Not let them Take Over!

The Agenda

Suggested Components for this Meeting

Part 1 – The Introductions

Part 2– Your Findings and Summary of their Needs

Part 3 – Offerings, Features, Benefits and Solutions - Point form

Part 4 – Installation and Terms and Conditions

Part 5 – Questions and Answers

Part 6 - Break

Part 7 – Pricing Review

Part 8 – Summary (*Your Call to Action*)

Ten General Tips for Meeting

1. It is a good idea to provide an agenda c/w timeline
2. Point out that there will be several mini-questions and answer periods at the end of each segment and a larger one at the end of your presentation.
3. Start with the introductions and the reason for the preliminary meeting and then move into the main part of your presentation.
4. Structure the first minutes following the introductions for the most important parts.
5. These parts will include your overview point form outlining their needs and your solutions (your offerings).
6. This point form part of the presentation will be followed by a more detailed explanation of your offerings and review of terms and conditions.
7. Be prepared to accommodate any questions that do come up
8. Do not let the whole meeting become a question and answer meeting.
9. If there is a lot to cover that may take longer than 25 minutes, it might be an idea to do it in two parts.
10. Perhaps say you will be stopping part way through for a short Q & A.

End this First Main part with a Q&A

This is an appropriate time for a break especially if there is only the pricing summary information to follow.

Although there will be no final pricing at this point, this will be a very budgetary review of the financial package, payment schedule and your terms and conditions.

This will be an Unofficial Trial Close

For Key Personnel

If any key personnel from your prospects company are present, they may have set a time limit for attending the main presentation.

If they know approximately how long it will be until pricing is covered, they can decide if they wish to stay for the break and review pricing.

If upper management is present at this meeting, you should always provide them with the entire package including pricing for this trial run at the start of the meeting and explain again the concept of the meeting. Go through your contact to do this or get permission.

Explain your timing for handing out pricing and terms and conditions to avoid premature discussion from them. They will fully understand the need to prevent a meeting, from getting out of control.

Benefits of a Q & A

- Discovery of those opposed to you, your company or your proposal (offerings)
- Able to ask questions of any skeptics
    - Publicly reveal their objections
    - Publicly solve them
    - By raising these issues publicly, you can avoid or at least minimize back room discussions and the sabotage of your quotation after you have gone.
- **Able to discover and respond to:**
    - Hidden animosity for your company
    - A hidden agenda and reasons that someone may have for promoting your competitor

- Able to Obtain information on other needs they desire that were not previously mentioned
- Often Exposes features that your competition is offering
- Often can indicate where you are positioned regarding price or preference.

Often an informal Q & A increases trust and credibility and is your best opportunity to re-position yourself for your final presentation.

The Break

The break can provide a time when you can speak with upper management if they decide to stay. Ask your contact first.

Often management will leave the more detailed portion to others and will discuss these details including pricing separately with their own people later.

The Dress Rehearsal Details

Overview

We are now into the details of the main components of your meeting. We have broken the meeting into the eight parts.

It is best to keep these separated as components and show them separately on your agenda as listed except for the designated part 8 which you will just call Action Required or Summary.

The Eight Parts and What to do

Part 1 – The Introductions

- Provide a brief history of your Company.

- Ask in advance who they want to start the introductions.

- If it is you:

  o Introduce your company members that are present and their functions as well as any key suppliers.

  o Then Introductions of Customers employees and their functions

  o **Note:** Their upper management can abstain if they wish

Part 2 – Customer Needs Review

- Provide a review of your findings to date in point form.

- Provide an outline of what you see as their needs, specifications or requirements from those meetings.

- Confirm these are what they are looking for.

- Ask if you have missed anything?

- Is there anything new that has been added?

- Should anything be removed or shown as an optional extra?

Wait for a Response

- If there are additional items, write them down.

- If items are no longer needed or part of the project, remove them

- Provide answers if you can.

- If you cannot provide complete answers say you will get back to them and provide the information prior to or in your final proposal whichever they prefer.

Part 3 - Your Offerings, Solutions and Benefits

- Provide your solutions, products, services, or equipment recommendations in point form.

- Supply any Drawings necessary for Clarity

Part 4 – Question and Answers

- Keep to the allotted time. This can get out of hand quickly.

Part 5 - Installation and Terms and Conditions

- Provide a description of the Installation (if any)

- Provide a review of your Terms and Conditions. (remember your built-in objections rebuttal)

- Open the meeting to Final Questions and Answers before the break.

- Provide your Detailed Support Information and Data

- Provide Full product or Service details and specifications.

Part 6 – Break

You might provide a light snack, coffee, donuts (depends on time of day - same as final presentation) check with your contact for approval first.

During the Break is the time to hand out any budget pricing.

Part 7 – Budget Pricing

Provide copies to your contact and let them hand out to the others of their own choosing.

Let them control who is qualified as you do not want to place this information incorrectly.

This is the time to also provide a copy to give to upper management if they have not been in attendance.

Part 8– Summary (Your Call to Action)

Have we now addressed all their needs?

What changes are required?

Re-state what additions have occurred?

Re-state what can be eliminated?

Most Important Question – *"How do we look?"*

Suggested Meeting Guide

Preparation

- Set up and test any equipment being used in your presentation prior to your meeting.

- Ask for perhaps 10 to 15 minutes ahead of your meeting start time for this.

- Set out coffee and snacks.

- When people arrive for a meeting – some will agree with the reason for the meeting, some are agitated and feel it is a waste of their time.

- There may be background issues internal conflicts some are less enthused, and many will doubt you.

This informal 10 to 15-minute set-up time, and providing the coffee and snacks is invaluable for breaking the ice and easing tensions and opposition.

The Time Allotted

Make your initial agenda time line to suit the original time they have provided for you. We have provided the example of 60 to 72-minute timeline.

Make your agenda time line scalable. Show the times you have allowed for each part of your agenda. This makes the prospect aware of what will take palace and how long you have allowed for each part.

If they decide to extend any part of the agenda, they will also realize what happens to the time line.

Tell them your plan and give them the option to expand any area that the feel needs more time to cover. They can change the time but do not just let things get out of control or you will be rushed at the end.

The 60 to 72 Minute Time Line

Part 1 – Opening Introductions	3 to 4 minutes
Presentation Start	
Part 2 – Needs	8 to 10 minutes
Part 3 – Offerings and Solutions	12 to 14 minutes
Part 4 – Q & A for Parts 2 & 3	4 to 5 minutes
Part 5 - Terms and Conditions Review	8 to 10 minutes
Part 6 - Break – Informal Q&A -	8 to 10 minutes
Part 7 – Pricing Review	11 to 12 minutes
Part 8 – Summary (Call to Action)	<u>6 to 7 minutes</u>
Total Meeting	**60 to 72 minutes**

Summary of the Dress Rehearsal

By making the prime message of your meeting a point form presentation you will be able to deliver a clear communication that is easily understood and fully absorbed.

- The greatest danger that can occur is to get totally bogged down in too much unnecessary detail in your initial part of your presentation and lose the clarity of your message.
- This will confuse the reasons why they should choose you.
- It is essential that you capture and maintain the client's interest during all parts.
- If you do this correctly, your prospect will want to take part in the discussions and be anxious to hear your final proposal.

There is usually more than one meeting for a large project or large piece of equipment and the dress rehearsal is a critical one.

Your client will usually want to review the details of this one as well, before having the final meeting.

This part is Considered the Appetizer

If you have Presented, the Right Components

You will be there for the Main Course

Evaluation

It is here; when you are finished, that you will get a reaction to your solutions and equipment concepts.

If you have provided a budget price you can also get a reaction to this as well which will allow you to have another check point to gauge your position and chances to obtain the order.

You are now ready with all the facts to start the assembly of your final presentation.

THE FINAL PRESENTATION

The Overview

How to Assemble the Final Presentation

It is time to put your final presentation together for the order. Your dress rehearsal should have provided all the missing and key components from your discussion and possibly uncovered some decision-making tips.

You can now proceed with more confidence in what your client is looking for.

What comes first?

- Price or Solutions and Benefits?
- The customer always wants price.
- It should always be – Solutions and benefits.

Why Solutions and Benefits first?

Pricing is often the first place in a proposal that people will turn to (if it is available) especially when you are making your final quotation.

If you have pricing as part of your main proposal package they may disengage immediately from your explanation of Solutions and Benefits.

Why Pricing Comes Last

If pricing is presented first:

- There has been no explanation of what is included in the price.
- There is no justification for the Price yet.
- No solutions have been discussed.
- No benefits have been discussed.
- Terms and Conditions have not been discussed.
- What is included has not been outlined.

Result

All they see is the Price and there may be total justification if your price is higher.

- o It may have a lot more benefits with a better Return on their investment
- o Your quality may be higher
- o Your delivery may be better
- o You may include more things in your terms and conditions or installation than your competitor

All these benefits could be lost because you have not been able to show them first and show value.

People will be Thinking only of the Price

And Not the Value

If the Price is Presented First

It is important to be able to provide a description of your main features, benefits and solutions to meet their needs; before you cover the pricing aspect, or there is no value-perceived to justify the price that is provided.

This is very important to remember and is one of the main reasons to keep pricing separate from the rest of the package. It needs to be handed out at the appropriate time and to the right people.

There will always be pressure to go to pricing first. Stand your ground and leave pricing until later or you may *"Pay the Price."*

If you prepare your contact properly and establish your procedure right from the beginning, there should not be a problem.

Suggested Meeting Components

Part 1 – The Introductions

Part 2– Summary of their Needs

Part 3 – Your Offerings, Features, Benefits and Solutions

Part 4 – Questions and Answers

Part 5 – Break (snacks, coffee, tea or soft drinks)

Part 6 – Installation Responsibilities, Terms and Conditions

Part 7 – Short Q & A part 6

Part 8 – Pricing (Equipment and Installation), ROI, Incentives

Part 9 – Final Q & A

Part10 – Summary (your Call to Action)

The Meeting Details

Overview

We are now into the main components of your Final Presentation Meeting. We have broken the meeting into the ten main parts shown above.

It is best that you treat these main parts as totally separate components and show them separately on your agenda as well.

Part 10 on the agenda you hand out is labeled

Summary - Not Call to Action

Respect for their Management

If any key personnel from the customer are present, they may have set a time limit for attending the main presentation.

If they know how long your meeting will be, they can decide how long they will need to stay to hear an important part.

You should always immediately provide upper management (through your contact) with the total presentation package including agenda and all parts including pricing, ROI and their terms and conditions.

Explain the Approach

You should explain that in your normal presentation process you cover the total package, the benefits and solutions and terms and conditions first before presenting price so that the pricing makes sense.

If they stay for the Entire Presentation

That is Good

The break can provide a time when you can speak with upper management if they decide to stay. Go through your contact.

Pricing is also best to come next after the break.

This allows those people who have a say in the product and any applicable terms and conditions (but do not get involved in pricing) to take part in the break and food and informal Q&A.

In this way, they will not feel excluded. They will be more likely to become a supportive friend behind the scenes.

The Meeting

Who should you Bring?

As the potential new suppler, you also may want to have a few your own people there to assist you. Perhaps your management; engineering or service personnel will be there to answer questions.

Possibly bring key suppliers that may be part of your proposal package.

Rules of behavior

It is critical that all those attending including suppliers and everyone from your company including your managers fully understand that there is only one person in charge of the meeting and that person is you.

They may speak only when called upon by you or asked by the prospect. They will say their part and immediately turn the meeting back to you when they are done by saying your name.

This must be a totally agreed upon fact before anyone attends the meeting. (Including your superiors)

Note: Have a "Pre-Presentation" meeting with your support group to cover everything including this protocol.

Often others; especially your managers or engineering, may want to take over the limelight once they get started.

1) It should be an absolute rule that it is **"Not Allowed"**

2) You are to be totally in charge from start to finish

3) If you (as the sales person) lose control of the meeting; *"as the authority figure"*, you are doomed when it comes to asking for the order or controlling this part.

Lesson Learned

- I learned this the hard way with meetings disrupted by overzealous engineers, suppliers and even my manager.

- The client began directing all further questions to these support people who: for the most part, were not qualified to ask for the order or answer objections.

- The entire sales process was out of control and it became extremely difficult to regain my position as the authority figure to get the sale.

- Do not let this happen, or you may be leaving without an order.

The Agenda

Part 1 – The Introductions

- Ask in advance who they want to start the introductions.

- If it is you then:

  o Introduce your company members that are present and their functions, followed by Suppliers and description of their involvement.

  o Then Introductions of Customers employees and their functions.

  o **Note:** Their upper management can abstain if they wish.

Presentation Start

Part 2 – Needs

What to do

- **As a last-minute detail; the day before your meeting,** you will have called and asked your contact if there is anything new or if there are there any last-minute changes because of your final review meeting, and make any adjustments required.

Point Form will be noted below as (PF)

- Provide a review of your findings during your earlier meetings. (PF)
- Do a quick review of their needs, specifications or requirements from those meetings and confirm these are what they are still looking for. (PF)
- Include and mention any changes that occurred because of your Dress Rehearsal. Ask if anything else has been added or if anything has changed since your last conversations.
- You should be clear to continue; but, surprises can occur. Be ready to handle them and make the changes to your final package while you are there.

Part 3 - Your Recommendations

- Provide a point form summary of your offerings, solutions and benefits.
- Supply any Drawings or visual aids necessary for Clarity.

Use PowerPoint, slides, literature or drawings. Be very thorough and cover all the important areas.

Part 4 - Questions and Answer Session

Here you will also control the meeting and you will either answer the questions asked or designate one of your company members or suppliers to answer it, if they are better suited.

Again, they should do their part and turn the meeting back over to you by verbally saying your name. *"Back to You (your name)"*

Part 5 - Break – Use this time also for an extended informal Q & A. It is also mingling time and opportunities for multiple discussions.

Keep this part under control and a maximum time as outlined or you will lose control and be unable to get the momentum going again easily.

Wherever the meeting is taking place you will have made proper arrangements for the food part in advance.

Menu Suggestions

a) **Start of the day** - Have coffee, tea, soft drinks and water. Provide donuts or an alternative healthier fruit snack.

b) **Mid-morning or midafternoon** keep it simple: a cheese tray, cold meats, bread, and cold drinks

c) **Lunch** – Sandwiches, veggie or cheese platter, cold meats and bread, coffee, soft drinks, cookies or treats (discuss with your contact)

d) **Afternoon** – Same as Mid-Morning

Part 6 - Installation and Terms and Conditions

At this point you will review Installation (if any) along with terms and conditions which are usually tied very closely to any installation.

Have a point form description of the installation for quick review.

Have a detailed description of Installation for backup support.

Have your terms and conditions relating to the project clearly defined and show everything that you have included and what is not included. (remember your built-in condition rebuttal)

Often the terms and conditions can make the difference in getting an order or losing it. Your competition may have left out costly items that you have included that might be overlooked.

Part 7 – Questions and Answer for Part 6

Part 8 - Provide Pricing

Your Q & A has ended and once the non-attendees for the pricing part have left continue.

1. Financial Information
   a. Equipment and Installation Pricing
   b. Optional Prices
   c. Payment schedule
   d. ROI, Information
   e. Incentives available
2. Provide your Terms and Conditions relating to pricing
3. Provide any Testimonials that are relevant
4. Having some good pictures and visual aids can increase the perception of value.

5. Have charts showing pricing details, incentives, leasing rates, Options and ROI.

Break your pricing summary into components by providing as many options with add-on pricing as possible. This way they feel they have control and your base price will look better as well.

By providing options separately you give the client control over any extra costs for added benefits.

In this way, you can discuss the benefits and features of the options and add-on to show the added value for each of them. If it is Applicable and Results are good, show any ROI for any Options as well

End of Formal Presentation

Part 9 – Final Questions and Answers for Everything

Part 10 – Summary (Your Call to action - Closing

- Ask for the order using the appropriate closing method.

- Answer any objections using the 5 Step process.

- Usually you will get only get an indication of your chances to get the order; but if you do get one, Thank them for the Order.

Meeting Time Lines

Set up and test any equipment such as projectors or sound systems that are being used for your presentation. Do this prior to your meeting. Ask for perhaps 15 – 20 minutes ahead of your meeting start time for this. Set out the coffee and donuts first.

When people arrive for a meeting

Some are emotional, some are glad to take part, some may be agitated, some are enthusiastic others may be complacent. There may be background issues internal conflicts some are less enthused, and many may not know you and will doubt you.

This informal 10 – 15-minute time with coffee and donuts while you are getting set up is invaluable for breaking the ice and easing tensions and opposition.

The Breakdown

Make your agenda time line scalable. Show the times you have allowed for each part of your agenda. Make sure the prospect is aware of what will take palace and how long you have allowed for it.

If they decide to extend any part of the agenda, they will also realize what happens to the time line. Tell them your plan and give them the option to expand any area that the feel needs more time to cover.

The 72 to 90 Minute Time Line

Sample Time Line – Adjust to suit

Part 1 – Introductions -	1 to 3 minutes
Actual Presentation Begins	
Part 2 – Their Needs	10 to 12 minutes
Part 3 – Your Offerings, Features Benefits -	12 to 14 minutes
Part 4 – Questions and Answers First Half -	<u>5 to 6 minutes</u>
Total time Parts 1 to 4	**28 to 35 minutes**
Part 5 - BREAK –	8 to 9 minutes
Presentation Continues	
Part 6 – Installation Duties, Terms & Conditions	10 to 12 minutes
Part 7 – Short Q & A for 6	2 to 4 minutes
Part 8 – Pricing, ROI, Incentives -	<u>14 to 16 minutes</u>
Total time Parts 6 to 8	**26 to 32 minutes**
Part 9 – Final Questions and Answers	5 to 7 minutes
Part 10 – Summary (Call to Action)	<u>5 to 7 minutes</u>
Total time Parts 9& 10	<u>**10 to 14 minutes**</u>
Total meeting time line including Break –	**72 to 90 minutes**

Summary of the Final Presentation

Trial Closings

Throughout the meeting, you will be asking things like:

- Is that right?
- Is that what you wanted?
- How are we doing so far?
- Does that solve the problem?

These questions are very helpful to see if your presentation is on track and may prevent surprises at the end of it.

Whenever pricing is discussed, you must always ask how you look as a minimum requirement with an expectation of a response. Asking for the sale is what this is all about and your closes will help you get the order.

Make Your Best Effort to Close

Ultimately, you may need to leave it with the decision makers, to discuss before they give you a final answer. Asking how you look, will (if answered) provide a strong indication of where you stand and could give you another chance if you are not solidly in there.

Leaving it for a final decision is often the case on large purchases so you should not panic if this happens.

Our Part 2 on Qualifying and Closing has provided many ways to ask for the order while you are there.

Our part 3 Overcoming Objections will provide you with the necessary information for completion of the sale.

Extra Time

Because this is a final presentation the length for any part could be even longer. It is important to take a short break approximately every 20 to 25 minutes. After 25 minutes the attention is much lower and sometimes not there at all.

We have already discussed making your time line scalable and showing allotted times on your agenda. Leave it open but ask the prospect if any area needs to be extended

THE CALL BACK MEETING

The call back is when you have left without a sale after your earlier final presentation. There may have been a reason or condition why you could not proceed at that time, or maybe you were just not good enough to close that day.

Other reasons:

- There may have been areas for you to re-consider or re-structure in your quotation

- They could have needed to talk to someone else or wait for more quotes to come in.

- They needed time to think it over or discuss it with all of the people involved.

- Perhaps the Main Decision Maker wants to see you one more time before they decide.

Now any Previous Conditions have been met

- You have reviewed your presentation and made any requested changes.

- You have called to arrange your Appointment

If No Changes Were Requested

Find out how much time they will be setting aside for your meeting, who will be attending and how many copies they will need. The answers that they provide to these questions will often reveal what your chances will be.

Be Totally Prepared

- To Answer any Questions about the Project
- To Ask for the Order
- To Answer any Objections

If Changes Were Requested

If changes were requested, inform them that you have made them, and are looking forward to showing these improvements to them.

Use the Word Improvements - Do Not Call Them Changes

People Hate Changes

1. Make sure that you have followed these steps before your visit,

    a. Prepare your new proposal so that it is up to date.

    b. Make sure your agenda fits the time allotted for your visit.

    c. Provide the right number of copies plus some to spare.

    d. Tag any areas in your proposal that have (changed) been improved with a removable sticker.

2. Prepare a list in point form of the (changes) improvements that you have made and all the areas you want to discuss during your visit.

3. Leave some space between each item in your review copy so that you can write down any additional comments.

4. Put it on your letterhead, and you can even call it "Appendix A" or something appropriate. You may want to attach it to your quote.

When you arrive: "You thank the prospect for seeing you again."

Then you say:

"So that I do not take up more time than you have set aside, I have prepared a summary of your main concerns that we discussed on my last visit or (our last telephone conversation)."

"I have made a copy for you so that we can review these areas quickly together."

"I have also revised our proposal to reflect those improvements and placed these removable stickers in each location of the revision."

If they are Receptive

Do not rush through your presentation like a runaway freight train. Confirm again how much time they have set aside and begin your presentation.

You have already asked how much time they are setting aside, who will be there and how many copies they will want.

Hand them your Agenda with Time Line

Start reviewing the changes (improvements). If questions are asked, provide your answers. After each item, ask if they need more clarification, or if that satisfies their concern and/or meets their needs.

Go through the whole proposal and when you finish, you ask if there are any new areas that may have developed since your last conversation.

If there are No Additions or Changes Required

Ask again if today's meeting has answered all their questions and concerns.

If they say Yes

Choose your Appropriate Close

And

CLOSE IT!

If there are Additional Changes

Address them and make every effort to solve them when you are there. If you leave them unanswered, you could lose any further opportunity to get the sale. If they are major changes then you will need to arrange to come back with the new changes if they are willing for another **Call Back.**

SUMMARY

The greatest satisfaction in perfecting presentation skills is that you will have optimum control over the potential outcome of your sales efforts.

You will have confidence in knowing that you have a plan, a track to run on and a way to obtain the greatest leverage for achieving the sale.

You will have the upper hand by knowing exactly where your presentations are headed and that you are in control.

You are now equipped to make any of the different types of presentations that you will need.

END OF PART FOUR

DIRECT SALES 101

PART FIVE

FINDING PROSPECTS

and

Generating Leads

The Marketing Part of the Selling Process

Where and When to Look

How Get your First Appointment

Written by

Wayne E Shillum

Introduction

When the word prospecting is mentioned in general conversation we almost immediately think of the act of panning for gold. We see a person crunched over at the river's edge washing away the debris to find the glittering pieces of gold.

When the word prospecting is mentioned while discussing *"**Direct Sales**"* we often think of the following:

- Making countless telephone calls

- Knocking on doors (both household and businesses}

- Addressing and stuffing envelopes or sending large quantities of faxes or mailers (often called junk mail) to the marketplace

- The internet - emails, newsletters, blogging and social media

- Newspapers, Radio, or TV

Here too we are searching for the glittering pieces of gold.

Prospecting is The Marketing Attachment to Sales

We say marketing attachment because attracting prospects is what **Marketing** is supposed to be all about. Marketing plans are designed to find prospects and use the best way to get the attention of potential clients or customers.

It is usually in a form of advertising to create a reason for the prospect to act.

Marketing is Finding Strangers

And Turning them into Interested Prospects

If done right, marketing should have *"call to action"* that causes the potential prospect to contact your company.

When this happens, the role of marketing has achieved its initial purpose. Once the prospect is attracted and a lead is obtained, the true function of sales starts to take shape.

Sales is Taking an Interested Prospect and

Turning them into a Buying Customer

Statistics show that approximately 80% of small to medium sized businesses do not have or use a marketing plan. They also do not have a marketing department of any significance.

That is why the responsibility of *"attracting and creating client interest"* has traditionally been left to the sales department in many companies.

The Sales Term used for this is *"Prospecting."*

Very often sales people do not take the time to learn and master the very important skill set of prospecting, that they have inherited.

The results are often very bad. Finding prospects becomes a nightmare and many people new-to-sales will leave the profession in frustration and disappointment.

Once Thing is for Certain

Prospecting can involve the highest amount of negativity in the selling process.

If an owner wants to obtain the most productivity from their sales department, there should be a significant company involvement in the marketing of their offerings.

When a marketing department does exist in a company, they will usually be responsible for advertising and promotions that will build the company image and attract prospects.

Many types of businesses take care of the total effort in bringing the client to the point of contact with the sales person. While employed by these types of businesses, the sales person will have little need for being able to prospect.

Retail sales is such an example of no prospecting required by the employee/sales person. There are also many other types of direct sales companies that will also perform this task for the sales department.

What about the 80%

As stated earlier, 80% of businesses involved in Direct Sales have little to no marketing plans in place. They will leave the finding clients part, totally up to the sales department.

It is often a big mistake that is made by many businesses, not to get involved in the marketing/prospecting part of the process. The owner will hire a sales person to handle both prospecting and sales and feel they are covered. They will have very little to do with finding prospects.

In doing this, many are placing the success or failure of their business in someone else's hands and fail to provide very much support. The Reality is, that they have a vested interest in the success of their sales people and should participate wherever possible.

This part of our training has been written for those sales people who will need to find potential customers as part of their job and selling responsibilities.

It could be an owner or an employee who is the sales representative. In either case; owner or employee, this skill set will be absolutely required for whoever is looking after the sales/marketing/prospecting for the business

Where Companies do get Involved

If two separate areas are involved (marketing and sales), finding clients should always be a cooperative joint effort.

There should be continuous feedback from the sales department to indicate what marketing is working and what is not.

- Left on their own, marketing does not always provide the sales department with qualified leads.

- If the sales department fails to communicate and inform the marketing department as to what is working and what is not, the problem of unqualified leads will continue.

- Thus, time is wasted by visiting prospective buyers who have no need or any real interest in a company's product or service.

- In some cases, the prospect will have absolutely no idea why the sales representative is there to see them.

Examples of how Bad Leads happen

Leads are often generated by a totally separate marketing arm in a company.

It often involves a telemarketing department and the telemarketer is looking to make as many appointments as they can get, to fill the daily quota set by the company.

The important step of fully qualifying the lead is left out by the telemarketer.

The sales department is sent on a wild goose chase, where there is no need or interest. It also could be the result of a bad marketing campaign where the wrong message has been sent or the wrong market has been approached.

Thus, these efforts fail to provide quality leads for the sales department to begin their part of the process.

Conclusion

Therefore, sales people should have a significant involvement in the marketing process when it is done by the business.

This involvement will mean better control over the effectiveness of the company's efforts, to get qualified clients, and reduce wasted time by the sales representative.

Success in Selling Starts with Qualified Leads

The Challenges of Prospecting

One should never underestimate the challenges of prospecting. It takes a lot of effort and often very thick skin. It requires the knowledge and use of the first four parts of our Training series.

Part One "The Essential Elements"

This prepared you for the task ahead outlining all the ingredients needed for you, your company and your prospects. It provided the framework to handle Prospecting successfully.

Part Two "Qualifying and Closing"

This part showed you how to qualify your prospects and discover needs and ask for the order.

Part Three "Overcoming Objections and Conditions"

This part showed you how to keep going; overcoming the roadblocks and questions, from start to finish and to secure the order at the end.

Part Four "Meetings and Presentations"

This part showed the importance of communication and how to structure your sales Presentations.

These skill sets will be needed before you can successfully do the first part of your job in "Direct Sales" which is finding prospects.

The Basics of Prospecting

The Overview

Since 80% of small and medium sized businesses do not have a full marketing plan in use; it becomes the added responsibility of the sales department, to generate leads and find prospects.

Sometimes, the owner or sales manager will decide what form the marketing (prospecting) will take, and it becomes the sales representative's job to carry out their requests.

If management is not up to date on what works and what does not work; then you as a sales representative, may be asked to waste time on prospecting methods that no longer are very productive.

This Example is still being done

Sending sales reps out to find customers does not work if the sales representative is expected to develop a territory by making in-the-field cold calls to see prospects immediately

Knocking on doors, without appointments or previous contact is no longer acceptable by prospects.

Today, random cold calling without previous contact, is simply a *"Waste of Time,"* if one expects immediate appointments.

However, cold calling and leaving information for Future follow up without asking to see someone, can be a very productive way to get started.

To the uninspired owner or manager of a sales department, the next may be one of the easiest instructions to give to their sales people.

"Get out there and make some Sales Calls"

"And get some Orders"

Cold calling is one of many prospecting methods that needs to be modified to suit today's type of purchaser.

Unfortunately, many companies will still send their sales force out to a very cold reception, resulting in poor to little success, and then blame sales for the poor results.

Random Cold Calling

This method will become a nightmare to find anyone who will immediately see you or be willing to listen. In addition, finding a company that has a reception area will be difficult. A telephone in the lobby has replaced most receptionists.

If there is a receptionist; the chances of being able to get past them to see someone, will be next to impossible without a previous appointment. Even getting a name can become an exercise in futility.

It will become very demoralizing for the sales person who is subjected to this type of prospecting, unless it is modified to suit today's purchasing practices.

Purchasers in the Business to Business (B2B) marketplace as well as today's Business to Homeowners (Consumer) (B2C) are no longer receptive to the old form of cold calling.

Outdated

In the past talking to random sales persons who were making cold calls, was how purchasing departments learned about existing and new products and services.

Now, they simply search for information on the internet and call the companies if they are interested. In some cases, they will make first contact because of successful marketing. (advertising or the branding efforts of a business)

If you use the old method of cold calling, you will not be very successful. If it becomes what is expected of you as a sales person, think twice about staying with that company, unless they will listen to other ideas.

Knowledge is Power

It is important to know what does not work and avoid these methods.

Today's Prospecting

Marketing methods are continuously changing and prospecting and attracting clients is marketing. Other more productive forms of prospecting, have now replaced the random no appointment "in-person" cold calling efforts for immediate appointments.

Once you learn these new and more productive prospecting methods, you will find it easier to locate your potential customers. This is when your actual real sales activity begins.

You will make the appointments, see the client and begin defining the needs or problems to solve. You will then prepare and make your sales presentations to get the order.

Some Changes Occurring

Many companies who are selling products or services still combine prospecting and sales. The growth of social media marketing and other specific forms of focused advertising, are now proving to be more efficient and cost effective.

When it comes to paying salaried sales personnel plus the added cost of their expense accounts to do both marketing (prospecting) and sales, there are good economic reasons for change.

Some companies have begun to separate prospecting from sales for better selling efficiency and for this economical control

Effective Efforts

This can make the sales person more effective and productive by allowing them to focus on pure selling. Unfortunately, it also has created a new problem of making sure that it is a team effort and the sales person is being supplied with *qualified* leads.

For our purposes, we will outline the various methods available and leave it up to the company or individual sales person to decide who does what.

Whether it is called Marketing

Prospecting or Generating Leads

It has the Same Purpose

We are looking for Potential Business

Prospecting Objectives

In your search for prospects, there are the basic objectives that you will need to consider.

>
> **First Objective** – Use the right prospecting method
>
> **Second Objective** - Determine if there is a need and interest
>
> **Third Objective** – Set your introductory appointment

1)Using the right Prospecting Method

Your success in this part will come from your research and learning about all the prospecting methods available. Certain methods will be better suited for your target market.

Your job will be to choose the right ones for your prospects. We will be providing a few ways to achieve successful prospecting results.

There will be Prospecting Methods

- That can be done only during normal business hours
- Some can be done in off-hours
- Some you will do completely on your own
- Others will involve people in your company or suppliers
- Make best use of your time and resources to achieve the optimum results that you can.

2)Determining a Genuine Need and Interest

This part of your prospecting will be looking for needs or problems to solve. This could mean finding more prospects doing the same types of things that your existing customers are doing.

It could also mean finding other uses for your products or services.

3)Setting Your Introductory Appointment

Once you have successfully completed 1 & 2 you are ready to set your first appointment. Use of your closing method *"Alternate of Choice"* is the best way to set appointments.

The Law of Numbers

The law of numbers could be loosely described by the statement: "If you throw enough mud at the wall, some of it will stick".

To be successful in the process of prospecting, requires that you use the most effective methods known to your industry. Time, research, persistence and experience, will show you which ones to use and when.

After you have established essential traits required for a good prospect and acquired the necessary skills; the following is one example of the expected outcome as related to the law of numbers.

Telephone Solicitation Call Statistics

Out of every 100 predetermined eligible people contacted; normal results for telephone sales prospecting efforts will usually be:

- You should find 8 to 10 people who are interested
- Out of these, you should get 4 to 6 presentations
- Of these, you should get 1 to 3 sales

Once you know your potential market and the means of qualifying the prospects, you can rely on this rule or law of numbers (percentages) for certain prospecting methods.

Use the law as a base minimum to determine your prospecting efforts, and to set your own pace for the goals you have established.

Examples based on Law of Numbers

- If you want 1 - 3 sales, you need a minimum of 100 sales calls
- If you want 3 - 6 sales, you need a minimum of 200 to 250 sales calls

These examples are based on statistics when relating to telephone prospecting. Attitude, enthusiasm, and the right approach will get the results. Experience will increase your success percentages.

There will be a similar statistical outcome for any of the prospecting methods you will use. Once you find out what any of these methods take to get a sale, then you can determine what your efforts need to be for your sales targets.

When to Prospect

In this outline for Prospecting we will deal with mostly B2B (Business to Business) methods for your personal efforts. Most B2B sales persons will use the telephone to make appointments

Most B2C (Business to Consumer) businesses will utilize telemarketing or other forms of company related prospecting to obtain appointments.

We do not advocate cold door knocking for either B2B or B2C as an effective way to get in to see prospects if it is the first contact.

When Calling by Telephone

Choose a calling schedule that does not upset an existing or potential prospect. This means respecting the times of day when your prospect may be busy.

These busy times are Usually

- At the start of every day when people are getting organized for the work ahead
- At the end of the day when people are attending to the last-minute things they need to wrap up.

Note- The times shown below are based on a company with office hours that start at approximately 8:30am and end at approximately 4:30pm.

A Sample B2B Work Schedule

7:30 to 9:30 Use this time for traveling, planning, quoting, making promised telephone calls only. You can make in-person sales calls that have been previously arranged.

> You can also use this time for Network Prospecting with your peers.
>
> (Perhaps an early morning coffee)

9:30 – 11:30 Use this time to do all types of Prospecting and it is prime time for seeing your sales appointments face to face.

11:45 – 1:15 Use this time to have lunch, travel, and work on quotes, summarizing the morning, planning the afternoon, or meeting your customers for lunch or your networking peers for coffee or lunch.

Note: Some companies do not look favorably on employees if they accept lunch invitations from sales people. Ask first if it OK.

1:15 – 3:45 Use this time to do all types of Prospecting and again is prime time for seeing your sales appointments face to face.

After 3:45 - Use this time

- To attend previously arranged or appointments requested by customer
- For summarizing your day's efforts, planning future prospecting, preparing of quotes and doing peer network prospecting.

Note: There is always a little flexibility in schedules and some companies may have different work start/stop times. Make the required adjustments to suit.

Work with the above agenda and establish your own time lines. Always respect your prospects time.

Common Courtesies

1) Each morning no new contact should be made before 9:00 - 9:30 to allow prospects to get their day started.

2) For afternoons make your last appointment start time no later than 3:30 so that you have sufficient time to complete it, leaving time for your client to finish their day. (unless otherwise requested by client)

3) On Fridays, do not try to make appointments to start later than 3:00 PM.

Here we are showing *Respect* for the prospects time. No one likes to be approached with a solicitation call first thing in the morning especially Mondays.

No one likes to be approached after 3:45 especially Fridays unless it is important, or they have requested it.

Build Your Knowledge

Knowledge for Getting Started

a) Your Company and its Offerings

Find out everything you can about your company. When it started? Who started it? Who is running it now?   Learn its history and how it has changed since the beginning

Most companies will offer some type of training for their offerings (products or services) and this is where you will concentrate on building your knowledge.

Find out what products or services you will be selling and everywhere their offerings are being used and why people use them. Learn what all the benefits are, and where you are positioned in the marketplace regarding quality, price and performance.

b) Your Company's Marketing

Ask what marketing is presently being done by your company and the extent of any marketing plan that may exist.

- What they are presently doing?
- Do they have a web site?
  - How are they marketing the site?
  - Are they happy with its results?
- What Social Media Groups do they Participate in?
  - What are they doing in them?
  - Are they happy with the results?
- What else have they tried?
- What is planned in the next three to six months?
  - Can you participate in the planning?
- What are you initially expected to do regarding their marketing efforts?

- What support from them can you expect?

c) Competition

- Find out who your main competitors are

- What are their offerings, their benefits and weaknesses?

- Find out where they are positioned regarding quality, price and performance compared to your company.

- What Type of Marketing are they doing?

d) Customer List

- Get a list of all your Customers

- What products/services are they purchasing?

- What is their purchasing Volume per month/per year?

- Who is your contact? Their Manager? The owner?

- When did they become a customer?

- Why did they become a customer?

- Why are they still a customer?

- Have they recently had any complaints or issues?

Note: Do the above items (a - d) immediately upon being hired or you will miss the opportunity as a new employee to gather this knowledge with the company's blessing.

Starting to ask these questions after you have been employed for 2 or 3 months will upset your employer. They want to see new sales activity by this time.

Once you have completed finding out about your existing customers immediately continue with parts e and f). You can combine these calls with other prospecting efforts.

e) Appointments with Existing Clients

Make appointment and visit your existing customers as soon as you can and find out:

1. If they have any concerns or problems with your products or services?
2. If you can do anything to improve your services?

If there are any changes to office or plant operations, manufacturing, quality that are being considered that will affect your products?

In doing this research you will start building trust, respect and loyalty.

You will also:

- o Find out what reason may interest others in becoming a client.
- o Find additional business opportunities.
- o Obtain leads for new clients
- o Build your references list
- o Discover any areas of concern and provide answers to these problems.

Note: Your actions here could prevent the loss of that customer if nothing has previously been done to correct a situation.

Do these tasks as quickly as possible and do not make these meetings a huge project that might interfere with your quest for new business.

f) Establish your Prospecting Plan

One of the greatest areas of failure; as we have already mentioned, is "doing what does not work."

Many business owners or sales managers make the mistake of requesting prospecting methods of their sales department that do not work efficiently or even worse – do not work at all.

The further that people are removed from the actual selling activity; the more likely it is, that this will happen.

Requesting a form of prospecting without understanding how or why it is supposed to work will usually result in failure.

In this Part 5, we will describe many prospecting methods, so you can understand and decide what can be utilized best for your own prospecting efforts.

- Some will work well.
- Some work better than others.
- Some may not work for your offerings

It will be up to you to find where your efforts will be

This knowledge along with some type of analytics will usually show you which direction to take.

Always ask both new and existing prospects how they found out about your company; unless you made first contact.

Summary of Your Needs:

- Knowledge of your target market
- Knowledge of your products or services
- Knowledge of your company
- Knowledge of your competition and their offerings
- Knowledge of what works and what does not work
- Knowledge of Prospecting
- Knowledge of the Key Elements
- Knowledge of Closing
- Knowledge of Overcoming and Answering Objections
- Knowledge of Sales Presentations

Learn every type of prospecting and establish as soon as you can – what works for you and almost more important – What does not work!

Company Prospecting

Overview

It is best to totally get familiar with what the company is prepared to do in assisting your efforts to find prospects. The following are some of the ways that a company can provide help in the prospecting process.

Do not become discouraged if you find they presently are not using many of these methods as part of their marketing plans.

We are outlining them so that you can get an idea of what could be done. Your part will be to suggest adding them and finding ways where you can support their efforts.

You will also better understand how your input could be helpful in making these things happen or work better.

Clarification

For our purposes, here, we are not offering readers an in-depth training of each method, but we are providing enough information to build awareness and to get one started.

Web Site

A company without a website is not part of today's business world. Web Sites have become an essential element in today's business world.

What a website does

It is a:

- Declaration that you are there and open for business.
- Focal point to send people to, for information about your company.
- Beginning of a company's branding process.
- Silent source of information for people to visit and learn more about the company's offerings.

You may have already checked to see if your potential employer had a web site in your job search. If they do have one, you have a base to work from.

If they do not have one, it would be a good idea to suggest getting things in motion to set one up when you are getting started.

How to get a Web Site Started

- Today you can secure a domain name and hosting for very little expense at sources such as *"go daddy,"*

- User friendly *"Word Press"* is available on go daddy where you or your company; with a little training, can totally control the administrative duties at a very reasonable monthly cost.

- **Word Press** is easy to learn and use and will allow you to start with a very basic site without having a lot of web-tech experience.

- Go daddy also allows you to operate your own hosting services at reasonable rates. They are easy for the newbie and their technical support staff is excellent and always there to help.

- **Yoast** is a WordPress plug-in that you can add. It will help attract people to your site. It is easy to use and will provide basic Search Engine Optimization (SEO) features to attract the search engines.

- **Akismet.com** is a great source for controlling Spam and unwanted comments and it is very economically priced.

The biggest mistake that a company can make is to assume that having a website will bring business on its own.

"Build it and they Will Come"

This is often the thinking behind establishing a website. Just being there simply does not do the job of attracting prospects.

A website must be promoted to attract potential customers. A website without promotion is like having 1,000 business cards printed for your use, and then just keeping them in your desk drawer.

If your employer is unhappy with their existing website, ask how they are promoting it. If it is simply just there, the following are some ideas that will start building traffic to the site.

The following suggestions will get you started and provide the basics, if your employer will not agree to having a professional service look after this part.

How to Promote Websites (DIY)

If you do undertake the Do-it-Yourself (DIY) task to develop a website, it should be done after hours so you will not interrupt your prime time for your sales efforts.

Search Engine Optimization (SEO)

SEO traffic building is a slow process and usually does not get immediate results. Be prepared for this building process. Learn all you can about SEO in **Word Press** and **You Tube** tutorials.

Building Your Web Pages

With the free *"Word Press SEO plugin" "Yoast"*, you just need to follow their easy instructions to build your site's web pages so that they will start attracting the search engines and building traffic.

Start with their basic service. You can always add the more advanced levels later, after you are more experience and *up-and-running* for a while. There are also many other SEO plans on-line that one can utilize.

Company Blog (Post)

Again, it is a slow building process. Some statistics say you need 100 posts before any real results happen. "Yoast" is also a great tool for this as well.

Our Purposes Here

This section is not meant to train one "how to blog." It is simply to make one aware of these blogging features.

You will improve your blogging with persistence, time and experience and will see the results if you keep doing it.

Corporate blogs are often used to enhance the communication and culture within a company. They also can be used to express thoughts externally for marketing, branding or public relations.

Niche blogging can also be used to focus on a niche market of a company.

If no one is doing any blogging (posting information) on the company website, perhaps you might offer to start a blog. Base your activity on presenting your ideas and outlines to management for approval first, before posting them online.

Blogging is Free

Except for the time involved there is no cost; and in time, it will eventually attract people to your site.

Once started however; it should follow a schedule and not become a hit and miss situation. If infrequent or scattered posting (blogging) happens, the would-be-follower soon becomes discouraged and will no longer look for your posts.

If you make use of your SEO knowledge and place the appropriate Meta tags and key words in your blog, you will attract search engines and people looking for information on these subjects.

Google Analytics is an excellent plugin for tracking

Provide an RSS feed link on you web page so that people can subscribe to your blog posts. Learn how it works, how to set it up and make it available. Word Press has great learning tutorials.

As you expand your blogging knowledge, you will find new ways to co-operate with other non-competing bloggers in your industry with promotions and extended readership.

Cards, Letterhead

Do not forget to have your company put your website address on all their cards, letterheads, emails, all advertising and every piece of correspondence that the company sends out (even shipping labels).

Wherever the Company Advertises and is Visible

The Website Address Should Be There

News Page on your Website

If you have a page for company announcements, upcoming events or new discovered uses for your offerings, this will build traffic.

Unlike a blog this page is like a news channel whereas a blog is more of an opinion source.

You can post your news letters on your web news page and archive them for anyone who wants to refer to previous ones. You can categorize them by subjects for easy search and find.

By placing general news from your industry on this news page you can develop a following of *"where to go"* to find out what's happening.

The buzz created will make you and your company an authority and bring new clients to look at what you have to say or offer.

Paid Traffic PPA

PPA – Pay Per Action. Paid Traffic can be extremely productive. Before you begin your involvement in paid traffic, make sure you fully understand this activity and what attracts people to your site.

A lot of money can be wasted with no results if one jumps in and starts without enough knowledge of how this works.

Ideas should always be tested and split tested and proven at lower cost levels before up-scaling takes place. This will help prevent promoting a bad idea that could become very costly and end paid traffic as a type of prospecting for you.

"Google AdWords keyword tool." This is a great source for finding the right words and phrases to attract potential prospects. Use it for paid traffic or even on your blogs or website.

PPA (Pay-Per-Action). This is a general term and is where you pay to attract people to your site. The tools used are PPV or PPC.

PPV (Pay Per View) can be fractions of a penny and upwards depending on the subject and company advertising for you. You will pay for everyone who views your offer.

There are many companies offering this **PPA** service, so do your homework here as well. Remember you pay for viewing not traveling to your site.

PPC or (Pay Per Click) is more expensive, but here you pay only if people click on your advertising and clicking will send them to your landing page or website.

Make sure you have a great offer and call to action to turn lookers into buyers or at least provide names and addresses of prospects for your future follow up.

Offering to send free information or your newsletters when they provide their email address is one way to build a list of potential clients.

Do your research and start slowly to see what will work best for you.

PPA gets their attention and can start their journey to your site or landing page; but after that, it's up to your offer or advertising to make things happen.

Tracking of your results to see which type of promotion is working best for you is also available with these PPA companies. There are also independent analytical services to track your results as well.

Do your research as it is very important to have these ingredients working together in harmony.

Auto-Responders

Consider implementation of an email response service that will send your email messages to your list of prospects and customers. They can also automatically respond with information to prospects who provide an email address.

Make sure you are familiar with and follow the changing restrictions regarding the sending of emails.

Make sure the recipient has the option of requesting your email newsletters or advertising correspondence as well as being able to discontinue them at any time.

Most auto-responders comply.

The auto responders are usually very affordable and will look after a whole email program such as news letters or company announcements.

Two available services are: *"AWeber"* or **"Get Response"**

This could become an excellent source of handling and keeping in touch with all new and existing prospects for you. Email is very cost effective; especially if it is controlled by you.

Once you have your qualified lists, you can easily send out information to your prospects and existing customers.

No Time or Not a Technical Person

If you do not have the time to learn or you are not a technical person, there are many places available online that offer training and software to make your involvement easier and more efficient.

There are also many web development companies who will build your site and manage it. This can be expensive and may cause your company to question proceeding in the "web site promotion" direction.

There is no excuse for not getting started. If the cost of using a developer is an issue, offer to do this part yourself with input from your employer.

Get started as these services can always be added later

SEO Companies

There are many SEO service companies for you to choose from at several cost levels. This can be good if your company is willing to pay for these services.

If you want more than the basic SEO activity from DIY efforts, often it is better to have the experts look after this area and not waste sales time learning how.

Email Advertising

Emailing is still a very effective means of prospecting, if you have an accurate list of companies that are typically interested in your type of product or service.

Many people now have their email address on their business card. Some companies may list a general email address on their web site or at least provide a contact form.

Most times a first attempt to reach the client; if not requested by the recipient, can end up in the spam category.

It is best to have a means by which the potential client will request information.

The "Call to Action"

Their request allows you to send without becoming spam

One way is to share promotions with other non-competitive people servicing the same marketplace with different products. You send their promotions with your emails and they do the same in return with their email promotions.

The restrictions have made the automated repeat email sending a little more regulated, and it has made it better and more effective for those who use it right.

Getting Permission to Send

Obtaining permission (the opt-in form or call to action) to send repeat items is good in this case.

Here the prospect provides their email address along with permission. Each item sent to them will also need a means to discontinue receiving them at any time.

You should have "an invite" to get your news letters or other free information placed on your site. Ask the viewer to provide their email address to receive either.

Summary

- Once they request your newsletters or information publications, you can continue sending them until they ask you to stop.

- Make sure you always have good content and helpful information.

- Give them a reason to call – a call to action as it is so accurately called.

- Provide an RSS feed link so that people can subscribe to your posts or social media site updates.

- With each email include a reminder that they have requested this information and have a right to discontinue at any time.

- The use of certain words in your headings can cause your emails to find the spam waste bucket.

- Learn which words to avoid using. Checking your own spam is one place to discover these words. (*Also, google "Stop Words List" has more information on this*).

- The use of an analytical program can be very helpful in showing you what is working and what is not.

- There are excellent free ones with Word press and Google Analytics.

Social Media Networking

The term social networking is not new. The term has been used for over 100 years.

Social networking can be made up of individuals, organizations, or businesses that are connected by one or more specific types of common interests.

When the concept of social networking is used on the internet, it removes the barriers of time, travel and proximity. Your audience potential is worldwide, and contact is instant, unlike travel related networking.

Social media networking is a very useful tool for any company to attract customers.

Your company should become connected to the common ones and those sites relevant to their industry. They will be visible, and people can request updates and see them when they are posted.

Often social networking power will come from individuals at the center of the group's activity and is not necessarily attached to a level of management or authority in a company.

If you can become that center and authority in your company, your peers and prospects will respect and trust you.

Some Main Sites

- FACEBOOK
- TWITTER
- LINKEDIN

There are many choices, so do your research. Find the ones best suited for your company and keep your involvement consistent.

Once Involved

Your company will have a chance on each to build a profile. Link back to the business web site if terms and conditions allow.

Use their business functions to attract potential prospects. These social sites are great prospecting tools and should be utilized.

Consider doing it yourself if your company is not involved

Often there are discussion groups on sites such as LinkedIn that may offer an opportunity to reach your target market. Get involved and get your message out there. Follow the rules or you will bared from using them.

Look for sites that relate to your offerings and join them. You should get permission from your employer if you are promoting your company on them.

If you are doing it as a personal exposure vehicle on your own, you will probably not need to get permission, but it is still a good idea to at least inform them.

Trade Shows - as an Exhibitor

An excellent source of leads can be obtained by being an exhibitor at trade shows. The biggest drawback to this type of prospecting for your employer is that, shows tend to be expensive.

Trade shows make it very easy to spend dollars on gadgets and gimmicks and other things that have little or no effect on your overall results.

Experience will help reduce these costs considerably and improve the shows ROI (Return on Investment). Encourage your company to participate in such events.

Many companies (potential prospects) attend shows to secure information for their purchasing.

Companies often send people who will be involved in decision making for any upcoming projects or find new sources for their existing needs.

Trade Show Tips

One of the factors to make trade shows a success is to be an active and receptive person.

Bring lots of simple but well-designed advertising aids to hand out.

Always have someone standing out front and greeting people as they go by. Sitting in the back of your booth and waiting for people to come to you is not very effective.

Be enthusiastic and friendly when handing out information. This will demonstrate how well you would service your potential prospect should they become a customer.

Take names and get their business cards and ask for email addresses.

The people who just display promotional material, and sit back, expecting the visitors to take the initiative; will leave the prospect with a negative feeling.

They may think that they are now experiencing the level of service they can expect from that supplier.

Other Benefits of Trade Shows

- Another asset in being an exhibitor in trade shows is the image-building you receive by interacting with potential customers, and the involvement with your peer group.

- You and your employer become a visible and important part of your industry.

- It gives you the chance to network from the prestigious level of a Trade Show exhibitor.

- Often these shows will provide the possibility of putting on a seminar about your products or services. This is a great avenue for providing exposure and building trust in your company.

Become a leader in your industry and someone that your clients will look up to as an authority on the products or services that you are promoting.

Telemarketing

If your company has any number of outside sales representatives, it may also have a telemarketing department to arrange calls for their sales representatives.

This allows the sales representative to devote more time to pure selling.

Cost Effective

With the increasing costs for gas, the travel time along with the ineffectiveness of cold prospecting, many companies have or are considering telemarketing to lower their overall lead gathering costs.

Cold telephone calling in the form of prospecting, is often something that many sales representatives who are on the road hate to do anyway.

Personally, I found making telephone calls myself, to be a very effective prospecting method. Provided I started with a pre-selected group chosen by myself, the results were very productive.

Areas of Caution

Leads produced for the sake of the telemarketer getting the required appointment numbers, can become a real danger.

It is important for you as a sales representative to be able to follow up and qualify the lead, confirm the interest and appointment, re-set it or cancel it. Qualification increases efficiency and closing ratios.

If your employer has telemarketing in place, make sure you have a way to provide feedback on the quality of leads you are getting. Your input into what you are looking for in a prospect is essential.

Make this involvement part of your sales agenda or you may find that you are too often involved in the proverbial wild goose chase.

Direct Mail

Direct Mail is the type of mail that is sent to very specific people and companies. It involves addressing and stuffing envelopes and applying postage.

Use a good source for recipient company information and up-to-date employee contact names. There are many Trade and Business Directories available online and at local libraries.

Be Specific

This is not a mass mailing as postage is involved, and you should be very specific about the type of company and people you are sending your direct mail to.

There are sources and programs that will allow you to choose the main parameters of your search and even print labels of all the companies found.

Unless you streamline your selection process, and choose your target market carefully, your approach may be too general. It will produce mediocre results and it can become very costly.

If not done correctly your company could look at the Return on Investment (ROI) and feel that it is too expensive to continue.

Once you have the experience in identifying good potential prospects, go through these lists and select the type of company, and the level of management that you want to receive this information.

The selection part of these companies and names is best done by you and works well for your "Off hour Prospecting"

Company Assistance

Give these lists to a secretary in your company to address each envelope, add the information, apply postage, and send the letter directly to the people you have chosen.

Make sure a list of names and telephone numbers has been made and is available for follow up.

You can assist by stuffing the envelopes after hours. It is a satisfying way to create the feeling of teamwork, if you show appreciation to the others involved.

Keep the Information Simple and to the Point
Too many Words - Will go right to the Trash

Direct mail is a great method to provide extra prospecting capabilities, without taking time from the most productive part of your day which is 9:00 to 5:00 for making appointments and seeing your potential customers.

Time Consuming

Direct mail is a time-consuming method, and what better time than after hours to establish your list of potential prospects.

Make time for a small amount to be done each day/week. Small daily or weekly mailings will hardly be noticed. This applies to your office help and applies to the cost factor.

It also will create leads on a steady pace that you can handle. Set your goals and stick to them. After a short time, you will see the results with increased inquires.

The Follow Up

Use your list of the places you have sent this information to c/w names and telephone numbers. Wait 3 or 4 days and follow up with a phone call. Smaller mailings will make this easier and more efficient.

News Letters

If your employer is not actively involved in any kind of newsletter, start doing one yourself (with permission). We have outlined information in the section "Personal Prospecting."

Mass Mailing - No Name – No Address

If your company has a product that is widely used or multiple products, this can work well as a third level prospecting method.

This was something I did, when nothing else seemed to be working.

It would also produce leads from the most unsuspecting areas. That is why I used it. Keep the mailings controlled from a cost standpoint. Bi-weekly or Monthly mailings are far better than one huge mailing.

What works?

This also gives one a chance to see what is working and what is not. There is no telephone follow up here

Over the years, I found that dumping a huge quantity of this type on the marketplace at once; whatever the delivery service was, did not produce very good results.

It often seemed like the larger the quantity was; that I sent out, the lower the percentage of results. Releasing mailers in smaller quantities over a longer time span seemed to increase the success levels in the response factor.

The Downside to this Type

Unfortunately, mail without a name and stamp, is often treated as junk and often does not reach its intended destination.

There is no accountability by anyone and most people know it. We have also all heard the stories of huge quantities of mailers found in dumpsters that were never delivered.

The overall results and the ROI per new customer obtained will determine if this method makes any sense to your company.

Choose a reliable delivery source and make sure your information shows your website's address company telephone number and your email address.

Most importantly, it must have a good call to action or offer.

Do random checks for delivery and let your delivery source know you will be doing them. After all, you are paying them to deliver your mailers and it will defiantly increase the delivery rate and your return.

Paid Media

Paid media can become very costly and not all will work for your employer's offerings. Tread very lightly before you suggest any of them.

Usually a good sign of their effectiveness might be if your competition is using one or more of them.

In the following areas, we suggest that you do your research and obtain the advertising costs. Also, find out the advertising strategies attached to each method.

Do this in non-prime-time for prospecting. Fully put together the results on your own before you start suggesting the use of any to management.

Find out what the benefits are for each and why the source feels their method would work for you.

Newspapers

Call or visit your local newspapers and ask for their advertising rates. They will usually have a package outlining everything you would need.

Their reach will also usually include other newspaper groups that they are involved with, outside of your community. You can usually pick and choose the communities you want to reach, by selecting these other groups individually.

Trade Magazines

This can be a very effective form of advertising if the magazine is focused on your industry. If it is a good source, there will be many competitors there as well.

Study the magazines for several issues and see what is being done. Make sure that whatever you do looks equal to, or better than your competition. You will immediately be judged on what you do because you are a new player.

Have Quality Content and a good Call to Action

Radio and TV

Contact your local radio and TV stations and ask for an advertising portfolio for small business.

Find out what support they would provide in putting a campaign together for you. Even if you feel you would not use these sources, knowledge is the best way to make your decisions.

Bill Boards

Often bill boards will work for a short period. After a while they can just become part of the scenery background. Changing information on them periodically or changing location, can reduce this "blending-in" aspect.

Mobile Cards

If you are part of a larger community where they have taxis, buses, park benches or benches at transit stops, you will often see this type of advertising.

Often it is used by professionals such as real estate agents or by businesses offering products or services to consumers.

Webinars

The term webinar is a short form for a Web-based Seminar. It can be a presentation, lecture, workshop or seminar that is transmitted over the web through a host.

There is usually notification and a sign-up process with the time and access information sent to the email address of the participants.

Prospects will view the activity on their computer screen and in most cases, they will listen with the speakers connected to their computer. Usually they have an option to use a telephone for audio.

Live or Recorded

Webinars can either be live presentations or previously formatted and recorded for viewing or listening.

Often there will be a live chat line for questions and responses to various parts of the webinar presentation.

If the webinar has been recorded, you or your company can use it for repeat broadcasts or convenient viewing in different time zones or to suit the schedules of the recipients.

Placing your past recorded webinars on your website, can provide a continuous source of prospect attraction. They can also become great background attention aids at trade shows.

If the company is not involved in any kind of webinar activity, suggest starting with a trial webinar and if successful build it into a bi-monthly or monthly activity.

Open House

One way of building relations with your clients as well as attracting new ones is to have open house demonstrations of your products and services. Have your internal office staff participate. Keep it informal to create a comfort level with the people attending.

Presentations to Organisations

There are many opportunities that exist in local organizations or groups doing promotions or holding events. Look for ones that could assist in your company's exposure. You could offer to be a guest speaker at such an event especially if it is relevant to your offerings.

Social Events by a Company

Often these events can take form in the way that combines a light breakfast, brunch or lunch while presenting a training session or information seminar for one's products.

If the company has a conference room

It could be a venue

There are many other available venues that cater to this type of event so do your research.

Other Events

Often less formal entertaining events for suppliers and customers such as a company golf tournament or BBQ can be a very effective way to show appreciation for customer support and their business.

It also Builds Loyalty

By Showing Appreciation

As a sales representative, this will give you the opportunity to meet with clients on an informal basis and build a relationship.

They can also be a great relationship builder with your suppliers and become a great place for an informal customer/supplier meeting.

Personal Prospecting -DIY

Overview

This will probably your main source of leads if you work for one of the 80% who do not have or use a marketing plan. There may be some sort of advertising being done but it is usually not consistent or organized.

Usually you will get some secretarial back up for letters and proposals for your prospects. There could even be assistance in putting together some mailing campaigns.

If you are fortunate they will participate in some of the areas mentioned in the previous chapter.

For the Most Part

It will be like developing your own mini-marketing plan which is what we will be outlining here.

The following prospecting methods are primarily focused on what you; as the sales representative, will be doing.

Office Personnel

Leads from Your Office

Keep in close contact with your receptionist, order desk people, purchasing, shipping, your service department, and your engineering staff.

They are often the people who develop relationships with your customers and suppliers and will hear of projects, problems or needs that will benefit your efforts.

The Office Lead Source

Everyone in your company can become great sources for information on new projects. Get to know everyone in your company, because not only is everyone important; but, they could be a source for sales leads.

If they like the way you have treated them, and you have shown appreciation for the way they are assisting your customers, you have probably developed a great source for leads in your own company.

Your company support staff is usually in touch with your customers and suppliers monthly, weekly and sometimes they talk daily.

Often your office support staff will hear about projects sooner than you might from your own contacts. People like to talk and sometimes boast about their own company's progress.

These people are often on the inner circle of gossip and news in your industry. You will in turn hear about these projects often before they are announced publicly to the industry you are in.

Looking for a Good Person to take to lunch?

Try Someone in Your Company

Do it to show appreciation for working with you and your customers.

They will be happy to share information and leads if they like you and appreciate your demonstration of gratitude.

Remember that while you are getting commissions on your efforts, they do not see anything for their involvement in your commission earnings. (unless there is profit sharing)

Sometimes co-workers become jealous of your earnings especially if it has involved their assistance. Rewarding them when you are successful goes a long way to keep a harmonious working environment.

Rewarding for Help

Taking them out for lunches as well as other perks like tickets to sports events or other entertainment activities will go a long way in creating that extra effort from them.

Do not leave anyone out of the group that you work with

Pay for a night out dining at a local restaurant for them and their partner. Often, they may work late while their partner is waiting at home.

This Method Shows your Appreciation

For their Partners Understanding

Note: You need to be earning some serious commissions to begin doing this, and keep this activity going.

Do not start and then stop. Do not go overboard. Maybe do a monthly thing for someone different each month. Small and often, is better than, large an infrequent. Keep the perks similar in size for everyone.

Maybe do a Group thing for the Whole Office

Remember this can also be a tax write-off

Suppliers

Do not forget the people who supply you with products or services.

We will discuss this further in Peer Networking

Telephone Cold Calls

Calling Previously Selected People

This method is being affected by the changing attitudes of buyers. In today's business environment, many potential prospects do not want to be disturbed, unless they have made the first contact.

Make sure you have a good presentation as it is hard to get past the gate keepers.

If you are persistent this can often be a surprisingly good source for leads because fewer and fewer sales people are making cold calls on the telephone.

Make a list of places you can call when you have spare time. You can make your lists in none prime time or off hours and on weekends.

Always have 50 – 100 names of places complete with names and telephone numbers you can call. Set your minimum call list and Maintain it

Again, the law of numbers will produce some good appointments.

When Nothing else is Happening

Sit down and Make some Telephone Calls

Try This Approach

- Introduce yourself, your company and the product/service you are promoting.

- Ask if they have heard of you and if this is something that they would be interested in seeing or hearing about.

- If yes, make an appointment

If no Appointment can be made

- If they say no - ask them if you can send or drop off any information. If they still say no - thank them and hang up.

- If they say yes send me information, get their name and title.

- If you are not sure of the correct spelling of their name, call back and speak to the person on reception.
    - Say that you just talked to (name the person) and are sending or dropping off some literature for them.
    - Ask if you can get the correct spelling and proper title of that person?

Send your information and they will be eligible for a follow-up call to see if they got the information, have any questions or will make an appointment to see you.

Blogging (posting)

Blogging often provides commentary on a subject. Some will function as an online viewpoint on something in your industry. It could become an information source.

Others will perform more of an online branding source for a company, its offerings or even individuals within the company. A typical blog may contain text, images, and links to other blogs, web pages or other media types related to its topic.

The ability of readers to leave comments is often part of many blogs.

Note: If you allow comments, there should be some type of screening process to eliminate public viewing of the unethical or obscene comments.

Often leaving some critical comments in, will show readers that this is an open forum. Often by doing this, you raise the overall level of reader trust.

If you develop a following they will become a great asset and good source of leads.

They will see you as an authority figure and want to read what you have to say about your industry, and even ask you to provide feedback and answers for their needs or problems.

If you Start a Blog

You must be consistent and establish a routine that works so people know when to expect your next post.

Choose a date that is easily identified; such as the last Friday of each month, the first and third Monday of every month or the 1st and 15th.

Establish it and Stick with it

Pace yourself and do not try to do more than you can easily handle.

Keep a few previously prepared posts on file to use in an emergency when you do not have the time to do one. In Word Press you can even schedule future posts over 3 – 4 months. This way; you can plan a series, and let things happen.

Post Office

If your employer will not provide this service, consider doing it yourself. It can pay big dividends if your products provide the right *Return on your Investment* of time and cost for materials.

a) News Letters to Past Contacts

A method that often works well is sending a monthly newsletter by the postal services directly to your past contacts who did not buy.

This becomes an excellent additional way of keeping a presence without the need of making continuous follow up phone calls. Do not make the mistake of following up after such a mailing or you will defeat the purpose of this subtle informal contact.

Past Prospects do not feel threatened by postal newsletters; especially if they know there is no call coming after it.

They are not threatened because they can choose to read them or ignore them, and they know that you will be none the wiser.

After a while they may even look forward to them

A hard copy is more likely to get filed for future reference or circulated immediately. Often it will re-kindle someone's interest.

The main thing that happens here is that you keep your company and products/services in front of your past prospects, in an easy and non-intrusive way.

For them it's like getting a post card from an old acquaintance, so keep the newsletter short, informative and friendly.

We Suggest via Post Office

This is because often emails get deleted without even being looked at, because purchasers and management get so many of them. Once they are deleted they are gone forever.

Most often there is more chance of being seen, being circulated or being filed if it is hard copy.

Always present something different or new, along with your standard messages. Often something totally unrelated to your offerings will create buzz and a following.

Even something like recipes for salads, BBQ cooking, or desserts work well. A humorous story can often do more than promoting your own offerings.

Provide Valuable Information

Make sure that you include helpful industry related information as well, that they will want to keep this on file for future reference.

It is amazing how newsletters can rejuvenate lost sales or create renewed interest in a product or service.

With every newsletter that our company sent out, we always experienced some sort of activity immediately following its distribution. It is more effective to leave the contact initiative in the hands of your prospect to call you.

Sometimes the timing was just not right when you last called, or maybe a project may have been indefinitely delayed and has just been put back on the front burner again.

Non-Prime Time

Sending newsletters is prospecting that can be done during non-prime time.

Keep adding these non-prime time prospecting ways to your off hours prospecting potential.

Build your Lists. You need to keep as many active contacts as possible and distribute the newsletters on a regular schedule. When any name is no longer valid find out who replaced them.

This is an Excellent Way

Of Renewing Possibilities as well

b) News Letters to Existing Customers

Existing customers can be great references and can become prospects for new business. Your company has gained their trust and respect, or they would not be customers.

Send the same style of newsletter addressed, stuffed and with a stamp for postal delivery. Do it as you did for non-customers. Part of the best Sales Prospecting is Mining your own Satisfied Customers.

Have a different grouping and format of information that is specifically sent to your existing customers. Thank them for their business. Inform them of important events in your company, or the industry.

Become a source of news, and you will keep everyone's attention, and support. They will also talk about you to others in a positive way.

There is a follow up for your newsletter with existing customers and it is a little different.

Often an informal in-person drop in call immediately following distribution of a newsletter, is demonstrating just good plain customer appreciation.

Make it a business/social visit to see if your company is looking after them. A newsletter and visit after can often lead to a new sale or prospect referral.

c) News Letters to Suppliers

Do not forget about your Suppliers. They are an extension of your contacts and will expand your reach.

They are people who have a vested interest in seeing your company successful because it will mean more sales for them. Here make your key contact(s) the recipient of the postal hard copy.

Emailing

News Letters

Many people read and prefer emails as a source of contact, so do not ignore this method. Do it along with your post office mailings of your newsletters, not as an either/or choice.

News Letters can easily be incorporated into an automated mailing service (auto-responders) that we mentioned earlier. Use your automated email service to send out multiple copies of your electronic news letters to others in the same companies who you have met or worked with.

Sending a copy to everyone by post office would become very expensive.

Easier to Include Everyone

Many additional people will play a part in any decision making for your offerings. In this way, they do not feel that they have been left out of the loop and will be more prepared to support your cause.

People React Favorably to Being Remembered

This also really works well if your company has multiple products that will appeal to different departments. Usually your prospects have many people who can influence the purchasing of your offerings.

There is no cost to send the additional emails and therefore no excuse not to send them.

Group Emailing

Separate your emailing into different groups as some emailing could be more specific and for a group or several specified groups.

We have listed four groups as an example. Further groups can be made depending on your products or services.

The Four Groups

1) Past Contacts and Non-Customers

Send an email to the main contact as well as the extended contacts you may have worked with to try to obtain their business. This is very good for extending your influence as well.

2) Existing Customers

Sending email newsletters to office managers, plant managers, department heads as well as engineering, key plant and office people, maintenance people, shipping and receiving is like mining in pure gold.

You can get many of these email addresses from your own company staff and your main customer contact.

3) Suppliers

Do not forget about emailing your suppliers. Again, they have reasons for wanting to see you successful.

Sending email newsletters to their office managers, plant managers, department heads as well as engineering, key plant and office people, maintenance people, shipping and receiving is also like mining in pure gold.

You can also get many of these email addresses from your own company staff or your supplier contact.

4) Your Own Company

Never forget your own group of co-workers. They above all may appreciate being noticed and possibly even mentioned and thanked in your emails or newsletters.

Summary of Emailing

The greatest part about emailing is that it is virtually free. Along with building your initial lists you will need to keep it up to date and keep adding wherever you can.

Do not ignore this method of Prospecting as it allows you to reach these sources in an instant through your automated emailing service.

There is no paper cost, no printing costs, and no mailing costs – just your time spent. Yes, there is usually a small monthly service fee for the auto-responder but when the results are reviewed, it is very low.

What Other Method

Could be more Efficient and Cost Effective

And Environmentally Friendly as Well

Customers Referrals

Referrals will materialize, if you have serviced your customer well, and provided the confidence level that will usually be required for them to provide your name to others.

It takes a little more for them to provide names of referrals to you instead of just passing it on and allowing the people to contact you.

When they provide you with the name, it will mean you have been successful in building a substantial amount of trust.

The only way you can really prepare yourself for this type of lead, is to look after every client to the best of your ability. Most times you will need to ask for referrals even with a high level of customer trust.

Social Visits

Drop into existing or past customers whenever you are in their area. It is amazing how one of these unannounced – *"Hi how you are drop-in calls"* - can make your customer feel appreciated.

Yes, a Social visit

Show interest, ask how things are going, and share industry information. This will be more of a social visit than a sales call.

We Stress a Social vs. Sales Approach

Say hi how you are or how are things going? How is the family? Wait for an answer. Maybe have a short discussion updating recent business and personal activities, and then be on your way. If they are busy just leave your card.

Such visits can be an excellent source of leads. While you are there; if the opportunity presents itself, it never hurts to ask if they know of anyone else who could use your product or services.

Do Not make it the Reason for your Call

Occasionally you may find out that they are expanding themselves or are having problems with other competitor's products and may need your assistance.

This can lead to supplying new offerings or more of your existing products or services. You will be surprised by the business that can come from a social visit.

Achievements – Birthdays – Seasons Greetings

Achievements

Often a company will achieve something special or reach a milestone such as 25th anniversary. Show your interest in the customer by dropping by or sending a congratulatory letter, card or gift.

Birthdays

Every individual likes to be noticed. If you know that it is someone's birthday, send or drop off a card. Keep a list of your client's birthdays or special anniversaries if you can.

Show that you care, and it will be appreciated. Keep adding to your list.

Season's Greetings

Drop by existing and past customers during the December holiday season. It will make them feel good and important to be remembered and appreciated.

Maybe leave a small gift for the office or plant manager like a cheese platter or chocolates. Not too large to upset any rules or not too small or you will appear cheap. Address it *"To office or plant personal."*

Your appreciation, friendship and interest in how well they are doing, will come back many times over.

Do it mainly as a thank you and a call expressing appreciation for their past business. The act of kindness and gratitude will not go unnoticed or unappreciated by both their office and plant employees.

Peer Networking

One of the best ways for getting good sales leads is by establishing contact with non-competing sales and service people in other companies, who are calling on the same type of companies as you are.

Peer Sources for Networking

- Your own suppliers are great sources for peer networking and they have a vested interest in your success.
- Your co-workers in your office and their contacts
- Other non-competitive sales people servicing your industry
- Owners and managers of your customers.

In my most successful selling years, my suppliers provided me with over 80% of my leads that developed into sales.

They also became the recipients of leads from me. Even better they also shared in the business obtained by supplying their products for my projects.

If your lead source is a supplier that your new prospect trusts and respects, it is perhaps the most powerful and qualified lead you can get.

Begin Building Right Away

When starting out, unless you already have friends and contacts in the industry, peer networking will take time to develop.

Start building your own network as soon as you can and keep building throughout your entire career.

Where to Find Them

You will meet your peers at trade shows, seminars, conferences, social activities, and often when attending a joint project meeting held by your own suppliers or even customers.

To increase lead sources, ask your customer who supplies them with other products that are non-competitive to you. You can then develop them as a lead source.

You could say: *"I often am asked who I might recommend for (*name the product*). If you are happy with your source, would it be possible to get their name and number so that I might contact them to establish a relationship.*

Once you get a Name

Call that person and Introduce Yourself

Tell them where you got their name. Meet with them for a coffee and discuss how you can help each other. They are also looking for contacts to network with, so this is usually not difficult.

Make sure the lead source is reliable and is respected, because you will be mentioning their name to your customers.

Some Pointers

Many people will already have contacts with whom they network, so it may take some time to win their confidence.

Sometimes the loyalty of a peer is attached to where they get the most benefits, like leads or spin off sales.

Be aware of Where their Loyalty lies

The best way is to start building peer lead sources; is to be the first to provide leads to them, for their offerings. Be careful at first, build the relationship slowly, until you are sure you can trust them.

You do not want them to take your important contacts to your competition. Provide some smaller leads first and wait and see how they handle them.

When you finally break the barrier, and get a lead from them, make sure you thank them, and do the best that you can to justify their gesture of good faith.

Look after Their Prospect Well

Get permission to use the name of your lead source, or even better, have them introduce you personally.

Servicing Leads

This is not something to take lightly, because you will only be judged by the results of the last lead you handled. Nothing will make a lead source disappear faster than, not looking after their lead properly.

This is called networking, so always be prepared to always keep doing the same in return, or this method will soon dry up.

Nourish it; Stick with it even though it takes a while to develop. When it is done right; in my opinion, the return your invested time beats every other type of lead sourcing.

Peer Networking is always About
Building and Maintaining Trust.

Peer networking is one of the most powerful introductions to a potential client. It is also like mining pure gold, and there is nothing better for your success.

Social Networking

There is another form of networking that many people use to obtain clients. It is referred to as social networking. It occurs usually during lunch time, after hours during the week, and often weekends.

Some sales people look for different social functions where they may attend and meet potential prospects or lead sources. Others may join organizations such as Chamber of Commerce or associations related to their industry.

It could be a trade show for other products, an exhibit or anywhere you mingle and meet people. It could be a golf tournament or benefit put on by a supplier or client.

Usually at these events, people tend to relax and let their guard down. They talk about their families, their hobbies and what they do in their spare time. Often friendships are generated and continued in the workplace. Some will become customers or lead sources and even lifelong friends.

Always Behave at an Acceptable Level.

Party Animals get their Attention but Rarely get the Business

Cold Calling in Person

a) Extra time when in the Area

When you are out seeing the prospects that you have made appointments with, you will often find yourself with extra time especially if there is a cancellation or a call ends quickly.

Always carry plenty of promotional material to leave with other companies in the area.

Yes, we did say cold calling does not work. But in this case, we are not going to try to see anyone. We are just leaving information, getting a name (if possible) and telephone number to call back. It is cold calling with a twist.

Be Resourceful

Many sales people get angry at a no show, or a shorter than expected no-results-meeting. They do not take advantage of the extra time that has unexpectedly become available.

They go for a coffee or early lunch or may head back to the office or even home, instead of using this BONUS time and continuing to work at getting future prospects while in the area.

Surprisingly; unplanned cold calling like this, can pay off big. Every potential prospect uncovered, is one that you would not have otherwise obtained.

In addition, you still have the original prospect to contact again later.

The Approach

When you make this type of cold call:

You say "*I was making a call at (your call) and I noticed your company and I was wondering what your company does?*

If it appears like someone who could use your offerings:

You say "*I do not have time to see anyone right now; but, could I drop off some information about our company.*

If they say Yes

You continue: "*May I ask who I would speak to about (whatever your offerings are) when I do my follow up.*"

Try and get a name then leave

Do not try to get in to see the person! Even if you did manage to see the prospect, people do not like this type of interruption without an appointment. It will affect future attempts to see them.

This low-key Approach

Is far more Effective in the long run

If you do not get a name when you are there check any directories you may have, or on line. Follow up the next day and ask for that person.

You say: "*Yesterday I left information for the person that looks after (your Product). Who I would ask for when I call for an appointment?*"

If you did get a name, ask: "*Do they have a title?*"

Once you have a name, the prospect is now eligible for a follow up telephone call.

b) Targeted Companies (visual signs)

This Type of approach is a planned and targeted one. Companies who may use your offerings will sometimes show visible signs that you can see from outside.

Some Examples

- If you sell liquid paint for industrial spraying equipment, it might be as easy as looking for factories that have exhaust stacks to remove contaminants from their building.

  o Paint stacks are usually identifiable and distinct.

Other types of exhaust stacks could mean a company that is welding and would be a prospect for welding equipment and supplies.

- Exhaust stacks could also mean a potential need for air make up units.

- Even the company name will usually tell you what they do. You can Google the name on your phone and find out while you are in the area.

When you approach the receptionist, (if there is one) ask if they do any kind of welding, or painting or whatever the process is that needs your offerings.

You Say: *"I was just making a call down the street and noticed the exhaust stacks on your roof."*

Using the type of offering you have as the example

You ask: "Would your company do any (your example).

If they say yes

You say *"I do not have time to see anyone right now; but, could I drop off some information about our company.*

Continue: *"May I ask who I would speak to about (your offerings) when I do my follow up."*

Try and get a Name and then Leave.

Do not try to get in to see the person! Even if you did manage to see the prospect, people do not like this type of interruption without an appointment.

Just like example a) this low-key approach

Is far more effective in the long run

If you do not get a name when you are there check any directories you may have, or on line. Follow up the next day and ask for that person.

If you do not get a name, Call the next day.

You say: *"Yesterday I left information for the person that looks after (your Product). Who I would ask for when I call for an appointment?"*

If you get a name, ask: *"Do they have a title?"*

Once you have a name, the prospect is now eligible for a follow up telephone call. Do this cold call approach whenever you can, and this extra time could allow 3 or 4 calls and maybe the discovery of a new prospect.

You will learn the Signs or Type of Companies to Look for

Trade Shows as a Visitor

If you are not fortunate to have your company participate as an exhibitor in a trade show for your business type or industry, do the next best thing.

Become Visible as a VISITOR

Network with all your peers and leave information with potential prospects.

Opportunities may be characterized as silver or second best as compared to being an exhibitor but participating as a visitor is still a great source for prospects.

You can socialize with existing peers and obtain new peer net-workers. Make sure your approaches are non-intrusive and do not interrupt the exhibitor's opportunities to speak with their own potential clients.

Approach them Only if

They are Not Engaged in a Conversation.

If you are talking when a prospect approaches them, politely step back or leave. Come back again if it is appropriate.

Prospecting Summary

The To-Do and Not-To-Do List

Do Follow up - One important thing that you should be doing in all forms of prospecting is following up. If you have obtained a name and you have not yet called that potential client, follow it up.

This backlog often happens after a trade show, where there can be so many leads obtained at once. Often a form of thank you for visiting your booth is a good beginning. It acts as a reminder as well.

There is no point in taking the time or incurring the cost to get a name, and then not use it. Having a huge list of potential clients remains just that, until you make the call, to turn them into a viable prospect.

The worst thing that can happen is that they can say NO we are no longer interested. It is more important to get a no and remove it from your list, than to leave the approach unfinished.

Thinking about your uncalled leads and feeling guilty can drag you down quicker than the No's you might get.

Failure to Follow up

Many people fail to follow up. These names are the most important part of prospecting, but they are of no value unless you use them.

The effectiveness of a lead diminishes very soon after it has been provided, so do not wait too long to follow up or the opportunity will be gone.

Do - Find what prospecting methods work best for you.

Find five or six methods that suit your personality and offerings. Use them constantly.

Be creative when sending or dropping off information. Provide something that will catch their attention and arouse their interest and cause them to call or check you out on your web site.

Do Smile - Show Enthusiasm and the Right Attitude. Smile when you talk on the phone.   Do this, and it will be transmitted to the person at the other end. The smile when talking to a person is always felt.

Be Enthusiastic - It is one of the greatest tools you can use, and it is contagious. The more enthused you are, the more enthused will be your prospect. Always keep enthusiasm present.

Norman Vincent Peale once said: *"Enthusiasm releases the drive to carry you over obstacles and adds significance to all you do."*

Do See the Right Person - Every product or service is usually handled by a similar type of position in any company.

- If it is office supplies you are selling, it is usually the office manager.
- Repeat plant supplies are most often handled by a purchasing agent.
- You might see the production manager or general manager if you are introducing new products for their manufacturing process.

The people who do the day-to-day purchasing are often "not" the ones who will select your new product.

Find out all the people who are involved in making those decisions to make a change. Your own experience will soon teach you who these people usually are.

Talk to your manager and ask who it was that they initially contacted when presenting their product or service to your existing customers. This will usually be enough to get you started until your own experience takes over.

Do not leave people out - If you are seeing a decision maker who is completely different than the person that does the day-to-day ordering, do not leave the day-to-day person out of the dialogue.

Most often, they will have two or three accepted sources for the same products or services. If you alienate them; even though you are shown as a source, they could ignore you or could undermine your future sales possibilities.

Do not - Use prospecting methods you dislike - Do not use a prospecting method that makes you uncomfortable, or you hate doing because you will rarely be successful, and your attitude will come across to the customer.

- Say that you will be making some calls in their area (whenever) and would they have 10 – 15 minutes to speak to you about (your offerings)?

Wait for their reply, **if they say** "OK", make the appointment. Thank them, repeat the scheduled time, and then say you are looking forward to meeting them.

If they are not interested in an appointment, ask if you can drop the information off next week when you are in the area for them to look at when they have time.

Then say you will call a few days after to see if they have any questions. Again, do not try to make a follow up appointment at this time as they have already said no.

Calling to see if there are questions

Will provide the Opportunity to ask for an appointment

c) Customer Referrals

When you call, you will already have a name from your customer.

Introduce yourself and your company and say: *"Company X is a good customer of ours and is very happy with our (offerings).*

(Say the person's name) suggested that I should call you to see if we might show you (what you offer).

Say that you will be making some calls in their area (*next week or whenever*) and would they have 10 – 15 minutes to speak to you about (your offerings)?

Wait for their reply, if they say "OK" - Make the appointment. Thank them, repeat the scheduled time, and then say you are looking forward to meeting them.

If they are not interested in an appointment, ask if you can drop the information off next week when you are in the area for them to look at when they have time.

Then say you will call a few days after to see if they have any questions. Again, do not try to make a follow up appointment at this time as they have already said no.

Calling to see if there are questions will set up the opportunity to ask for an appointment.

d) Pre-Planned In-Person Cold Calling

This is cold calling in person with a twist. You are not trying to see anyone. You are doing this to set the reason for your next call and too get a name. If there is a reception area introduce yourself and say:

The approach "I was making some calls in the area and your (company name, materials outside, exhaust stacks, find something) suggested to me that your company might be interested in (whatever your offerings are).

Finish with: *"I do not have any time to see anyone right now and I realize that it is best to make an appointment, so I would just like to leave some literature for whoever might take care of this area. Would that be alright?* **If they say yes**

You Ask: *"Who would I ask for when I call for an appointment?"*

Note: If there is just a telephone in the lobby call the reception and say the same as above. Make sure at the end for either way, that you have all the information you will need for follow up.

SUMMARY

Prospecting is your Avenue for Success.

If it is part of your job, and you are good at it, you will have the keys to achieve all your sales goals. This part 5 has provided you with some of the tools and the ways to find your prospects, future customers and clients.

Start with these and Always Be Building

If you know how to create your own leads, you will always have a large inventory of potential customers and opportunities for sales.

Even if your employer supplies leads, you should learn the methods outlined in this part. Prospecting is a skill set that will always be of enormous value in applying for any sales position.

Without this skill set you will remain unable to be self-reliant in your undertakings as a sales person. Without this ability, you will always need others to create opportunities for you.

Selling should be all about setting your own goals, creating your own future and pathway to success.

By learning and mastering the information in this book you will indeed become self-reliant and a self-starter.

That's What the Direct Sales Profession

Is All About

END OF PART FIVE

Wayne E Shillum - Author

www.ingramcontent.com/pod-product-compliance
Lightning Source LLC
Chambersburg PA
CBHW062025210326
41519CB00060B/6984